MR. PRESIDENT

A Spiritual Journey

Colin D. Mallard

Wild Duck Publishing

MR. PRESIDENT
A SPIRITUAL JOURNEY

by

Colin D. Mallard, Ph.D.

Published by

Wild Duck Publishing
P.O. Box 909,
Kapa'au, Hawaii 96755 U.S.A.

Copyright Colin D. Mallard 1996

All rights reserved. No part of this book may be reproduced in any form or by any means without permission in writing from the Publisher, Wild Duck Publishing,

Cover design and illustration by Lightbourne Images, copyright 1995

ISBN 0-9646040-5-1

Library of Congress catalog card number: 95-90227

In Grateful Appreciation

For my father, who instilled
in me a love of Philosophy

For my mother, who showed me love and devotion,

For my son, who still teaches me

For my wife Stephanie, my loving partner and best friend.

Thank you Anne and Norman,
Tai Chi buddies
and more

And Mac,
Thank you for your assistance with this project, and for sorting out
the confusion between football and baseball teams.

Special thanks to Channing
for his invaluable assistance and friendship.

And Madhukar, good friend
thanks for your encouragment, insistence and love.
A lovely satsang indeed!

Thank you John, David,
Fran, and Ana,
for you were the book's first reality check.

Thank you Ruth.

"...a riveting book of our times...Read it and grow!"
Leona Mayers, Camille Publications, Arlington Texas

"Truly and inspiring and hopeful book. A must read by all."
EAGLEye Nanaimo, British Columbia, Canada

"Mallard crafts a message for today. Penetrating gradual unfolding of the secrets of life."
The Book Reader, San Francisco, California

"The time is now. Your imagination is my inspiration."
David Tarnas, Hawaii State Representative

Ah Ramesh, the wily one,

The light

The moth could not escape

When a country is governed with tolerance,
The people are comfortable and honest.
When a country is governed with repression,
The people are depressed and crafty.

When those who love power are in charge,
Ideals are high, and results are low
Make people happy,
And you lay the groundwork for misery.
Make people moral,
And you lay the groundwork for vice.

Thus the sage is content to serve as an example,
Not to impose his will.
He is pointed, but doesn't pierce.
Radiant, but easy on the eyes.

Lao Tzu

Introduction

India is known as the land of the "Mahatmas," the enlightened "great souls." Here, saints are not so unusual. For Moslems, Hindus, Buddhists and Christians alike, the term "Buddha-hood" refers to liberation from pain and suffering. It is also known as "God-realization" or "enlightenment."

The Indian public regard enlightened leadership as the highest form of leadership possible, something greatly desired. The nation's history is replete with accounts of enlightened leadership, from time immemorial. Perhaps the most recent spiritual teacher, statesman and leader in modern times was Mahatma Gandhi, a man who for most Indians was one of the founders of modern India, and a counselor to its people.

It would not, therefore, have been surprising to read a story of enlightened leadership by an Indian author. Imagine my surprise when I read *Mr. President,* and learned that it was a Western author, a friend of mine, who had written it. The idea of enlightened leadership in Washington had never crossed my mind. The thought of such a possibility was nothing less than staggering, comparable to the quantum leap in thinking which brought about the theory of relativity, and the attendant consequences for mankind.

To think of the United States, even the world, being guided by the sure hand of enlightened leadership is beyond comprehension. Only the actual, real life event would halt all speculation on such matters, and surprise the world with its wisdom and farsightedness.

The thought has been introduced to the world, the book is written. May it be a forerunner, in the near future, of enlightened leadership in Washington, of the caliber and stature of Moses.

Realistically though, I've little doubt as to how the American and Western public would react to such leadership. Believers in the Christian conception of God would speak of blasphemy. There would be those who would rather see the president crucified than follow his farsighted and insightful guidance. Their personal beliefs in God would be challenged and they'd react as do most people who feel threatened by new ideas. To pursue this line of thought could well be the basis for yet another book.

There's no doubt in my mind; this book will create controversy. In the story of *Mr. President,* the author points in clear and unbiased terms to the facts which form the basis of hostilities between Israel and the Arab world, implicating their resolve with the unusual thinking of President Tremaine. Tremaine willingly exposes himself to personal risk in an effort to address the needs and suffering he sees before him. He points to the difficulties of modern democracies and the rise of fundamentalism. This new perspective on the Arab

Israeli conflict will, no doubt, create controversy in Jewish, Christian, and Muslim communities.

The fact that Israeli president Rabin was assassinated by his own people. The fact that Israel has existed as a nation, largely at the behest of the United States and its president, suggests the book should be made available in both Israel and other Middle Eastern, Arabic countries.

Colin has a Ph.D. in Eastern Philosophy and this, coupled with his interest in politics, makes him someone to be listened to, his ideas considered. But, more important than his educational background and abilities is the fact that his spiritual 'knowledge' is unshakably established, which is undoubtedly the foundation of his book and his life.

This book and its president must be regarded as an altogether different dimension of presidential leadership. It represents a possibility, inconceivable to the general electorate and politicians alike. Why? Because such perception, insight and knowing, exhibited by Tremaine, are not learned or acquired through any kind of training. Such wisdom can only be bestowed by the grace of the Divine. Only when wisdom is experienced directly within one's being does it have power and legitimacy. Can such wisdom really be shared in the political arena? Perhaps, but only through the form of "selfless service," depicted, for instance, in the story of Tremaine. Tremaine serves truly and totally because he has no personal stake in anything. His actions are for the good of his people, his country, and the world. While alive and thriving, operating on full throttle, he is dead to himself.

President Tremaine is at once both spiritual and human. He's a man who has sinned, a man transformed, an honest man in his personal life and his life as a politician.

Mr. President offers the reader a glimpse into the life of an unusual man, a presidential candidate, a man who might appear somewhat alien, foreign, and outlandish to some. But that's exactly the quality that is needed today. The time for one-dimensional, shallow politicians who are motivated by personal gain, fame and power is over. After reading this book, citizens will discern more clearly between the substance and the froth, between the human qualities of presidential candidates and their respective promises.

It's certain that a president will be elected in 1996, and it's equally certain that President Tremaine, will be alive in many people's hearts as the first enlightened presidet of the country.

May the year 2000 make the dream of an enlightened American leadership come true, if God so wills. After all, since the idea appeared in my friend's book of today, perhaps the manifestation is not too far away.
Inshallah!!!

Madhukar
Bombay, India
December 19, 1995

Preface

Many novels are purely entertaining, the content beyond recall a month after reading them. *Mr. President* is a novel complete with excitement, suspense and pathos. It is an illuminating book, not easily forgotten. It induces a thought process, a questioning about human behavior, about relationships between individuals, and, in the larger sphere, about the connections between people of different religions and cultures. David Tremaine, the new America president, creates turmoil as well as hope with the pragmatic honesty of his governing. He brings the same honest approach to the age-old conflicts of the Middle East.

The story is not simply confined to those in high places, but involves men and organizations dedicated to violence to secure their objectives, and on the other hand, those men and women seeking peace and comfort through understanding and love, though they themselves suffer the agonies of violence.

War, violence and inhumanity are still rampant across the world. Though the solution to it seems remote, bold and honest leadership can accomplish much, as the case of Tremaine illustrates. However, such leadership can best operate in societies where support is given by those people who themselves are imbued with the necessity to share and care, to be tolerant and understanding, to have reverence for life, and above all to behave for the common good—beyond both political and religious dogmas.

I urge all who govern or aspire to, to read this book—from presidents and prime ministers to municipal councilors and non-government community leaders. It brings a message of hope for the future, to those who have become skeptical of human behavior.

A powerful message for self-honesty and honesty with one's fellow human beings suffuses *Mr. President,* and is both heart-warming and thought-provoking. It is a message to be translated into reality.

Not often does a father have the opportunity to praise his son's achievement publicly. In this instance I do so with respect, gratitude and love.

Derrick Mallard
Victoria, Canada
February 11, 1996

Shall we begin?

"When a building is under construction, a plumb line is used to ensure the walls are true. In life it is difficult to know what is real."

"Why?"

"Because we live with shadings of truth. We portray life the way we want it to be, not the way it is. Often we are disappointed. A truthful man describes life as it is; he is never disappointed. Only a man like this can distinguish between the real and the imagined. He is like a plumb line."

"How can we know what is real in this day and age?"

"Let me tell you a story of an American president and a Sufi sage. Not unlike the Roman Emperor Marcus Aurelius or the Indian king Janaka, they were men of wisdom, men who had awakened."

"What do you mean by awakened?"

"Life is like a novel and we are the author. While writing, we are immersed in the plot, a participant in the drama. Our consciousness is focused, our formlessness defined. We've forgotten who we are. Awakening is nothing more than remembering."

"What is so special about awakening?"

"Nothing. When we go to a play it's easy to be immersed in the events on the stage. When the play is over we go home. Imagine being an actor so immersed in the play you forget who you are. You genuinely suffer from events talking place before you. When you remember who you are, you still play the part but no longer are you overwhelmed by sorrow, nor seduced by desire. You see life as it is; great entertainment!"

"Are there really those who are truthful?"

"Of course."

"What makes them truthful?"

"They know who they are and so are not afraid."

"I doubt whether a man such as you've described would ever become president."

"I agree, but if he did, how might it be?"

CHAPTER 1

It was Friday morning, the day after Christmas. Above the mountains to the east, a fiery sun burned in a cloudless sky. The street still in the shadow of tall buildings, was a hive of activity. Local merchants opened their stores, sliding back the iron grates, removing shutters, and wheeling out the display carts loaded with produce. Along the street, traffic was heavy, impeded by trucks unloading fruit and vegetables from the kibbutz. Haggling was a way of life in most Mediterranean cities and Tel Aviv was no exception. Another busy day had begun.

The bus, filled with passengers on their way to work, pulled onto the street and joined the rush of traffic, its klaxon horns adding to the din of early morning. Through an open window a young girl watched, mesmerized by the activity of the shop-keepers, red hair blowing in the wind from the moving bus. It was still too early for the breeze to stir off the water, clearing away the fumes of diesel, gasoline and oil.

Above the cacophony of sounds, doves tumbled in play.

Then, with a thunderous roar, the bus blew apart. A bright sheet of orange flame shot upward, sending metal fragments and body parts in every direction. The force of the blast shattered windows up and down the street.

A dreadful silence followed. Then the moans and blood-curdling screams of the injured riveted the attention. Lurid yellow flames with black smoke flickered in the empty shell of the bus. Nearby several cars lay on their sides; one spun slowly on its roof. Next to the destroyed bus, a large truck leaned at an odd angle, crushing the car beside it. The driver was dead, his head bloody on his chest.

People in the street ran in every direction. A nurse ran, too, but toward the bus. Climbing up the side, she pulled herself into the burning wreckage to check for survivors. In moments she was joined by others, and as quickly and carefully as possible, they removed the injured before flames could reach them.

The red haired girl lay pinned beneath the twisted seats, a shard of metal protruding from a bloody shoulder beneath a shattered collar bone. Two men lifted the twisted seat. A third bent down, and together he and the nurse lifted the girl off a metal spike. She groaned and passed out. Ripping pieces from his shirt, the man handed them to the nurse. She glanced up and found herself looking into the green eyes of her husband.

Bunching up the pieces of shirt, she stuffed them into the bloody wounds and quickly bound them tight. Then carefully they lifted the girl over the side to waiting hands and safety. In the distance, sirens wailed. Looking around the bus, she saw that no one was left alive. She climbed down to see what else she could do.

....

That evening, just before sunset, a well-dressed man went to a phone booth on a busy street. Like any other businessman in that section of the city, he went unnoticed.

However, what he said did not. With the phone to his ear he waited. He heard a click, and a woman's voice came on the line. "Good evening," she said, "can I help you?"

"Yes. Listen closely. That bus this morning— it was the work of Hamas. We will never allow a dishonorable peace. We are not afraid to die. Allah is great!" The man hung up the phone, turned and hurried away. Joining a crowd in front of the synagogue, he adjusted his yarmulke, and entered the building.

CHAPTER 2

David had agreed to speak at his alma mater. He arrived in Boston in the late afternoon, leaving enough time to shower, get something to eat and look over his notes. Other than the Secret Service agents, he was alone. Sandra had remained in Washington. It had been hectic around the funeral and she'd asked to stay behind.

Half an hour before the speech David and two Secret Service agents drove to the university and entered the chapel from the rear. An arched corridor joined it to the School of Theology on one side and the School of Philosophy on the other. A most appropriate arrangement, David had always thought.

The chapel itself stood back from the large trees on Commonwealth Avenue, making a spacious quadrangle in front; behind, the Charles River slipped quietly to the sea. The building was designed in the tradition of a European church with sandstone, stained glass windows, high Gothic arches and flying buttresses.

Sitting back, David looked over a sea of expectant faces. Dr. Menzies, the president of the university, stood at the podium introducing him. Floodlights lit the stained glass in brilliant colors and gave the chapel an almost festive air. He'd not been here for more than two decades; he'd been a graduate student at the time, living in an apartment on Commonwealth Avenue, several hundred yards from where he now sat.

Twenty-two years ago, at three thirty in the morning, he awakened to the tolling of the chapel bells. It was a prearranged signal, and in less than a minute he flew down the stairs and into the cool night. For days he'd slept in his clothes, anticipating what he hoped would never come. As he'd raced from the apartment, he saw unmarked cars lining the deserted avenue in front of the chapel. In the open quadrangle, more than a dozen police cars were parked haphazardly, some with doors still open. His heart pounded and his mouth was dry.

A small crowd gathered at the entrance. He raced across the empty street and pushed his way through the crowd to the top of the steps. Light spilled through the open doors into the darkness. Blocking the entrance were members of Boston's finest.

The chapel was packed, and the quiet sobbing of a woman hung in the tense silence. The center aisle was clear, but at the end of each aisle a marshal blocked the way, preventing anyone from leaving. As David watched, three federal agents emerged from the stairs behind the altar. They half-lifted and half-dragged a young man down the aisle toward the open doors where David stood.

It was Stephen, the young soldier to whom David and four other students had offered the sanctuary of the church. Stephen's shirt was torn, and he was missing a shoe. One of the marshals held him by the hair, pulling his head back. Two others flanked him, holding his arms pinioned, the fingers bent as though they would break. The men were red in the face, unused to such exertion.

Stephen was white, deathly white. His black, neatly cropped mustache and hair accentuated the pallor. His dark eyes were large and frightened. He was obviously in pain. As he was pushed, lifted and dragged down the aisle, the refrain "We shall overcome..." burst from a thousand throats. Those in the chapel swayed from side to side, their hands crossed and joined in front.

Efficiently and forcefully police officers cleared a path through which Stephen was quickly propelled. Reaching the bottom of the steps, they dragged the young soldier across the courtyard and into the open door of a nearby car. Quickly marshals and police filed from the chapel and entered the waiting cars. With roaring engines and screeching tires, the cars sped away.

It was over in a matter of minutes. The refrain of the song filled the sad night, while the tolling of the chapel bells signaled an end to the Marsh Chapel sanctuary. For five days Stephen sought sanctuary from the church, refusing to join his unit scheduled to leave for Vietnam. He believed the war was wrong and wanted no part of the killing. To this end David and four fellow students, in the tradition of the medieval church, took it upon themselves to grant Stephen sanctuary in the university chapel.

Dr. Menzies turned, and with a smile gestured David to the podium. "Please welcome Dr. David Tremaine, President of the United States of America." Thunderous applause filled the chapel.

With a jolt David returned to the present. He stood and shook the outstretched hand then waited at the podium for silence, glad of the few moments to collect his wits. Setting aside his notes he gazed into the young faces before him. When silence returned, he began to speak.

"One day in Bombay while riding in a taxi, a friend I was with asked me, 'What did the yogi say to the vendor at the hot dog stand?' I looked at him and laughed, but couldn't think of an answer. 'Make me one with everything,' he said."

David waited for the laughter to subside. "Sitting here, I found myself remembering the last time I was in this chapel. It was more than twenty years ago and our country was engaged in a war that many believed was a terrible mistake, a mistake that cost the lives of Americans and Vietnamese alike. Some went to war to serve their country; others refused, and by refusing, they also sought to serve their country. To this day, too many Americans consider those who went to war patriots and those who did not, traitors or cowards. I was in the latter category. Convinced that the war represented a terrible and costly mistake, I found myself in active opposition to it.

"After graduate school I watched a decline in the integrity of those who served in government. The resignation of Richard Nixon signalled the beginning; Iran Contra continued the legacy. Since then. service has too often been perverted by selfish interests. I despaired that government could ever again be what our founding fathers had foreseen and hoped for. And so it was that I turned my back on political service. The interest always remained, however, and I was an ardent observer and enjoyer of politics with its attempts to govern, create and implement social policy. To be an active participator in it was the furthest thing from my mind. But then the gods intervened and presented me with the unexpected, an opportunity to be president.

"The Republicans had held the White House for twelve years and showed little inclination to surrender it. It was generally accepted that their hold on power was so strong that no Democratic contender would risk either the expense or his good name for what seemed like certain defeat.

"When Emerson agreed to stand as the Democratic candidate, he was a token representative, put forth to provide a voice of opposition to the Republicans. A small cog in a meaningless ritual of futility, called the presidential race. That was not how he saw himself, however. He was a good and honest man. He spoke truthfully of what he saw. I knew him for years and had a great respect for him. When he asked me to accept his nomination as vice president I felt sure we would not, indeed could not, be elected. However, after giving it some thought I accepted his invitation.

"Emerson might have regretted his choice of a running-mate because of the firestorm of controversy which greeted the nomination. For as you may remember, my stance on Vietnam was brought to the fore, and in the headlines I was charged, judged and condemned. Though I offered to withdraw from the ticket, Emerson stood beside me. 'You and I,' he said, 'signify the healing of old wounds, wounds brought about by differences of opinion concerning a war: you, a representative of those who opposed to it, I a representative of those who fought in it. Unquestionably both of us were interested in the well-being of our country.'

"During the campaign, disgust with the government was apparent. The administration tried to deflect attention from the Iran Contra scandal, but as more and more details became known, the administration's election campaign faltered. For the first time, whispers of a possible Republican defeat began to circulate. Some of the early Democratic presidential hopefuls, those who had held back, were kicking themselves for not having entered the race after all.

"When the Japanese government collapsed in scandal two weeks before the election, few thought much of it. Engrossed as we were, in what had become a quixotic tilt at the windmills of power. But as revelations from Japan spilled into the papers and dominated the news, the administration's duplicity constituted a betrayal of the public trust. As we all know, the cost to the country was enormous in both jobs and finances. Exactly how much money filtered to the leading lights of the Republican administration may never be known. These events determined the election and took the Republicans down to a crushing defeat. So, in a way, it was defeat, not victory, which brought Emerson to the presidency.

"Though it might be nice to believe otherwise, we were not elected for what we stood or because we were Democrats. We were elected because anything seemed better than the government before us, and the past twelve years of Republican rule that led up to it. But, the fact is we did stand for something. Emerson had, in his own unique way, injected the simple values of common sense, decency and accountability when he spoke to the electorate.

"For the twelve months of his presidency, he worked to restore the integrity of government and the nation as a whole. As you know, he met with constant criticism and was ridiculed and reviled by the press and the disgraced opposition. Through it all, he never lost sight of his goals nor his sense of humor.

"For a year he sought to educate the American people. He saw it as his job. He knew hearts and minds had to be weaned from petty thinking and selfish actions. He knew that neither the House nor Senate would pass constructive legislation without the collective will of the people instructing them to do so. To that end he spoke often with the American people, explaining what he sought to do with the decisions he was taking. Carefully he attempted to prepare the people for the changes that would come, both the wanted and the unwanted.

"Not once did he avoid issues; not once did he gloss over the difficulties. He said, 'I'd rather we anticipate the worst and be pleasantly surprised, than anticipate the best only to suffer disappointment. People are tired of being told things aren't so bad, only to discover they're worse than anyone expected. We must be honest with people. In the end it is the only way to restore the nation's health. We can no longer afford to put off what must be done today.'

"I think the American people began to respect and appreciate this little man with a big heart. At least, they began to realize that he spoke truthfully whether they liked it or not. There was a stirring in the population, which, from my perspective, showed a willingness to wake up and face the difficulties before us.

"On that Tuesday when he knew he was dying, he and I talked through the night. At three in the morning he gathered his wife and two daughters at his bedside to say good-bye. When the coming sun lit the eastern sky, he slipped into unconsciousness and died several hours later. I left his side determined to carry out the work we had begun.

"In this chapel, more than twenty years ago, five students took it upon themselves to grant 'sanctuary' to a young soldier who refused to follow the orders of his commander-in-chief. He was a young man with hopes and dreams like you, but one who said, 'I cannot in good conscience take up a gun to kill those called my enemy in a cause I consider hopeless and terribly wrong.' I don't know what happened to him. I only know his sincerity and clarity left an indelible impression upon me.

"As a nation we're beset by problems that will only be resolved when we as a people are willing to face facts. As a nation and as citizens of the world, we can combine our creative abilities to resolve the difficulties before us. Our nation is beset with violence and crime, yet we have little comprehension of its cause. Despite the fact that we're one of the most technologically advanced nations in the world, too many of our citizens lack even adequate medical coverage. There are problems of poverty, racial inequality and misunderstanding, violence and crime.

Only by understanding the root of these problems will we be able to do anything about them. Patience and persistence are needed, for what we face was not created in a day.

"A transition is under way in the new global market. It is a time of unprecedented change, unprecedented opportunity, and unprecedented challenges. The old definitions of work are changing and we must adapt, learn to be creative and skillful again.

"We live in a democracy, and from an early age we've come to believe it's the best form of government the world has ever known. But let me ask you a question. Does this democracy, in the form in which we practice it today, really help us to live full and productive lives? If we look carefully and speak honestly, the answer for too many of us is *no*. With that in mind I propose that we, as a nation, engage in a great undertaking; that we look honestly at our problems; that we seek the deepest possible understanding and apply the creative genius of the human mind by turning problems into assets, difficulties into opportunities. I urge you to take up President Kennedy's challenge: 'Ask not what your country can do for you, ask instead, what you can do for your country.' The invitation he extended still stands. Let us accept it.

"I would add, let us work hard to resolve the difficulties that face not just our own nation but the planet as a whole. We the people who make up the nations of the world are interconnected. Destruction of the rain forests affects us all. Our use of gasoline and oil pollutes not just the cities of our own country but the whole planet. Third world countries buy Japanese cars that are made more affordable because they lack pollution control devices. The result is a staggering cost in ill health and shortened lifespan for its citizens.

"We must care for each other. We *are* our brother's keeper. Modern communication brings with it a greater awareness of different cultures, while beneath our differences, the similarity of the human heart remains the same. The truth is that human beings, regardless of their nationality, their religion or their culture, are one single family: the family of mankind. We must not forget this. Thank you."

The students were on their feet and filled the chapel with applause. David stood quietly, waiting untill they sat down. "If you've any questions, I'll do my best to answer them." Hands waved in the air. David pointed to a well-dressed young man with brown curly hair.

"You have said in the past that democracy has certain flaws. Can you explain what you mean?"

"Yes. The United States has long been looked upon with respect for what is known as the American Dream. And what was that dream? Essentially, it held that those who worked hard would realize a reward commensurate with their efforts. If the quality of their work was excellent, if they were honest, accountable and hard working, they could expect to live reasonably well, free of economic deprivation, within a society that safeguarded the various freedoms so readily taken for granted.

"Although as a society we still lay claim to this dream, we've parlayed it into a nightmare. At a deep and fundamental level, we've lost the vision and replaced it with the idea of "something for nothing."

"In psychological terms this represents a failure to deal with reality. Because of this we've elected politicians who've been afraid to tell us the truth. Most householders understand that you cannot spend what you don't have. Yes, from time to time, we can and do borrow money to pay for the things we want. But, we promise to repay what we borrow in a reasonable time. If we keep borrowing, we eventually lose the capacity to repay the loan.

"We want and expect many things. We want insurance,

medical services, jobs, welfare, unemployment insurance and social security. Every time there's a flood or a hurricane and we expect government to help. This can be expected, but it costs money. And the truth is, we've been unwilling to pay for it. If a politician tells us it will cost "X" amount of dollars and suggests it be raised by taxes, we vote him out of office. If we attempt to downsize government, members of the affected bureaucracies, backed by the unions, find ways to prevent it.

"Recent administrations bought the affection of the people by giving them many of the things they wanted. The taxes collected did not meet the cost of the services provided. The result was, that government had to borrow money and increase the national debt. For the first time in our history, payment on the interest of the debt alone has become a drain upon our resources.

"Who's responsible for this? I know it's fashionable to blame the Republican administrations, but they fed us what we wanted. So the truth of the matter is that we the people are responsible! All of us. Like it or not, we're the ones who've coerced our politicians into borrowing money by threatening to vote them out of office should they increase our taxes, or tell the truth we do not wish to hear.

"We want something for nothing. It cannot work that way for long. We must grow up; it's time we stopped seeing the government as the enemy. We are the government, and in a representative government such as ours, the collective will of the people is reflected by its representatives.

"Lincoln said that democracy is government of the people *by* the people, and it's true; we govern ourselves. Recently, we've not done so well."

David pointed to a student in the front row.

"You said earlier that you had turned your back on government, that it had become corrupt and the idea of service had been lost. Then you say that we must stop seeing the government as the enemy. That seems like a contradiction. Can you explain what you mean?"

"Yes! The corruption of government and the perversion of the idea of service have occurred simultaneously, both in the population as a whole, and in government itself. When we send men and women into government service. We expect them to perform miracles, to solve our problems, yet we refuse to give them the needed support, respect and finances to do so. We want something for nothing. When we don't get it, we look for a scapegoat, and government officials are easy targets.

"We cleverly proclaim that 'only death and taxes are certain,' and smile with smug self-importance as those around us nod their heads in agreement. Within the population as a whole, we are dishonest. It is reflected in our government as well.

"There's no way around it: *We* are the government. Government like ours represents, for good and ill, the collective consciousness of the nation as a whole.

"If we have a flat tire, we must repair the tire, not the transmission. When we point honestly to the cause, we'll discover we point to ourselves.

"Yes."

David pointed to another student.

"You have said the human mind is the cause of our difficulties and also that it is one of our greatest assets. Can you elaborate?"

"In the process of life itself we encounter certain difficulties; such is the nature of life. When this happens, the mind develops solutions to cope with them. For instance, insects presented problems to certain agricultural pursuits. DDT was developed and solved the problem, or so it seemed.

"Then the solution became the problem because DDT got into the food chain, and we began to poison not just the insects, the plants and animals, but ourselves as well.

"We know that soil in flood plains is rich, so we cultivate it and even build our homes in areas susceptible to floods. We get flooded and then build levies to prevent the flooding to our homes. We prevent the flooding only to discover we no longer have the natural enrichment of soil which comes as a result of flooding.

"Rather than build houses on difficult terrain such as on mountainsides, we build them in river deltas then wonder why we've so little soil to grow the food we need.

"We irrigate desert valleys and produce good crops for a time, only to discover that because we blocked the natural flow of rivers, the valleys cannot be adequately flushed, and so our fertile land reverts to infertility again.

"Our emphasis on safety prevents us from taking care of ourselves in certain situations. We like the idea of being taken care of. We have unemployment insurance and welfare to help us over difficult times. After a while, we become dependent on it, and our creative abilities decline. Without these safety nets we'd be more ingenious in order to survive, better able to care for our families.

"The rise of trade unions helped put an end to the abuse of workers. Today the trade unions are a problem themselves. They've perpetuated such things as feather-bedding and contributed directly to the decline of productivity. They're instrumental in the loss of joy and satisfaction that comes from pride in workmanship.

"When Japanese products first came on the market, they were poorly constructed and earned the label "junk." Now Japanese products are synonymous with technical excellence and quality of workmanship.

"Even the Japanese success has led to its share of problems. Large trade imbalances have, in a certain way, temporarily upset the balance of global trade, negatively affecting certain countries. These countries will in turn respond to the situation and make improvements in the quality of their work and become more proficient in what they do.

"And so it goes, on and on. But, that's what makes it interesting. The examples I've cited demonstrate what I said. The mind is the cause of our difficulties, and also one of our greatest assets. We use the human mind to create solutions to existing problems, and in so doing end up creating others. Without this process, life would be dull and boring.

"Nature is subject to the cycles of the seasons, the cycles of ice ages and so on. We can see similar cycles exist in the affairs of humankind. Many of these cycles are from interactions of human minds with one another, on a large collective scale; and with the natural environment as a whole.

"The great civilizations of the Chinese, Greeks, Romans, Aztecs, Mayans, Indians, even the more recent civilizations of the Portuguese, Spanish, British, and even Americans are subject to the same cycles. They grow, flourish for a time, and then slowly wither and die. It's a reflection of the human mind over long periods of time and is referred to as human history."

A young woman with short brown hair and granny glasses stood up.

"You said we must come to understand our problems. Can you say more about that?"

"Real understanding must come by facing facts. By that I mean seeing things as they are, not the way we want them to be, or according to any particular social or political theory. The good scientist takes into account what lies before him. He does not discard that which fails to fit his preconceived notions. Sometimes he's forced to allow apparent contradictions to coexist. In time the mind resolves the contradictions by bringing about a new level of understanding.

"As a nation we can stop blaming others and carefully explore the difficulties we face. In so doing the solutions make themselves known. Those of us called upon to represent this nation through its government must be willing to transcend party lines and party prejudices. If a man is the best in his field for a job, he should be chosen without regard to his political affiliations. When the Republicans have good ideas, we must use them. It takes all kinds of people with all kinds of insight to resolve the problems before us."

"Can you give an example of seeing things as they are?"

"I said earlier that we face many challenges, some of which stem from greed and selfishness. To see what they stem from is insufficient. What is it that we seek to accomplish through our greed and selfishness? If we look carefully, we'll see that we hope to gain some measure of security, happiness, peace of mind, success or something that these words represent. Now this is where facing facts comes in. Does greed and selfishness grant us what we hope for? They don't, do they? By facing facts, we come to understand what doesn't work. After that we can begin to discover what does."

"Can you be more specific?"

"How many of you here have attempted to help in time of crisis, be it an accident, a flood or storm or even gathering in a harvest before a pending rain?

"I can see by your hands that most of you have had that experience. Now I ask you, was there a sense of satisfaction in what you did? For most of you, the answer is *yes*. So, from this simple example we see that the acts of greedy and selfish men do not bring satisfaction, while the generous acts of those who spontaneously seek to help, do. For this reason the Peace Corps has been an enduring and deeply appreciated organization, both at home and abroad."

"Mr. President, you said that democracy has several

flaws, and I only heard you speak of one. Are there more?"

"Because we accept majority rule in a democracy, we have a tendency toward mediocrity and at times broadly based prejudices. Prior to the Civil War the idea of slavery was subscribed to by the majority. Widespread acceptance didn't make it right. Today politicians are elected to represent our views. What if our views are limited, narrow and shortsighted? What if we're blind on issues of race? Must we perpetuate racism?

"To me, a politician is not only a representative of the people; he's also an educator. He must challenge people's ideas in such a way as to provoke a genuine exploration of issues. Like Socrates, he must be a gadfly to the people. He must help to uncover the hidden fears with which we are all beset and seek to address them.

"Keep in mind most of the difficulties we face come about because of human nature. Therefore, this education of which I speak must necessarily bring about self-understanding at a very basic level. With self-understanding, we may learn to communicate more effectively with each other.

"Though the majority may rule in a democracy, there must be appreciation for the minorities. On one side of the majority we encounter the fear and hatred that derives from misunderstanding. Here we see rigid belief structures and extremists such as the KKK, Neo Nazis, militias and so on. On the other side we encounter the clear seeing, the visions of the dreamers, visions the majority has yet to discover.

"More than anything else, let us convey to the people that *they* are the government. The government does not exist but for them. Therefore, *we* the *people,* both the governed and the governing, are the ones who must resolve our difficulties. No one else can do it for us. As I mentioned, we must give up this childish attitude of complaining that the government is the source of our problems, while crying that the same government is not doing enough when we're in need. We can't have it both ways.

"We can discover a better way to register the interests of the people than the ways we have at present. The Political Action Committees wield too much power, and the large sums of money they dispense corrupt too many of our elected officials. I don't blame the officials, for I doubt there are many who would not be tempted by such wealth."

"I disagree, sir." All eyes turned toward the fourth row where a dark-haired woman in her early forties stood and faced Tremaine. "Your point is well taken, but integrity and personal accountability are critical. Our system of government lends itself to corruption and must be changed. One way we can change it is by electing representatives of high integrity and holding them accountable.

"I have felt for a long time that no one can get elected to high office without becoming corrupt. This is where fundamental change is needed. How can a genuinely caring person who wants effective change get elected?"

"I appreciate your comments. No matter what kind of system we have, we'll not remove corruption completely. Corruption is found wherever human beings are found. It is the province of selfishness. But, there are things we can do that will make it less tempting. Let us as a nation address this question. Let politics attract from our midst, the flower of our people, those who sincerely seek to serve; let us once more discover the joy of selfless service.

"Thank you for being here this evening. I've enjoyed talking with you and look forward to more of the same. Thank you for your kind attention and the excellent questions you raised." With that Tremaine turned and shook Dr. Menzies' outstretched hand, turned and walked quickly down the steps and exited from the rear, accompanied by Secret Service Agents.

CHAPTER 3

It was late when David arrived at the White House. He still had difficulty getting used to the idea that this was home. He went straight to the bedroom. Sandra lay propped against the pillows reading. As he sat beside her on the bed, she took his hand, and kissed it affectionately.

"How did it go?" she asked.

"Pretty good. You'd think I'd know better than to take notes; I never use them. Anyway, it was enjoyable. I just talked, let them know what was on my mind. They seemed appreciative and asked good questions. I like that kind of thing."

"How long is it since you were last there? It must have been the late seventies, wasn't it?"

"It was. This time we met in the chapel which brought back a flood of memories. Anyway, it was a start, a break from the country's mourning. In fact, it was a good place to pick up where Emerson left off."

"I always enjoyed the intellectual give and take of students; they always seem less jaundiced and more open to the exploration of ideas."

David nodded, it was what he liked too. He looked at her, glad to be home and in her presence again. "How was your day?" he asked.

"We finished the living quarters the way I want them. I had lots of help, of course. I find the lack of privacy here quite annoying. We've got to do something about it."

"I agree!"

"Lacy came over this afternoon. We had tea and talked for several hours."

"How is she?"

"As well as can be expected. She's decided to move back to the farm. She's glad to be out of the White House and is looking forward to being in the country again."

"When do they leave?"

"Next weekend."

"How is she handling Emerson's death?"

"She cries easily and says she keeps looking for him, expecting him to show up. She said it's especially hard to go places where they used to go together, knowing they'll never do that again. It's sinking in that he's dead and not coming back."

"How are the girls?"

"She says they're doing well. Crying a lot. Sometimes they all cry! They talk about Emerson and the things they did together. They've been going through his personal effects. Did you know he kept a journal filled with poems he wrote?"

"I didn't, but I'm not surprised."

"He began writing in the early sixties while an undergraduate student, and the last poem he wrote was the evening before he died. Lacy said it's like a journal of his life. Over the years he read some of the poems to her, but she hadn't realized how much he wrote. Each evening for the past week, she and the girls have taken turns reading the poems. There's lots of tears, but I think it's good for them."

"Probably."

"Anyway, she was very helpful. She said she and Emerson had some difficulty getting used to the White House, and she thought we might, too. She was funny. Said she felt she was living in a museum, and was afraid to sit on the furniture. The only way she could handle it was that she and Emerson made it into their home."

"How did they do that?"

"They insisted on more privacy and changed some of the procedures. She said they met stiff resistance. The argument they heard constantly was 'this is the way we do things here.' Breaking that kind of thinking was hard, but they had some success. She suspected it would soon revert to its old form and we'd have to begin all over again."

"I can imagine."

"Well, that was my day. Are you ready to come to bed?"

"I'll take a shower then read for a while. I'm not tired. I've a meeting with the chairman of the Joint Chiefs in the morning."

He squeezed her hand and, getting up, went into the bathroom.

David luxuriated in the shower as though washing off the accumulation from his first week as President. He read for a couple of hours before going to bed. Coming back to the bedroom he found Sandra asleep, the book she was reading open on her chest. Gently, he put the book away and slid in beside her. She stirred and snuggled close to him.

He found his mind drifting back to their first meeting. He'd loved her from the start, although he'd not realized it at the time.

....

David had been invited to Vancouver to speak on a book he'd written. Because of the proximity of Whistler and Blackcombe, he rented a car and drove inland to the skii resort. He had the use of a friends condo for a week. Situated in the village of Whistler it was in easy walking distance of the lifts. He loved skiing. At the end of the first day, he was, as usual, one of the last off the run. The sun was obscured by the mountain when he reached the bottom. He carried his skis to the condo and put them away.

Afterward he wandered through the village. It had been several years since he'd been there, and he had to familiarize himself with it again. The village was crowded with skiers, with bright-colored clothes and red, windburned faces. Laughter, the murmur of voices and music filled the crisp air. Everyone seemed in a festive mood. It was one of the things he liked about skiing: it put people in a happy mood.

He entered a small English-style pub and ordered a McEwans. He sipped his beer slowly, glad to take the weight off his feet. His body tingled, and his face felt flushed and hot. He relaxed and enjoyed the pleasing effect of the beer as he listened to the friendly conversations and laughter that surrounded him. The pub was packed and yet, despite the crush of people, he felt alone, and was quite comfortable in being so.

She came out of nowhere and asked to sit with him, "No more empty chairs," she explained. She was tall, standing by his table, her head bent toward him. Light from the ceiling framed the dark hair with an aura of reflected gold. She wore a red ski jacket over a navy blue sweater that accentuated her unusually dark eyes. Eyes that were large, open and quiet. A hint of mischief lurked at the corner of her mouth. But it was the eyes that drew his attention. They seemed to sparkle from the light in the room while beneath the surface he sensed a quality of utter stillness. There was an ease about her which he liked at once.

They'd talked of skiing and the different areas on the mountain, about which he was unfamiliar. He learned she was a nurse working for a home health agency on Vancouver Island.

Before long their conversation drifted to a recent trip she'd made to India and Nepal. She'd gone to study Buddhism and art and had offered her services as a nurse. She spent nine months there.

"It helped me get a better perspective on life," she said. "I traveled in the north and spent a month in Benares, which is where those who are ill go to bathe in the Ganges before they die."

"Why did you go there?"

"Benares or India?" she asked with a smile.

"India."

"I think I wanted to get a perspective on Canada and my life here. I also felt drawn there and had the idea I might be of help. Now I see what a condescending attitude I had. How arrogant we are, how arrogant were our forefathers who settled North America."

"What do you mean?"

"I went to India thinking that as a Westerner I had something special to bring to the poor suffering people of this third world country. I think Christian missionaries must have much the same attitude wherever they go, too. As a result they fail to see what lies before them. In some cases, I'm sure, they must stand in the presence of enlightened masters with no awareness of who stands before them. The Greeks had a term for this; they called it *hubris*, which means, 'overweening pride.'

"I mistakanly believed that when people are poor and suffering, they can't be happy. I hoped to bring them a measure of happiness. So it was a shock for me when one day I realized that most of the people I met seemed relatively happy, despite appalling circumstances and terrible physical diseases."

"Was it hard to adjust to Western life when you came back to Canada?"

"It was. The last two months I spent in Nepal, six weeks of which was spent in a Buddhist convent in silent meditation. The village was small, and so was the population. When I came out I was shocked to find people everywhere. What had been a sleepy little village was now teeming and overcrowded.

"The Dali Lama was the next day, and thousands of Tibetans, Nepalese and Indians had come to the village to listen to him. So that was the first shock. When he came, I joined the others and listened to his discourses.

"Shortly afterward I was on a plane to New York for a connection to Vancouver. When I arrived in New York I found my father had changed my ticket. He wanted me to spend time with my sister, who was having a rough time. She lived in Toronto. So there I was, one day in Nepal, and two days later walking down Yonge Street with a sister who was bored with life and upset that she couldn't have everything she wanted when she wanted it. That was a shock. Life seemed completely unreal; I felt as though I was in a dream.

"India and Nepal affected me a lot. I learned that what was important had nothing to do with wealth or power, or our position in society, who we know or who we don't. For the first time in my life I was overwhelmed at the waste in our society, particularly in our cities. I realized we're cut off from nature, and have lost the sense of our own mortality.

"What also struck me was the realization that for many Westerners there is a deep and disturbing emptiness, untouched by anything we have. It seems to me that nothing in our culture will satisfy this hunger, not even the religious practices and beliefs of our churches."

"You seem pessimistic about all of this," David interjected.

"No, I don't feel that way. I think this hunger, this emptiness was necessary because it turned many of us away from Western thinking and Western values."

"How do you mean?"

"Well, the Beatles, with their music, long hair, irreverent ways and drugs, spoke to many of us of what we sensed as the hypocrisy of our society. We listened to them, and when they introduced us to the Maharishi, a window to India was opened."

"What makes you think that was important?" David asked.

"I think India has for a long time been the spiritual heart of the planet. The strange paradox was that among a large number of the Indians I met, there was a strong desire to live in the West and, failing that, to emulate Western values. They wanted to bring India into the fold of Western technology, hoping affluence would follow."

"Why do you think that is?"

"What I saw in India and Nepal was that the culture as a whole was deeply religious. That religiousness, however, was superficial in the sense that it represented a literal adherence to thousands of beliefs. The great spiritual truths were obscured by these beliefs and by the spiritual practices of millions of the people. In India there is a constant preoccupation with the outward observances of religious dogma.

"I think an increasing number of Indians are beginning to sense the emptiness of such a way of life. So what do they turn to in their search? Images of America. They believe materialism and technological sophistication can fill that emptiness.

"In the West, on the other hand, we've already tasted this fruit and found it does not bring lasting satisfaction. And, no matter how we attempt to repackage the rituals and religious beliefs of modern Christianity, they do not fill the emptiness we feel. The worldview of Christianity is too limited. The result is that more and more are turning to India, and some are finding what they seek.

"If there's so much superficiality of belief, as you've said, why would anyone want to turn to another superficial system?" David asked.

Sandra thought for a moment. "The answer, I think, lies in the fact that despite the prevalence of religious superficiality, there are probably more enlightened men and women in India than in any other country in the world. I know of very few enlightened masters in the Americas. Now, why is that? Perhaps the lack stems from the fact that in the West we have social and cultural freedom accompanied by a lack of freedom, in the realm of ideas and spiritual understanding.

"In India, on the other hand, they have the opposite. The power of the caste system is strong; there is little social or cultural freedom, whereas in the realm of ideas and spiritual understanding the mind is free to soar."

"What makes you say that we in the West lack the freedom to explore new ideas?"

"There is still fear in your society when it comes to exploring spiritual and philosophical ideas. Christianity is one religion among many. It arose as a direct result of the life and teaching of the enlightened Jewish master, Jesus. Before the time of Jesus there had been other enlightened masters, such as the Buddha, Lao Tsu, Ashtavakra and so on. All of these masters, including Jesus, spoke of the truth and attempted to stimulate in their listeners the direct understanding they'd realized themselves.

"The further removed the followers were from the master, the more the teachings assumed the characteristics of beliefs. But Christians and Muslims were unique in a certain disturbing way.

"They assumed their beliefs constituted the one true

description of the way. The corollary to this assertion is that all other teachings are false. This thinking denied them access to living masters because, according to them, the last great masters were Jesus and Mohammed.

The results of such narrow-minded thinking led these two great religious bodies into the inevitable bloodshed of the Crusades and conflict in the Middle East.

"All such rigid religious thinking has led, sooner or later, to religious warfare. The inquisitions that spread across Europe cost the lives of millions of people and were the direct result of intolerance for anything but accepted doctrines. Freedom of thought was prohibited on pain of death.

"People believed it was better for others to die at the stake than to be eternally lost in the fires of hell. Such thinking had a profound effect upon our European forebears.

"In your country it gave rise to the separation of church and state. In fact your Declaration of Independence, even the founding of your nation and the formulation of its constitution were a direct result of a deeply held desire for freedom of thought, in the pursuit of happiness. But even so, eighteenth and nineteenth century Christianity has left an indelible impression on the collective psyche of the Americas, North and South."

They'd finished their beer and David had invited her to dinner. She accepted, and they left the pub and walked to a quiet, secluded Italian restaurant he knew of. Once they were seated the conversation had continued.

"You say there's freedom of ideas and religious thinking in India which is not present in the West, and yet it seems to me there's been a rise of conflict between Hindus and Muslims."

"What you say is true, but the fact is that in India as a whole there's a freedom of thought concerning religious matters not found anywhere else in the world. I would say that the religious conflict between the Hindus and Muslims has basically two causes, as far as I can tell. One is nationalism and the other religious fundamentalism.

"When the British conquered India they conquered other countries as well. So for instance Kashmir, which is now considered a state in Northern India, was at one time a separate Muslim country more closely associated with Muslim Pakistan. When India received its independence, Kashmir was invited to be part of this process. The promise made to Kashmir was that Indian independence would bring Kashmir independence.

"The Indian government, to this day, has refused to honor its promise. So what is occurring is less a conflict between religious bodies than a war to gain independence. Kashmir is not the only trouble spot in India that, on the surface, looks like a battle between religious ideologies."

"I see. You said the other cause had to do with religious fundamentalism. What do you mean?"

"Religious fundamentalism is a rigid adherence to a literal interpretation of beliefs. There's a tendency to define reality in terms of right and wrong, good and bad, black and white. Even today, when there's a rise of religious fundamentalism, conflict and warfare seem inevitable. And so we see the excesses of a Khomeini, and the viciousness of Saddam Hussein against the Kurds.

"Even in your own country, the religious right is becoming more strident, and the killing of abortion doctors and bombing of clinics are just more examples of the same religious intolerance. In India such religious intolerance is quite small by comparison. Freedom of religious thought in India is appreciated.

"From a larger perspective, what I think is underway is an evolutionary process that will, in the end, bring together the social and cultural freedom of the West with the religious and spiritual freedom of the East."

After dinner David walked Sandra to her condo, which turned out to be near his. For a week they skied the mountain together and in lengthy conversations explored a wide range of subjects. The conversations seemed to stem from a deep commonly held interest in philosophical inquiry. David was delighted to find his conversations with Sandra had none of the superficial and argumentative speculations he'd sometimes encountered with university students. Her thinking seemed, instead, to be the result of inquiry and reflection. In her he found a wisdom and serenity he'd encountered before, but only on rare occasions.

She seemed unaffected by power, prestige, or the opinions of others. He watched her, fascinated, and saw how easily people gravitated to her. It was almost as if they didn't know why they were drawn, and wanted just to be in her presence. In those sunlit lovely days on the mountain, they became good friends.

....

Since his divorce four years earlier, David had a series of brief relationships, none of which was destined to last. For a while he was uncertain whether he was interested in another intimate relationship.

He liked his own company, tended to be a solitary man, and felt little need for companionship. For a long time he was undecided. Then one day, like the sudden tipping of scales, he knew that he would indeed be happy to welcome a woman into his life as his wife and partner, lover and friend.

He began to think there was someone waiting for him somewhere. Sometimes in certain places the thought would cross his mind, 'I wonder if she's here?' With the passage of time those thoughts subsided, and after several years of no significant relationship, he resigned himself to the pleasure of his own company. Shortly after that, Sandra walked into his life.

....

Friday was David's last day at Whistler. He and Sandra met for an early breakfast and hit the slopes as soon as the lifts opened. They skied all day, exploring the places they'd visited in six days of skiing on the mountain and stopping only briefly for lunch

In the late afternoon, they came over the crest of a hill and paused. Far below the valley lay in shadow. They leaned on their poles and drank in the magnificence before them. They'd spoken little all day, just enjoyed the thrill and exhilaration of a full day skiing.

"Let's sit a while" Sandra said, then turned and skied slowly to the lee of some nearby firs. David followed. She trampled a spot with her skis then removed them and drove them into the snow for a back rest. She sat on her hat and gloves. David did the same.

In silence they watched the shadows reach farther and farther up the valley. In the distance they could see Whistler Village. Blue wood-smoke lay curled in layers around the tops of the trees while the lights of evening twinkled through the gathering dusk.

The remaining rays of sunlight winked out as a golden sun slid below the ridge behind them. Already they could feel the gathering cold of night. Sandra turned and reached for David's hands. She looked at him and smiled.

"Thank you so much for an enjoyable day," she said.

That was the first time he knew he loved her. But he wouldn't allow himself to believe it. I hardly know her, he thought, and in the morning we'll go separate ways and never see each other again.

He helped her to her feet, and she stood before him pulling on her gloves. He caught a hint of the fragrance she wore. Her face was flushed from the wind and sun, her eyes bright and still. He leaned over and kissed her gently. She responded in kind. He wanted to tell her he loved her but couldn't bring himself to say the words before the ski patrol came over the hill on their last sweep of the day.

"We must go," she said. She turned and launched herself down the hill. He followed. David reached the bottom before she did and was stepping out of his skis when she came racing down the last slope. She came straight for him, flipped her skis, and sprayed snow all over him.

They stopped for a beer in the pub where they'd met. Both felt the impending separation; both keenly aware their time together was almost over. After finishing their drinks they went to their respective condos to shower and dress.

When David knocked on her door an hour later, Sandra was almost ready. She wore a long full denim dress with a red sash about the waist. While he watched, she pulled on thick, woolen navy socks and lambskin boots, then threw her parka over her head and slid her arms into the sleeves. Grabbing a scarf, she wrapped it around her neck. They stepped into the cold night and closed the door behind them. Then, arm in arm, they walked the short distance to the Hokkaido, a Japanese restaurant they'd picked out earlier.

Alone in the small elegant room of rice paper walls, they sat across from each other on small cushions on the rough tatami mats covering the floor. David picked up on the conversation they'd had the night they first met.

"I've been thinking about this idea of religious fundamentalism," he said. "I suspect it has little to do with religion in the first place, and more to do with narrow-minded beliefs firmly held. I've seen people in politics with the same kind of fanaticism. I've seen it on the left and on the right. And as you said, there's a tendency to define things in terms of right and wrong, good and bad."

"What do you think gives rise to it, David?"

"I think it has to do with the nature of belief itself."

"What do you mean?"

"What would you say is at the heart of belief?" he asked.

Sandra thought for a moment, shook her head, then said, "I don't know."

"Think about it carefully. What's implicit to all belief?"

Again she couldn't see what he was getting at, "I don't know."

"Suppose you'd never met me and a friend of yours said there's a psychologist she knows called David Tremaine and that he can help you with a problem you have. Would you believe your friend?"

"If my friend was noted for her honesty, yes."

"Good. Now suppose on your way to see me you stop for a cup of coffee and a close and dear friend, who has always told you the truth, comes into the restaurant. You get talking, and in the course of the conversation you mention you're coming to see a man called David Tremaine. Your friend looks at you oddly and says, 'There's no such person as David Tremaine.' What happens in your mind?"

"Doubt enters. I doubt the friend who first told me about you."

"Right. Now let's try another scenario. Your first friend tells you of David; you come, and we meet and we spend some time together. You leave, and on your way home, you stop for coffee. The same friend comes in, and you strike up a conversation. She says the same thing. 'David Tremaine doesn't exist.'" David watched her closely and saw the smile on her face.

"What happens in your mind? The smile gives it away, doesn't it?"

"I think my friend has gone over the edge."

"Is there any doubt this time?"

"No."

"Why not?"

"Because having met you, I know you exist."

"Then returning to my earlier question, what is implicit to all belief?"

"Uncertainty."

"Yes, uncertainty or doubt. Belief is not the truth. It represents instead, not knowing. This is understood at a very deep level by most human beings. So when it is pointed out, the truth of it is readily apparent.

"Now, belief may correspond to the truth, but for the believer there is no certainty. He simply doesn't know, and that's an important distinction."

"Why?"

"Because uncertainty produces insecurity. In order to overcome insecurity, we seek to get others to believe as we do in the vain and largely unconscious hope that if enough people believe in something, it must be true."

"That's interesting. I'd never thought of it in that way and yet it seems perfectly obvious."

"It does, doesn't it?"

"You know, David, I've always felt that truth is self-evident."

"Yes, when truth is brought to awareness, recognition takes place. But in the realm of belief, the believer has identified so closely with his belief that any challenge to it is felt as a threat to his identity. Because of this, such people become fanatical and in extreme cases dangerous."

"I think you're right." She smiled at him, and the smile

took his breath away. He loved talking with her. In fact, he'd enjoyed everything he'd done with her. She was a remarkable woman.

They drank sake and savored the delights of Japanese cuisine. It was a precious time for both of them. The shadow of the next day's parting lent exquisite richness to the moment. David watched her across the table. She was radiant. The waves of her dark hair shone in the light. She looked up, and their eyes met. Her eyes were almost black. So dark, in fact, that the pupil and the iris seemed to be one. Looking at her he sensed a deep silence, a sense of ease he'd never found in anyone else. That quiet serenity was always there, even when she laughed or cried. Perhaps this is what people feel drawn to, he thought.

"Do you mind my looking at you?" he asked, suddenly aware that his eyes were taking her in completely.

"No, not as long as you grant me the same enjoyment."

He smiled. She sat before him straight and strong, a light dusting of freckles covered her arms. The neck of her dress was unbuttoned at the top, and formed a V which revealed the gentle curve of her breasts. She reached across the table and took both of his hands in hers, kissing them.

"Let's go back to the condo," she said. "I've a hot tub, and we can ease these aching muscles."

David smiled and nodded.

Walking slowly, hand in hand, beneath the old-fashioned street lamps, they wended their way along the crowded sidewalk, absorbed in each other's presence.

At the condo, Sandra stamped the snow from her boots, unlocked the door and walked inside.

"Come in," she said. She bent down and removed her boots and socks then stood and hung her coat. David did the same. She led him through the living room to an outside deck. Sliding the doors back they stepped outside. The deck faced the mountain. A dark ridge of peaks stood against the brilliant stars glittering in the sky. A crescent moon delicately tipped the ridge to the east. On either side the silent firs stood unmoving in the cold night. She pointed toward a small bench against the wall. "You can put your clothes there," she said. "I'll get some towels."

David undressed and slipped into the tub. It took a few moments to get used to the hot water. Sandra returned, drapped in a large towel secured above her breasts. She put extra towels on the bench and reached up to switch off the lights. By the light of the stars and the bright snow, he watched as she slipped the towel from around her. For a moment she paused and he could see the lovely curving body silhouetted against the sky. Bending, she slid into the water. Her breasts hung full and round before they disappeared below the water. She sat facing him. A breeze stirred the nearby branches.

"Oh my, this feels so... good," she said.

"It does indeed."

They soaked in the warmth and their tired muscles relaxed. Nothing was said. Suspended in the still, warm water, they rested easy in the cold mountain night. Several times they emerged then slipped with tingling bodies back into the enveloping warmth. That night they stayed together, their lovemaking strong and tender.

....

It had been eleven years since then. Years of loving her deeply.

David kissed her while she slept. Funny, he thought, I had no doubts about her from the start. He switched off the light. In the darkness he gently caressed her nipples. She stirred. "Good night darling," he said. "I love being with you. How fortunate I was to find you."

CHAPTER 4

General J. P. Travis left the room, he was smiling and confident, the meeting had gone well. Since the death of Emerson the week before, he'd held lengthy meetings with the Joint Chiefs. He'd not wasted time, feeling it imperative to strike before the new president got his bearings. All of them supported keeping gays out of the military. *The military must not be corrupted by these weak-kneed fairies in drag,* he thought. *The military is a man's world, and as far as I'm concerned, it will stay that way.*

Although there'd been unanimous agreement in opposing gays in the military, not all of the Joint Chiefs felt as he did regarding the new president. Most of them held a respect for the office, if not for the man. Travis had an implacable distaste for this man he considered a draft dodger, a man who'd actively opposed the Vietnam war and who, through a quirk of fate, was now the president of the country— a country he'd long held to be the greatest in the world. Privately, he saw it as his duty to prevent any man who'd not done military time from exercising control over the collective might of the military forces of the country he loved.

He was prepared to offer his services in that capacity, distasteful as it might be. He, Travis, was willing to advise the president, to make decisions for him on military matters. He would be the real power, while the president would defer to his knowledge and expertise. Of course, he'd maintain the fiction that the president was actually the one in command.

McManus had warned him to be careful, that this man was not to be taken lightly. McManus was a fool, he thought.

Travis was hungry. He glanced at his watch. Time for a quick breakfast. From there he'd go to the White House for his appointment at ten. As he came down the steps, his aide opened the car door and held it while Travis got in. He gave the name of the restaurant and sat back complacently. It was a lovely summer morning. Trees were in full fresh foliage, while the grass in the parks was lush and green, accompanied by the smell of moist earth. A brisk wind had swept the pollution from the city, and visibility was good.

After breakfast, he was driven to the White House, arriving precisely thirty seconds before the meeting. Tremaine arose from the desk and approached Travis with a smile, his hand extended in greeting.

Travis had forgotten how striking the man was. He was six feet tall and weighed about a hundred and seventy pounds. He appeared slim and athletic, with brown wavy hair and the most unusual green eyes he'd ever seen. He was in his late forties, Travis guessed.

They shook hands, and Travis felt the man's strength. Two chairs sat in front of the desk and Tremaine signaled Travis to take one while he took the other. They sat comfortably and faced each other over a small elegant coffee. On the table stood a silver coffee pot, creamer and sugar bowl, two mugs and spoons.

The two men presented a strange contrast. Travis was in dress uniform, ribbons and medals prominent on a broad chest. His creases were sharp, his shoes like polished ebony. A big man over six feet tall, he weighed two hundred and twenty pounds. He had a short, iron gray, military haircut and the solid strength of a fifty-two-year-old man who'd seen his share of life. Tremaine was dressed casually in a pair of light brown cotton slacks, sandals and socks, and a white cotton shirt open at the neck.

"Care for some coffee, General?" Tremaine asked.

"Yes, that would be fine."

Tremaine reached over and poured coffee into the mugs.

"Help yourself," he said as he poured a touch of milk. He settled back in the firm comfortable chair and waited. Travis spooned in sugar and stirred brusquely. He sipped and savored his coffee, eyes momentarily closed. Suddenly he realized Tremaine was waiting for him.

"Travis, I'm not one to beat around the bush, we must address the issue of gays in the military. It was something Emerson was committed to, and I feel the same as he did. Before his death, there was little support for a new policy among the Joint Chiefs. How do they stand now? I need to know your thoughts on the matter."

"It's our feeling"— began Travis

"No, I want to know *your* thoughts on the matter," said Tremaine, interrupting him.

"My thoughts?" Travis was taken aback.

"Yes, your thoughts."

"I think the military is no place for gays, and I feel strongly about it!"

"Why?"

"Because I think it will seriously affect the morale of the men."

"How do you see that?"

" I think it's uncomfortable for most men to have other men look at them with sexual interest. Since you've not served in the military yourself, it might be difficult for you to understand how men feel when they live in close proximity and have little privacy. This is compounded during time of war. In time of war the men must have as few distractions as possible. They don't need the extra discomfort of other men being sexually interested in them, or being sexually attracted themselves. The same goes for female personnel."

"Wasn't that one of the arguments against women serving in combat?"

"Yes, it was, and as far as I'm concerned the argument still holds true. Women in the service are a distraction for men who must be about the business of war. Besides, women are not suited to combat. And even less suited are the men who, apart from having a penis, are in most respects women themselves. We've had to create separate quarters and segregate the sexes. It would require even further segregation to meet the needs of most normal men with regard to gays. I doubt whether there's a single heterosexual man who would feel comfortable taking a shower with a homosexual. Not one!"

"So you're suggesting that if gays were allowed to serve openly in the military, they'd have to be segregated much as women are today."

"Yes. But I would not recommend them being allowed to serve in the first place!"

"I understand. Our present policy is to refuse entrance into the military of those who openly declare their homosexuality. We also discharge those who are found to be gay. Yet it seems obvious that there have always been, still are, and will continue to be gays in the military who remain undetected. How does this affect your argument concerning the discomfort of men being looked upon as sexual objects by other men?"

"The men feel supported by their government and commanding officers if they know there's an active policy forbidding gays in the military. By denying gays access to military service, we don't encourage them to join, and so the number of gays actually serving is probably less than in an open system."

"I understand your point."

Tremaine sipped his coffee and seemed lost in thought. Travis picked up his mug and took several swallows. It was good coffee. He watched Tremaine closely without being obvious. It was the first face-to-face conversation he'd had with the man. Before today, his conversations had been with Emerson; Tremaine, though present, had remained quiet, not speaking a word. For that reason he'd concluded Tremaine would be easy to deal with. He wasn't so sure anymore.

"General, what do *you* think of gays yourself? What are your personal views?"

"I'm not sure they have anything to do with this," he said carefully.

"I disagree, our personal views deeply affect how we conduct ourselves professionally. Some men, knowing their bias, may bend the other way to compensate, while for others, professional and personal opinions are the same. I'd like to know your personal views on the matter."

"Well, gays make me uncomfortable. I don't like the idea of men looking at me with sexual interest."

"Why not?"

"I'm not sure... I feel uncomfortable, and I find myself getting angry. I think homosexuality is wrong and unnatural. It's obvious to me that from a physiological standpoint, men and women were made different sexually in order to continue the species, through the act of procreation. Homosexual acts cannot do that, and I find them unnatural and repugnant."

"You said you felt it was wrong. Is that from a religious

perspective?"

"No, I don't consider myself a religious man I do believe in God, but I don't attend church and haven't for a long time. I think things that are natural are largely right and things that are unnatural are largely wrong. There may be exceptions, but that's the way I see it."

"It's interesting to me that the dialogue going on in the country as a whole is similar to the one we're having. Most of the conversations take place from the perspective of gay and heterosexual men and not from the perspective of the women who also serve. Do you have any thoughts about why that is?"

"Not really, except that from what I hear, it is the men who feel the most uncomfortable with it."

"Some have suggested that masculine gay females make good soldiers because they're more aggressive, more masculine in their way of being. What do you think?"

"I really don't know, but it does seem to be true. Many women serving in the military do exhibit more masculine characteristics than their counterparts in the civilian population. Maybe that has to do with the fact that the military has, until recently, been an institution dominated and run by men. It could be they instill certain characteristics and women assume them. I doubt it, though."

"Some contend that gay men are not aggressive enough to make good soldiers. What do you think?"

"It seems to me that a soldier needs to be aggressive and in a sense 'macho,' and most of the gay men I've met do not exhibit those characteristics. My honest opinion is that gay men do not make good soldiers, period."

"I understand your point of view, but I wonder if it really bears scrutiny. It seems to me that some very fine soldiers were gay. Lawrence of Arabia is one of them, and he was a pioneer in the art of modern guerrilla warfare. His sexual preference didn't seem to inhibit his ability to instill allegiance in his men and didn't appear to interfere with his abilities as a soldier."

"I know there are exceptions," said Travis, "but I think they're few. Those exceptions don't change my opinion or the opinions of the other Joint Chiefs of Staff or, for that matter, the opinions of the vast majority of men in uniform who are serving their country today."

"As you know, Emerson considered the ban of gays a violation of their constitutional rights."

"Yes, I know, but I and most of us who serve in the military feel that the military does not fall within the jurisdiction of civilian courts and is not subject to the guaranteed rights of civilians. Military law and civilian law are two distinctly separate systems and must never be considered the same."

"Why?"

"Why? Because the military is inherently an authoritarian system with a chain of command that works from the top down. If civil law was applicable, a soldier could refuse to carry out a direct order on the grounds that it could jeopardize his life or the lives of those under him. Civil law can never be tolerated in a military establishment. Like oil and water, they don't mix."

"What are your thoughts on allowing women to fly combat missions?"

"I oppose it!"

"Again may I ask why?"

"For the same reasons that I oppose women being in the military in the first place. First of all, I don't think that by nature women are aggressive fighters. Second, they put other men at risk should they be captured. And, if captured they can easily suffer rape and sexual torture at the hands of enemy soldiers. This gives opposing military forces a great deal of leverage against a nation such as ours where women are respected, valued highly, and must be protected. Ultimately, we'd be more likely to sacrifice a man to an enemy than we would a woman."

Travis picked up his mug and took a long swallow.

"General Travis, I appreciate your forthrightness. I wish to talk to you on another matter now."

Good, Travis thought. He disliked having to deal with this issue. It was distasteful to him, and he wanted to get on with more important matters.

"More coffee?"

"Please."

Travis extended his mug and Tremaine filled it and then his own. Travis stirred in two spoonfuls of sugar then sat back to wait.

"Before we move on I want to know one more thing on this matter. If I issued an executive order banning discrimination against gays, would you support it?"

Travis was annoyed by the question but tried not to let his feelings show. Tremaine sat casually in his chair, but his eyes were fixed firmly upon the general's.

"No, I would not!" he said gruffly.

"Would you actively oppose it?"

"I would!"

"And what is your assessment of the other Joint Chiefs? Will they also actively oppose it?"

Here it was at last, he thought, the beginning moves of the showdown. Travis was glad he'd taken the time earlier in the week to gain the Joints Chiefs' undivided support.

"They will actively oppose it as well."

"How?"

"We don't really know at this time."

"Might it involve resignations?"

"It might."

"Once more I appreciate your honesty."

Tremaine sipped his coffee. He'd noticed the general

stiffening and could feel the tension in the man.

For a few moments they sat quietly. Tremaine appeared thoughtful, then put his coffee down and said, "It's no secret I did not enter military service so there's been speculation as to my fitness as Commander in Chief."

"Yes."

"I will need the assistance of men like yourself over the coming years. I will need your knowledge, your expertise and the benefit of your informed opinion. But it must be clearly understood that I will make the decisions and you'll have to follow them whether they contradict your informed opinions or the judgment of the other Joint Chiefs. I will expect you to follow the orders I issue. There'll be no hindrance or sabotage of those orders. If there is, I will not hesitate to fire whomever engages in such behavior. Is that understood?"

Travis was taken aback by the directness of Tremaine's statement. He'd felt the force behind the words even though it had been spoken quietly. Tremaine's eyes had not wavered, and Travis had been unable to avoid them. He had the uneasy feeling that Tremaine was reading his mind, or at least, assessing him, and doing so accurately. Travis felt off-balance, almost trapped. All his scheming would come to nothing if he could not dominate this president. And from the conversation so far, he was beginning to feel that he might not be able to do so.

"Yes, I think I understand," Travis finally responded.

"I don't mean to be rude, Travis, but on this point I'm not interested in what you think. I want to know if you understand me. I'll say it again. I will solicit information from you and the other Joint Chiefs. I will require your expertise and the benefit of your judgments. From that I will make the final determination as to appropriate action. I will issue the orders, and I expect you and the other Joint Chiefs to carry them out, do so faithfully, and in no way obstruct them. Is that clearly understood?"

"Yes!"

"Now you must understand something else. I have no interest in having anyone advise me by giving me what they think I want to hear. I'm open to all points of view, all input. All of us have a job to do, and we must do it well. Each one of us must speak the truth, as we understand it. Nothing less will be tolerated. If you can't give me what I ask, then you must consider whether you can serve me in this capacity or not. If you cannot, you must resign. I will understand. I do not ask of anyone what he is not prepared to give. Do I make myself clear?"

"Yes, you do."

"What is your response?"

"I will think about what you've said."

"That's fair enough. You have one week. I want you to convey to the Joint Chiefs the substance of our conversation today. We'll meet next week at the same time."

With that Tremaine stood, and Travis followed suit. The President saw him to the door. The two men shook hands.

"Thank you for your time, General, I appreciate your candor. I think we understand each other now. I'll see you next week."

Travis stepped into the hall, and the door closed behind him. He made his way to the entrance where the driver waited. He felt dazed by the events that had transpired. Thoughts tumbled through his brain. He ordered his aide to drive back to the office. On the way, he changed his mind.

"Take me to the Lincoln Memorial," he said.

"Yes sir."

A few minutes later they stopped in front of the immense statue of the seated Civil War president. Travis got out and instructed the driver through the window. "I'll walk back," he said, "Be ready for me at three. I have a meeting at the Senate."

"Yes sir."

The wind blew stiffly. Turning his back to the Lincoln Memorial, Travis walked toward the WashingtonMonument. On the way he took a detour and slowly made his way toward the Vietnam Wall. From a distance he could see the usual crowd of visitors, Vietnam Vets and their families. There was something powerful about this place. At first he'd disliked the monument, preferring the more traditional statues of war. But it had grown on him, and it was a place where many Vietnam Vets gathered. He himself had looked for names inscribed on the black marble, names of men he'd known during three tours of duty in Vietnam.

He knew more men who'd not returned than he cared to count. It had been a vicious war, one not easily forgotten by those who'd been there. He sat on a bench and watched the memorial through the trees. Somehow the presence of the wall reminded him that he must not forget the men who'd fought with him so many years ago.

To support a president who'd actively opposed the war was an anathema to him, nothing less than a betrayal of the young men who'd given their lives, and of the thousands who'd returned maimed in body and soul. No, he'd not support this man. He couldn't! Nor would he quietly go away. He'd oppose him in every way he could, of that he was certain.

He stood and straightened his shoulders. His mind was calm again, his direction clear. As he started to walk, a man in a wheelchair, dressed in army fatigues, came along the path toward the memorial. Unshaven and dirty, his eyes were wild and uneasy. A battered hat was stuffed on his head. Suddenly he saw Travis and recognized the uniform. Taking his hand from the wheel, he saluted smartly. Travis returned the salute. In that brief moment the man lost control of his chair and quickly gathered speed as he headed down the steep path. Several times he tried to slow the wheels with his bare hands. Travis jumped for the wayward chair grabbed it by the handles, slowed it then brought it to a stop.

"Are you all right?" he asked.

"Yeah," came the breathless reply. "Thanks for yer help."

"Would you like some help to the bottom of the hill?" Travis asked.

"Yeah, if ya'll don't mind. Name's Luke."

"Mine's Travis."

Travis held the handles and slowed the chair with his weight as they descended.

"Serve in 'Nam?" he asked Luke.

"Yeah, you?"

"Yeah, sixty-six through sixty-nine."

"Holy Geese, ya'll must've been fuckin' crazy. What was ya'll, a super patriot or somethin?"

Travis was stung.

"If ya'll spent three years there, ya'll must have been brass, high muck-a-muck. Bastards like ya'll sent the likes of me into the living hell of war. Follow orders, or be shot for disobedience. So what the fuck, what choice did we have? We followed yer fuckin' orders and a lot of us died.

"We were smart mother-fuckers then. Remember when a newsman asked that asshole general why they'd destroyed the hamlet? Y'all remember what he said?"

Travis shook his head.

" 'We had to destroy it in order to save it.' Well, wasn't that the goddamned truth? I was there in that god-forsaken Iron Triangle, I lost my legs there. One hell of a gift for being a patriot, serving this godforsaken country, following the orders of other men. And when I got back stateside, what the fuck did I get? Five years in a V.A. hospital getting shafted."

Travis'face flushed and his neck puffed up. He couldn't believe what he heard. Boiling, he looked at the top of Luke's head. He had the urge to tip Luke out of the chair; he wanted to punch the jerk out. They reached the bottom of the hill, and Travis stopped.

"You're on your own now," he said, and without a backward glance turned on his heel and headed back up the hill.

CHAPTER 5

Shamir adjusted the yoke across her shoulders and set out along the path. The fierce heat of day had subsided. She loved the walk to the wadi; it was always a welcome break from caring for her brothers and sister. While she was gone, her mother would prepare the evening meal, and her father would be home by the time she returned.

She followed the trail as it wound along the shore and over the low-lying hills. The ocean sparkled in the sunlight, and beneath the bending palms small waves brushed the shoreline. The trail turned and followed a shallow valley leading to the foothills. It was the end of summer and the grasses were brown and parched from lack of rain. Clumps of sycamore and poplars dotted the hillsides. The poplars at higher elevations already evidenced the characteristic gold of early autumn.

Shamir climbed steadily until she reached a curve where the valley turned south. Following the trail, she walked though a series of low hills before ascending a steep incline. She crested the hill and paused. Below, the trail sloped gently to the well with its pool of water shimmering in the light. Around the water's edge a sea of green grass created a startling contrast to the parched land. A cluster of palms stood at the abrupt end of a ridge extending from the mountain. Beside the palms a steep canyon cut into the hillside and vanished from sight.

She could see him sitting on the rocks at the edge of the pool, his sheep gathered at the entrance to the canyon, some standing, others lying down. He'd been there every evening for two weeks. She had first seen him one afternoon when she'd come to the well for water as she did each day.

At first she was afraid of him, but as she got to know him her fear subsided. Each evening he drew water and filled her pots. He wore the traditional clothes of a herdsman and his hair and close-cropped beard were white. Black bushy eyebrows contrasted with the white hair. His skin was dark like hers, but weathered. His eyes seemed to sparkle and emanated both great strength and gentleness. She'd been taught to avoid the eyes of men, but she could not avoid this man's. When he spoke, his voice was soft and rich and soothing. He said his name was Nassir and told her that he'd lived in the hills all his life. His ancestors, who'd built this well and others, had taken care of it for generations. He'd told her that as the seasons came, he moved the flock from place to place, visiting different wells. For two weeks she spent time talking with him, and afterward hurried home before abrupt darkness swallowed her surroundings.

The evening before, she'd told her parents of meeting the shepherd at the well. Her mother stopped eating and looked quickly at her father. Shamir caught the look and asked, "Do you know him?"

"What does he look like?" her father asked.

She described him. "Do you know him?" she persisted.

"Yes," her father answered. And then he told her the

following story. "Eighteen years ago, just before you were born, Nassir arrived one evening at sunset. He'd been traveling hard and seemed exhausted. We gave him water and shared a meal. After we'd eaten, we sat around the table relaxing. He looked at me and asked if I trusted him. I thought it a strange question, but I realized I did trust him. I couldn't explain why. Later, your mother told me she felt the same trust in him. Then Nassir looked at us and, taking both our hands in his, told us we were in great danger and must leave for several days, until the danger passed. We asked him to explain, but he wouldn't.

"We packed some food and a few belongings, and he took us, that night, into the hills. We walked until dawn, and just as light crept up the eastern sky, he helped us through an opening into a deep cave. Water skins hung on wooden pegs, and the charcoal remains of a cooking fire were surrounded by sheepskins and woven mats.

"For three nights we remained in the cave. In the middle of the fourth we returned home. We arrived at first light and could see at once that something was terribly wrong. Only the almond and sycamore trees remained standing, and one small shed. Everything else was a pile of rubble, with one white wall and an empty doorway marking the place where our house once stood. Several craters gouged the earth, and a strange smell hung in the air.

"Nassir assured us we would now be safe. We asked him if he knew what had happened. 'Israeli air force' is all he would say. For seven days he helped us rebuild our home, and before leaving brought us a pair of goats.

"I was furious over the destruction of our home. We'd done nothing to deserve it, and for the first time I felt the urge to join the guerrillas. I wanted to strike back; I wanted the Israelis destroyed. I wanted things to be the way my father and his father had described them, before the Israelis had taken the land and formed their own nation. A long-standing hatred had simmered inside me all those years. Now it boiled over, a silent, controlled rage. I wanted to leave right away, wanted to kill. Your mother begged me not to go, but I wouldn't listen.

"That evening, Nassir went with me to gather water at the well. We filled the pots and then he told me to sit down. He sat opposite me. For what seemed like a long time he fixed his eyes on mine. At first I was impatient and didn't want to sit, but I couldn't break the hold of his eyes. After what seemed like an hour I found myself filled with a strange peacefulness. I think Nassir had been waiting for me to feel this, for only then did he speak.

"'It's not your destiny to go to war. Your wife is pregnant, though she doesn't know it yet. Your first-born will be a girl, a lovely girl. She'll bring you great joy and, like all of us, she has a purpose to fulfill. You'll have three more children, and it's imperative you take care of your family. Not only must you take care of their physical needs, you must nurture them with a loving heart. That love is the gift required of you in this lifetime. Like a pure well, you must not allow it to be contaminated with bitterness and hatred. Do you understand?'

"He'd spoken quietly, and in the silence, his words touched my heart. I did understand. In that moment I saw that only love and understanding can put an end to hatred and the terrible bloodshed of war. As if reading my mind, he said softly: 'We're all brothers, all the children of the Exalted One, there are no exceptions.'

"The next evening he left. We gathered together as we had the first night he came. 'Much suffering comes from wanting something to be other than it is. It is Allah, the Exalted One, who gave us birth; it is He who brought us together. Each of us is part of a great cosmic dance about which we know very little. Keep in mind that everything unfolds as it should. There are no mistakes, only an insufficient understanding.

"'For this lack there can be no blame. As you come to accept the all-pervasive harmony of things, you'll discover the twin snakes of good and evil vanishing. Never again will their poison infect you. Then will come the realization that all actions are appropriate. Then perhaps you'll come to know yourself as the all-encompassing silence, the peace within which all universes, all things and all events take place.' He paused and looked at each of us separately.

"Then he said, 'I'll not see you again, but will one day meet your daughter by the well. When she tells you of our meeting, as she will, you must tell her of these events. Shortly after we meet, a new stage in your lives will come to pass. No matter what happens, never forget that you are deeply loved by some who walk the earth today and some who are yet to come.' Then Nassir stood and embraced us. I walked with him as far as the well and watched him disappear into the hills. We've never seen him since."

....

Now, as Shamir approached the well, her mind was suddenly in turmoil. She felt as if the very stability of the world she'd known was threatened. How could Nassir know the things he knew? She looked up and saw him walking to meet her. Reaching her, he took her hands and looked into her eyes. The turmoil subsided.

"They've told you, haven't they?"

She nodded.

"Come and sit down," he said then led her to the edge of the well.

They sat across from each other, and once more she felt the peacefulness in the eyes.

"Who are you?" she asked.

He smiled slowly, a radiant smile, and his eyes sparkled. "Just a friend," he said. "Shamir, before long things will change drastically. Life as you've known it will be swept away, and you'll enter the unknown. You'll need courage to overcome the fear that will hold you in its grip. When the changes come, there'll be many twists and turns, and in time you'll leave the shores of your homeland and come to a new one. There your surroundings will reflect the peace you've found in yourself. At that time you'll meet a man who will help you.

"You must never regret the past, only enjoy the present. For the past, be thankful, as the tree is thankful for the seed that brought it into existence, for the winds that caressed it and the waters that quenched its thirst."

"What do you mean, Nassir?"

"I'm sorry, Shamir, but I can't explain. My task is merely to inform you and be a friend to your family and you when the times come."

"Are you a prophet?"

"No, little one, I'm what is known as a 'seer'. I have the gift of sight. I know what is to come and the parts we play. I follow the impulses of the heart and never go astray. That's all for now; let's fill the pots so you can make it back by dark."

When they finished, he walked with her to the top of the hill, carrying her yoke. Carefully he set the pots down and stood looking at her.

"One day soon you'll see a stranger dressed in black. When you do, you must run and hide. Make your way to the well, and I'll be waiting for you. When you see him, under no circumstances must you go home, nor can you do anything to help. Just come here, and I will help you. You must go now." He lifted the yoke and placed it gently across her shoulders.

"Nassir, I'm frightened by what you say."

"I know, but it had to be spoken. I'll see you tomorrow. Have a good evening and give my greetings to your parents. Tell them all is well and not to worry."

When she got home, Shamir took her parents aside and gave them Nassir's message. She felt disinclined to tell them what else he'd said. She hugged her brothers and her sister as she put them to bed and found herself telling them how much she loved them.

She sat long with her parents at the table that night. The light from the lamp cast a warm glow and helped ease the fear lodged in the back of her mind. Late, she kissed her parents good night and went to bed. Outside the window a bright moon cast a tapestry of shadows across the uneven ground. In the silence she detected the sound of poplars, their leaves stirred by a vagrant breeze. She'd grown up here, loving the isolation.

In the morning she was up early and helped prepare breakfast. Her father arrived with milk from the goats just as breakfast was ready.

....

By mid-afternoon the heat was intense, and they napped. When Shamir awoke, it was already late. Her mother baked bread for supper. Shamir splashed water on her face and emptied the water pots ready to get water from the well.

Kissing her mother, she set out, the pots swaying as she walked. As she turned away from the shore and headed into the hills, she looked back. She loved her home with its white-washed walls and orange, tiled roof. It was like a precious gem nestled in the convergence of low hills, surrounded by stands of trees, gardens, and the sparkling blue ocean.

Suddenly she caught a movement on the hill behind and above her home. Something stirred a cloud of dust. As she listened, she heard the sound of a high revving engine. Whatever it was, was moving fast.

Then she saw it: a military jeep with four men inside. With a squeal of brakes, it pulled up beside the house, and the men jumped out and quickly ran inside. To her horror she saw one of the men emerge with her two brothers. As she looked, she saw he was dressed in black. Her stomach knotted, her heart jumped in her chest. She couldn't catch her breath. Nassir's words rang in her mind. Her family, she must help them. She heard a scream from the house, and the sound of a shot cut it short.

Above the ocean, two jets screamed directly inland. They came in low, guns blazing. She saw flashes of flame from their wings. Then in horror she watched her father racing up the shallow valley from the fishing boat. She saw the puff of bullets hitting the dirt and watched helplessly as they reached him and cut him down, his body jerking with the impact.

As if in slow motion, she saw a rocket detach from the belly of the lead jet. On a tail of fire, it slammed into her home, with a loud explosion and burst of flame. The roar was deafening; the concussion from the explosion knocked her down. Her ears were ringing as she pulled herself to the edge of a large rock and looked down. The war planes were gone. All that was left was the thunderous roar from their engines and the smoldering rubble where her home once stood.

As she watched, she saw more trails of dust coming down the hill toward the smoldering ruins. As they reached the bottom, men disgorged from jeeps and quickly fanned out beneath the trees. She watched for a few minutes, terrified. Then with a deafening rush, small rockets lifted into the air. Streaming flame behind them they came toward her, passed overhead, and vanished beyond the hills.

She picked herself up and ran as fast as she could. As she

rounded the trail and started up the steep incline, she saw Nassir running toward her. She flung herself into his arms, sobbing uncontrollably.

"Are you unharmed?" she heard him asking as he looked her over. Satisfied she was, he held her tightly.

....

Yigall and Joseph found their places at the table. Standing behind their chairs, they waited for the Rabbi's blessing. The families had gathered to celebrate the boy's bar mitzvah. It was a big event, and all the members of the settlement joined in. Days had been spent preparing the hall; the food had taken a week. The boys spent the afternoon listening with fascination to the older men who congregated at the end of the hall, smoking their pipes and telling stories. The women had put the finishing touches to the food and all was now ready.

Quickly, the murmur of voices and sounds of laughter, subsided. The boys listened to the familiar words of the blessing and, when it was finished, seated themselves to the accompanying scrape of chairs. In that same instant, two rockets slammed into the hall. With an ear-shattering roar, bricks, mortar, wood, metal, tiles, and bodies hurtled in every direction. In the appalling silence, flames flickered among the ruins. Groans and cries of pain mingled with the sound of falling rubble. Smoke and dust were everywhere–choking, gagging, acrid smoke.

Yigall knew he was hurt but felt no pain. He squeezed his friend's hand; there was no response. He looked over to see if Joseph was all right. A deep cry of revulsion and fear burst from his mouth. In the light from the flames, he saw the stump of Joseph's arm, the hand still holding his in its grotesque grip.

CHAPTER 6

Day after day, night after night, the Israelis flew into Lebanon, destroying everything that moved within twenty miles of their northern border. Troops, tanks and guns crossed the border pounding villages into rubble. Gun boats patrolled the western shoreline, destroying fishing settlements and sinking every boat they found. Within days, a flood of refugees streamed north toward the war-torn city of Beirut.

Squads of Hizballah guerrillas fired hand-launched missiles across the border into Northern Israel. They moved quickly, never staying in one place, sometimes taking cover in the tide of humanity flowing north. Syrian and Jordanian troops mobilized along the borders with Israel. Lebanon appealed to the UN Security Council for help.

....

Tremaine spent the day in the briefing room being apprised of the fighting now raging in Lebanon. He solicited and received suggestions and options from foreign policy experts and National Security advisors, Doug Kersey, the Secretary of State, and Jonathan Makarios, his personal advisor. At five o'clock he pushed his chair back and left the meeting saying, "I need a break."

The briefing had been thorough, the suggestions and options helpful. Now he must be alone with the information and ideas. Then, when it was time, he'd know what action to take.

Tremaine stretched.

"Doug, I'll meet you back here in an hour."

He pushed his chair in, and walked out into the fresh air. He set out on a good brisk walk.

....

When he returned to the briefing room, David found Doug waiting for him.

"Let's walk a little," he said.

They walked in silence for a while. The intense heat of the day had subsided, and now a full-bodied warmth bore upon it the fragrance of roses.

"Doug, in case there's any question in your mind, I want you to know I'm pleased to have you as Secretary of State. When you were appointed, it was an appointment that Emerson and I both made, an appointment we were both happy with, and I still am. I wanted to make sure you understood that."

"Thank you. I'm glad to be of service. I've enjoyed working with you and look forward to continuing."

"Good. Now concerning the new crisis in the Middle East, it's time to implement a new policy along the lines we discussed previously."

"I think you're right," Doug said.

"You'll go to Israel tomorrow. After you meet with Prime Minister Levin, we'll talk further. I'll brief you this evening at nine. Come to the Oval Office."

"I'll be there."

David put his arm around Doug's shoulders and gave them a squeeze.

"I'll see you this evening at nine. Now go home to your wife."

....

Three days later, Michael Levin and his Foreign Secretary Joseph Goldstein entered the Oval Office. Doug Kersey and Jonathan Makarios stood with Tremaine. They shook hands all around and made the introductions.

"Have a seat." Tremaine nodded toward the chairs around the coffee table, where fresh coffee and fresh-baked pastries were arranged.

"Coffee, gentlemen?"

They accepted. Tremaine poured coffee, and Doug passed the pastries. Tremaine added a touch of milk to his coffee then sat back and waited. He'd never met the Israeli Prime Minister or his Foreign Secretary before. They looked tired.

Looking out the window, Tremaine noticed a red rose hanging from a trellis. Caught in a shaft of sunlight, it bobbed back and forth, nuzzled by a soft breeze. Tremaine returned his attention to the Israelis. They'd been watching him, gripping their mugs tightly. They seem uneasy, David thought.

"Well, gentlemen, let's get under way." Tremaine turned toward Levin. "Mr. Prime Minister, you requested this meeting so I'll let you begin."

"Mr. President, we cannot accept your proposals. In fact, as a nation we are insulted by the suggestions conveyed two days ago through your Secretary of State, Mr. Kersey."

"I'm sorry to hear that. There was no intention to insult you or your countrymen. What specifically do you object to?"

"First of all, we object to your interference in our political affairs. We have a right to defend ourselves in any way we see fit. As you know, we're a country at war, a country that's been at war since its birth in 1948.

"From the very beginning we've been forced to defend ourselves from hostile neighbors. We live under constant threat of death and are subject to terrorist attacks all over the world. During the Gulf War, under pressure from Mr. Bush, we withheld our response to the Iraqi Scud attacks. But this latest attack by Hizballah cannot go unpunished. We will not stop our bombardment of Lebanon until the Lebanese government pressures the Syrians to call off the rocket attacks. The only thing our neighbors understand is strength. They're afraid of our strength, and that keeps us safe. If we appear weak, then we're no longer safe."

"I'm sorry, Mr. Levin but I cannot accept your assumptions. True, you've been at war since your nation was born, and its true you've had to defend yourselves. You think you must retaliate for every attack that comes your way. But this constant warfare is a symptom of something else. It will continue until there's a willingness on both sides to address the problems that underlie the hostilities..."

Angrily the Prime Minister interrupted. "Rockets slamming into a hall filled with innocent people and killing twenty civilians is not a symptom, no matter how you look at it!"

"I'm sorry, but I see it differently. If you let me finish, I'll do my best to explain. So far you've lived by the gun and I'm not saying it's unwarranted. But violence hasn't solved the problem, merely perpetuated it, and this violence now jeopardizes the safety of the world.

"The mass of armaments in your region beggars the imagination. And because of your power, some of your neighbors feel they must develop their own nuclear weapons. That is frightening for the rest of the world. Your war with your neighbors threatens the well-being of every person on the planet."

"We're not the threat; we merely respond to the threats of those who would destroy us."

"I understand, but it sounds too much like spoiled children pointing fingers at each other, each accusing the other of starting it first."

Levin exploded. "Who the hell gives you the right to call us spoiled children?"

"Look," David continued, "Israel was established as a nation by the displacement of Arabs from land they'd held for the last fourteen hundred years. True, there was displacement by the Turks first and then more recently by the British. I doubt whether Israel would have come into existence without the support and assistance of the British government. As I see it, there was little concern or consideration for those who inhabited the land before you, those who were forced to move and make way for the new nation state."

"That's not true. Israelis have always lived in Palestine. The Zionism of the 1800s was the precursor to modern Zionism and was proposed and thought out by Jews living in Palestine."

"I don't disagree with the fact that Jews were living in Palestine all along. But these people, apart from their religious affiliation, had more in common with their Arab neighbors than they did with European Jews.

"Like it or not, the fact of the matter is that, with the establishment of the Jewish State, large numbers of Jews immigrated from Europe and settled in Israel. By doing so, they displaced the people who'd lived there for more than a thousand years. This is the issue that's never been adequately addressed.

"Until now, as you've said, you've had to defend yourselves. In so doing, you've established yourself in the region, and that is unlikely to change. Now it's time you address the legitimate needs of the people around you, those whom you've displaced."

"Why should we address these so-called needs? Our neighbors have sworn to destroy us. It's either us or them."

"That kind of thinking, in my opinion, fuels this whole conflict. The problems of the Middle East are like a weeping sore that does not heal; the time has come to treat it so that it can heal. To do so requires that one face facts and do away with ideologies and one's own pet points of view."

"You've no idea what it's like to live under constant threat from your neighbors, so how can you presume to tell us what to do?" interjected Goldstein angrily.

"We don't presume to tell you what to do; we presume to tell you what we're prepared to do. Please understand, I'm not pointing a finger at you while being oblivious to our own problems. I've no interest in that kind of hypocrisy. As a nation, some of our policies have in the past been hypocritical. That's about to change."

Levin looked at Tremaine. His whole demeanor was disconcerting. He, unlike his Israeli counterparts, was dressed casually. He wore a pale green short-sleeved shirt, open at the neck, and a pair of dark emerald slacks. He'd kicked off his shoes. He seemed relaxed and at ease, and his green eyes missed nothing. The two men with him were also dressed casually.

Tremaine continued. "I don't feel that we as a nation have been any better than you. The white man came to the shores of the Americas and systematically destroyed the culture, religion and lives of millions of indigenous people, people who lived on these continents long before the white man ever set foot here.

"To this day, large numbers of indigenous people are

treated as second-class citizens; they live in poverty and suffer from ill health, a high mortality rate, and very high suicide among the young. As far as I can tell, the same behavior occurred in Australia and New Zealand. What difference is there between the white man who came to the Americas and the white Europeans who settled Palestine and displaced the indigenous people who'd lived there for generations?"

"I don't see how you can equate the two situations; they're quite different. One of the differences is that we have a long-standing historical association with Palestine, which even your own Christian religion recognizes."

"You're correct in saying that the Christian religion recognizes the historical connection between the Jewish people and the area known as Palestine. But I think it's a fallacious argument."

"How can you say it's fallacious?"

"First of all, as I understand it, the historical Jewish people stemmed from Isaac's two sons, Jacob the younger, and his half brother, Esau, the older. Esau, through manipulation on the part of Jacob's mother, Rebekah, lost his birthright to his brother. The two tribes that derived from Jacob constituted the lineage to which most Jews subscribe.

"On the other hand, the lineage of Esau gave rise to the remaining ten tribes, and are the people known today as Arabs. They settled throughout the area known as the Middle East. In time, the Diaspora occurred, and the Jewish people were scattered throughout the world, the majority spreading into Europe. But who were they? Were they descendants of Esau and Jacob? No, they were only the descendants of Jacob. And what of the other ten tribes? They remained and integrated with others over a long period of time.

"Many became Muslims, having lost the religious roots originally associated with their cultural heritage. So, it could be argued that if anyone is to lay claim to the lands of the Middle East, it would appear to be the Arabs."

Levin was flabbergasted at the turn of the conversation. It was unlike anything he'd expected and a far cry from his dealings with the American presidents he was aware of that preceded Emerson and Tremaine. He felt angry and exasperated. He couldn't believe what he was hearing. Was this new president serious, or was he mad or maybe an anti-Semite?

David paused to give Levin a chance to speak. He knew his words had upset the Israelis and he felt sorry for them. They weren't getting what they hoped for. Neither man spoke, so David continued. "From another perspective, it is easily seen that the two tribes from which modern Jewry traces its lineage have been a warlike people themselves. They've had a history of occupying land others once lived on and justifying their behavior with the argument that God had promised them the land. That's good for those who subscribe to such a frame of reference, but what about those who don't? What of the people who are displaced?"

"Our history is a history of people chosen by God, people who were obedient to Yahweh and the Law."

"That's what I mean. It's internally consistent for traditional Jews— and meaningless and unacceptable for non-Jews.

"Many nations have made similar claims. The British colonial expansion was justified because the British were a Christian nation. Their missionaries set out to convert the people in the lands they conquered, with the best of intentions. They believed they were doing a service.

"And, I'm sad to say, our own country has acted in a similar vein in its war with Mexico, and in its meddling in the affairs of Central and South America. We've forced our way on others under the auspices of 'Manifest Destiny' and The Monroe Doctrine. The fact of the matter is that all people deserve to live and raise their families without regard to religious beliefs, and in comparative safety.

"As far as I can tell, there's been too much bloodshed in the name of religions that, as yours has done, lay claim to the 'one true God.' The Jew is no better than the Christian or the Muslim when it comes to such arrogance. I'm afraid such reasoning carries little weight with me."

"What are you getting at?" Goldstein demanded.

"What I'm getting at is that you support your position with the idea of tradition and the authority of God. This only holds weight with those who accept the same basic assumptions as you."

"What do you mean?"

"One person might say 'the fourth of July was a wonderful day.' Another might say 'the fourth of July was a terrible day.' They disagree based upon a shared basic assumption, which is that the day was the fourth of July. Without agreement as to the basic assumption the conversation becomes confusing and the source of considerable misunderstanding."

"I don't understand the point you're making."

"The British and the Americans, and perhaps most other Christian nations, accepted the same basic assumption: that the Jews who moved to Palestine from Europe had a historical right to do so.

They agreed that such a right justified taking land lived on and belonging to others. What I've done is question the very assumption itself, because we've all been blinded by what we take for granted. The Palestinians, the Lebanese, the Jordanians and so on, see all of this from a much different perspective. We'll have difficulty seeing their point of view as long as we continue to subscribe to these basic assumptions."

David watched Levin carefully. He saw that he'd cracked Levin's arguments; a slight opening had occurred. He doubted, however, that this conversation alone would be sufficient.

"I understand your point, but I'm not sure I can accept it," Levin said.

"Look at it from another perspective. As you know, the Buddhist and Hindu peoples believe in reincarnation. So from that perspective, what possible sense can be made of claims that argue a historical lineage?"

"What do you mean?"

"From the perspective of reincarnation, we've all taken our turn being men and women, black and white, Jew and Gentile, rich and poor, beggar and king. If such is the case, how can anyone claim he is descended from one tribe, one race, or from one sex?"

"You can't argue that we have no claim to the land we call Israel," Goldstein blurted out.

David looked at Goldstein. "Neither more nor less than others. The United States has, in the past, accepted the same basic assumption to which you subscribe. Our policies regarding Israel and its neighbors reflected this. As I said before, that assumption has now been questioned."

"So what are you proposing?" demanded Levin.

"I'm proposing that we will no longer blindly support your country's actions no matter what you do. We will support direct talks with the PLO and other Arab leaders."

"You'll what?" Levin snapped.

David looked carefully at Levin, giving him a moment to calm down.

"Arafat has been the only representative for many displaced Palestinians. He speaks for them. You may not like what he has to say, but you cannot ignore him."

"We will never recognize him nor the PLO."

"That's nothing more than political posturing. Insisting that you don't recognize someone doesn't make that person go away; it only leaves you ignorant concerning him. The fact of the matter is that he exists and he does speak for many of the people that, by your own admission, hate you and wish to destroy you. That hatred comes from something, as I've been trying to point out. If these problems are to be resolved, they must first be understood. What I mean is that we must each be willing to listen to one another. We must find out what it is that bothers our so-called enemies. What do they believe from their point of view, what frustrations do they have, what hopes and aspirations? Without that understanding, little can occur that is beneficial for those concerned."

"We'll never deal directly with Arafat. Both he and the PLO have as their stated purpose the destruction of Israel."

"Do you think that a lifetime of war has no effect upon a man? You've been at war now for more than forty years and you're no closer to achieving peace than when you first began. I'm sure you've lost friends and loved ones to this incessant fighting. The same is true of Arafat. He's a human being like you and me. All of us have loved people, some of whom we've lost through death, some through violence and war. Only a few, the most hardened and fearful, remain untouched by such events.

"What is it like to near the end of one's life, to look back at what one has accomplished, and behold forty years of bloodshed, untold suffering, and no end in sight? I suspect a man such as yourself, having lived for more than seventy years, must have had such thoughts from time to time. Your own people, your neighbors and your allies are weary of this war. The time has come to bring it to an end. Talk with your enemies; talk with Arafat."

"This is not open for discussion," Levin said forcefully.

"I'm sorry to hear that."

"You said you wouldn't tell us what to do but would tell us, instead, what you will do. We've heard only a little of what you'll do. You've indulged us in a history lesson that we don't accept. What's the rest?"

"You're right. I wanted you to be the first to know what lies behind our changing policies. We will sever all financial ties, curtail all trade, and cancel all military contracts with you. We'll no longer guarantee your loans. We'll support the enforcement of UN Resolution 242. We'll consider introducing our own troops into areas where you attack civilians of neighboring nations..."

Levin jumped up, knocking the chair over. He was furious. "How dare you say such things? You'll not get the support of your congress, and I doubt your Joint Chiefs will go along with such actions."

"We'll see," said David, his voice firm. "You asked what we are prepared to do and I'm answering you. I want you to understand our point of view on these matters and be prepared for the actions that follow."

Levin his anger now under control, picked up his chair and sat down. "Go on," he said.

"What I'm explaining is a range of actions we're considering if things don't change."

"Yes, yes, get on with it," Levin snapped

Tremaine chose to ignore Levin's tone of voice. "We'll actively support the resolutions passed by the UN after the 1967 war. No longer will we function in a hypocritical manner. No longer will we support and enforce sanctions against Iraq and Somalia while ignoring the sanctions against you. Our policies from now on will be more evenhanded.

"On the other hand, we're prepared to use our good offices and goodwill to bring a lasting settlement. We'll do our best to defuse this powder keg that threatens us all."

Tremaine looked at Goldstein. He could feel the anger in the man.

"Speak your piece," he said.

"Your perspective reminds me of most anti-Semites I know. A more sophisticated one, that's true, but an anti-Semite nevertheless. This is nothing more than blatant prejudice."

Tremaine saw Levin's discomfort with his Foreign Secretary's statement. He did not take Goldstein's statement personally. He understood his feelings; he had, in the past, been in similar positions himself. Looking at Goldstein and then at Levin, he addressed both men.

"What you think of me is your business. I've no interest in being an anti-Semite. Nor do I have any interest in being a reverse anti-Semite. My only concern is to speak the truth as I see it, without fear of what others might think."

"What do you mean by reverse anti-Semite?" asked Levin.

"Racism is, as we know, a blatant form of prejudice associated with a person's skin color or nationality. The outer expression of prejudice becomes familiar and those who try not to appear as racists deliberately refrain from actions that might appear so. Such people are more interested in how they look to others than in the right action."

"What's that got to do with us?" Goldstein demanded.

"That your country was formed after the Second World War was no accident. Had it occurred at some other time, its founding might not have come about so easily and with so little regard for the people you displaced.

"We know what the Nazis did to the European Jews. We Americans, and I'm sure the British, too, felt guilt over those events. We should have been more willing to see the signs of what was happening. We did not want to believe the reports we heard, and as long as it didn't touch us directly, we were reluctant to get involved. Going to war is not something to be undertaken lightly.

"I suspect there was considerable guilt over what occurred during the Holocaust and, for that reason, among others, we supported the establishment of the State of Israel and turned a blind eye to those who were displaced. We've continued to turn a blind eye to actions your country took that we felt were extreme.

"It's abhorrent to me that in your own press and in ours, the death of one Israeli is considered a horrendous act while the death of twenty or a hundred Palestinians is reported with as little concern as the death of so many rats. I'm not accusing you of what we are not guilty ourselves. We did the same during the Vietnam War. Life is life, and is equally precious, regardless of the nationality or the color of the skin.

"Getting back to the Holocaust: it was uncomfortable for us to speak to you, after what you'd been through.

"That's what I mean by a reverse anti-Semitism. I don't care if you label me an anti-Semite—that's your business and has nothing to do with reality. I'll continue to speak the truth without regard for a person's skin color, national origin, or spiritual tradition. Now, if you don't like it, I'm sorry; but that's your problem, not mine."

David paused for a moment then continued.

"Of one thing you can be sure. This administration will speak the truth as we see it. We will do our best to express our views with clarity and the reasoning behind them. We will actively seek to understand those who disagree with us. We are open to all points of view. Understanding does not occur when one is unwilling to listen or consider points of view other than one's own."

Levin didn't like what he'd heard this afternoon. He was tired and wanted a break, something to eat and a good rest. David sensed the exhaustion of his guests and knew it was time to bring the conversation to a close.

"Why don't we take a break for a while? You can get some rest and then, please, share dinner with my wife and me. We'll eat at eight if that's acceptable to you."

The invitation was accepted and the Israelis left. David walked to the window and stood looking into the garden. Large black clouds boiled threateningly over the city. Lightning flashed and thunder rumbled close by.

"What has happened here today will send shock waves through the Middle East," Doug said quietly.

Tremaine turned and looked at Doug and Jonathan.

"It strikes me," said David, "that what's being worked out in the Middle East today is the old conflict between the half brothers, Esau and Jacob."

"I'm not familiar with that story," Doug said.

"Oh, I'm sorry. The story goes that Isaac had two sons, Esau the elder and Jacob the younger. In those days the father, as head of the household, bestowed his herds and certain belongings upon the eldest son. This was an expression of the father's blessing. It was not something done lightly. Isaac decided the time had come for the ceremony to take place. Esau went out hunting to find the ingredients to make his father's favorite dish. Jacob's mother, who was not Esau's mother, had schemed to have her son receive the blessing instead.

"Isaac, getting on in years, could no longer see properly. She prepared Isaac's favorite dish herself, and while Esau was out hunting brought Jacob to receive Esau's blessing. She was able to fool Isaac into thinking Jacob was Esau."

"How did she do that?"

"Esau was peculiarly hairy, and so Jacob's mother covered her son Jacob with goat skins. When Jacob entered carrying Isaac's dish, pretending to be his half-brother, Isaac was surprised his son had returned so quickly. Unable to see, he reached out and touched his son. Feeling the hair, he was convinced that

Jacob was Esau.

"Isaac bestowed the blessing and his herds upon Jacob. When Esau returned, he prepared his father's meal. When he entered his father's presence, they both learned of the deception. Esau begged his father to rescind his blessing and bestow it on him instead. Although Isaac would have loved to, he felt bound by his oath. He loved his son dearly and was angry over the deception. He believed that once a man's word was given, it couldn't be changed.

"From that time forth, there was great animosity between the two brothers. In fact Jacob had to flee in order to escape his brother's murderous rage. As the story goes, God changed Jacob's name to Israel and told him he'd be the father of a special nation."

CHAPTER 7

"We must leave quickly," Nassir said., "Come with me." He turned and headed back along the trail. Shamir followed. She felt dazed, unable to fully comprehend what had happened. As they came to the top of the incline, she heard the frightening sound of rockets passing overhead.

"There are men in these hills; we must not attract their attention." Nassir had turned toward her, making sure she heard him above the noise. She nodded. For half an hour she followed him. They passed the well from which she'd drawn water for so many years. She noted absently that the flock was gone.

Nassir was moving fast, and she struggled to keep up with him. Finally they came to a valley leading toward the rocky peaks of the mountains to the northeast. Nassir headed up its slope. The going was rough, and she could tell by the lengthening shadows that it was almost evening. For an hour they climbed quickly.

Then, above her labored breathing, she heard the sound

of gunfire somewhere behind them. She turned to look, but Nassir grabbed her by the hand and pulled her toward an outcropping of rocks and stunted oak. She scrambled as hard as she could. At last they reached the protection the rocks afforded. Nassir pushed her down and peered out from behind the rocks and through the trees.

Out of breath and lying flat, she pulled herself to the edge of the outcropping and looked over just in time to see two jets far below, lifting out of the valley they'd followed earlier. Hugging the hills, the jets streaked toward them. In the failing light she saw flashes of fire from the guns on their wings.

Whoever the jets were firing at must have been following the same valley she and Nassir had been climbing. As they watched, one of the jets exploded in a huge ball of flame. A moment later they heard the sound and watched pieces of flaming wreckage tumble lazily through the air. The remaining war plane peeled off and, at high speed, turned back toward its prey. Guns blazed long beads of brightness in the sudden darkness. Then, as quickly as they'd come, the aircraft were gone. Only a hushed silence remained.

Shamir and Nassir looked in the direction from which the jets had come. In the distance to the west, a light winked on and off. Above them a ridge of mountains formed a black silhouette against a carpet of scattered stars in the sky above them. Suddenly, to the south three bright lights lifted out of the darkness and arched across the night sky to disappear over a ridge to the south.

"What's that?" Shamir whispered.

"Rockets being fired across the border into Israel. Come," he said and reached down to pull her to her feet. "We've got to get away from here. We must be far away by morning. If the planes catch us in the open, we won't stand a chance."

....

By ten o'clock that night, they were climbing along a ridge Shamir had seen earlier that day, before the light faded.

"We'll rest here." Nassir sat with his back to a rock. Shamir sat beside him. A cool breeze was blowing and brought with it the familiar scents of the high country. They heard a loud hoarse braying from a donkey somewhere to the north. For a while they sat quietly. Shamir caught her breath; the cool breeze on her skin was refreshing. Turning to the east, she saw a huge full moon rise from behind the serrated peaks above.

While Shamir beheld the beauty before her, in the pit of her stomach she felt a hollow pain, an aching, uncomprehending sorrow. Watching the moon as it lifted into the sky, she recalled the night before, when she'd sat with her parents and then, before going to bed, she'd kissed her brothers and sister as they lay sleeping. All dead! She couldn't believe it. Last night was a world away now. Her life would never be the same. Tears flowed down her cheeks. Nassir put his arm about her shoulders and for a while let her cry.

....

Shamir was exhausted when at last she saw the approaching dawn. She followed Nassir down a steep ravine into a dark valley. They were no longer following a trail, and she slipped in loose shale, but Nassir stopped her slide before she went over the edge. She found herself trembling.

"Not much further to go," he promised.

She looked at him in the subdued light and saw the exhaustion in his face. She got to her feet, and they continued. When they reached the floor of the valley, the going was easier. Eventually they came to a steep rock face.

Carefully, Nassir climbed a narrow goat trail that angled up the side of the wall. Shamir looked up to see where it went. In the faint light of dawn, she saw it disappear into a sharply inclined ravine a hundred meters above where she stood.

Carefully she worked her way up the trail until she reached the intersecting ravine. Nassir was waiting for her. She stood to catch her breath. The valley floor below was lost in shadow, while the rim above was bathed in the light of the rising sun. Rocks and boulders stood in stark relief while the grasses shone golden, waving in the early morning breeze.

Shamir turned to follow Nassir, but he was nowhere in sight. She looked up the ravine toward a cluster of giant boulders that had fallen from the rocky wall. She walked toward them. As she approached she saw Nassir sitting in the shadow, his back against the cliff.

"We've made it," he said.

"Where will we stay?" asked Shamir.

"Up there. " He pointed.

All she could see were more boulders protruding from the rocky wall and rising thirty meters from where she now stood, nearly seventy five meters from the top of the wall.

"Come," he said and climbed directly up the tumbled boulders. She followed, careful not to fall into the cracks. At last she reached the top, shaking from exertion.

Nassir lowered himself through an opening and signaled her to follow. As she did so, she found herself climbing down a sharply inclined tunnel that gave access to a large cave. Light entered indirectly from several sources at the back. As she looked around, it was apparent that the cave was lived in. Sheepskins were spread on the floor around a circle of firestones. Leather water skins hung on poles, and she noted cooking utensils and a variety of foods on ledges. On one side were two sleeping pallets with woven blankets covering them. At the back she could hear the sound of trickling water.

"Welcome to my summer home." Nassir smiled at her. "We're safe here; it's not easy to find. There's a spring of water over there," he said, pointing in the direction of the trickling water. "If you want, you can wash. I'll get us something to eat, and then you can rest."

They were both hungry and ate in silence. When they finished, Nassir pointed toward one of the sleeping pallets.

"You can take that one over there. I must go and check on the flock. My brother's watching them, and he is expecting me."

"Don't you need to get some rest?" she asked.

"Once I make it to the flock, I'll get some rest, but I need to be off before it's too hot. I'll be back at dusk. If you need to go out, be careful not to be seen; stay in the shadows as much as possible. Help yourself to food and water."

She watched him as he gathered dried fruit and picked up a water skin. Then he turned to her.

"I'm sorry to leave you, but I think you'll sleep well. You'll be perfectly safe here. I'll see you when I get back."

Slinging the skin over his shoulder, he disappeared through the opening. She walked over to the pallet and lay down. Before long she fell into an exhausted sleep filled with frightening dreams.

....

She watched helplessly as an Israeli war plane came directly at her, guns blazing. She awoke with a scream. For a moment she didn't know where she was. Then the memories of the preceding night flooded in, and she shook with great sobs. She missed her family. Vividly etched in her mind was the convulsive movement of her father's body as he was struck by bullets from the low-flying aircraft. She wanted to kill those who'd killed her parents, her brothers and sister. Sorrow and rage alternated in an endless cycle with the images and thoughts in her mind.

Finally she got up and looked around. It was already afternoon. She drank some water, found some dried fruit, and taking it with her, went through the entrance. She climbed above the opening and sat in the shade against the rocky face. She looked around. She had a good view of all approaches. Hidden in the shadow she would be difficult to see.

What could she do? Where would she go? What was to become of her? There were no answers to these questions. After a while her eye caught a movement far below, and she watched as Nassir emerged into the lower end of the ravine. Quickly he moved toward her then disappeared from sight, only to reappear from behind the rocks below. Reaching the top, he stood and looked around. Catching sight of her, he waved. She stood and went to greet him.

"I'm glad you're back," she said.

He looked at her closely, detecting the sorrow in her voice. He noticed the cheeks still wet with tears, the eyes swollen and red. He was glad she'd been crying. His heart went out to her. He knew what she was going through. Opening his arms, he let her head rest on his shoulder and held her as she cried.

....

They ate in silence. When they'd finished, they went outside. Once more she followed Nassir along a narrow trail leading to the rim above the valley. He helped her up, and they climbed higher into the mountain. Darkness had fallen by the time they stopped.

From where they sat they could view all approaches and would be aware of any movements beneath them. A warm breeze brought again the fragrance of old cedar. Overhead, the great dome was studded with millions of winking lights.

Nassir spread a blanket on a smooth rock and they sat back to back. An hour passed before Nassir finally spoke.

"Talk to me, little one," he said softly.

Immediately her eyes filled with tears. After they subsided, she told him of her day and the thoughts that bedeviled her mind.

"Let the thoughts come," he said. "They cannot be stopped. They come by themselves, don't they?"

"Yes, they do," she whispered

"Then let them come and let them go. Be toward the thoughts as you are toward the clouds that appear and disappear by themselves, leaving you untouched."

"How can I?" she asked. "I want to kill those who killed my family, but I don't know where to begin or how to go about it."

Nassir felt the rage in her and understood.

"In the morning you'll meet my brother. When you do, you'll see there's something wrong with him; he's simple."

"Was he born that way?" she asked.

"No, he was struck in the head with a gun by an Israeli soldier. It left him brain-damaged. He knows sheep though, and that knowledge seems unaffected. He's been a great help to me. He no longer has much need to be around people, and so the silence of these mountains is home to him."

"What happened to the soldier who hurt your brother?"

"My father killed him."

"When did this happen?"

"Forty years ago."

"Nassir, what happened? Can you tell me?"

"I will tell you. I've not told this story before, but I think it has bearing on your own. Perhaps you will learn from it. I once told your parents that their gift to life was the love they gave their children. It is their legacy to you. They have nurtured you with love and an inner strength. In this way have they molded you for what destiny has in store."

Shamir was puzzled by this statement but said nothing.

Nassir sat quietly for a few minutes collecting his thoughts, and then, as though seeing the events before him, he began his story.

....

"My family had been shepherds for generations, and the land on which they raised sheep lay in both southern Lebanon and what is now northern Israel. When the State of Israel came into existence, we had no idea of the changes about to take place.
"The British had broken the hold of the Turks and established their own rule. But none of it really affected the lives of the people who'd lived on the land for generations. None of us really expected any changes this time either.

"My mother and father had three children, my two older brothers and myself. Father worked the flocks with my uncle, who also lived with us. My mother ran the home, and as my brothers and I became old enough, we helped my father and uncle tend the sheep. We were sometimes away for days at a time. My mother spent time carding, spinning and weaving and had charge over the household. We lived in a small valley that sloped from the hills and gave way to the Mediterranean, much like the valley where you lived. We had almond trees, sycamore, and a tall, beautiful stand of poplar. It was a lovely place.

"We didn't understand at the time that our home was just inside the northern border of the new Jewish state. One morning I was to leave early with my father, uncle, and two brothers. We were moving the flock higher into the mountains. That morning

I wasn't feeling well. I felt light-headed and couldn't keep food down. I was disappointed I had to stay behind. I was ill for two days, but by the end of the second day I was feeling better. We expected the men to return any time.

My mother, Fatah, and I were sitting at the table. We'd finished supper and were talking by the light of the lamp. I loved my mother. She must have been thirty-seven at the time. She was a striking and beautiful woman with a lovely warmth about her dark almond eyes and jet black hair. We heard a sound outside and were about to get up, thinking the men had returned, when the door burst open. In the light from the lamp four soldiers glared at us, rifles leveled. They were Israeli soldiers. It was the first time I'd ever seen them, but I knew from the Star of David on their shirts who they were. While one of them covered us with his rifle, the others went outside and returned a few moments later.

"They tied my hands with cord and pushed me into a chair. I was shaking with fear. I looked at my mother. She was shaking too. Then two of the soldiers grabbed her, and the third started tearing her clothes off. They raped her in front of me, right there on the kitchen floor. When they were finished, they dragged us both outside. Several hundred yards away stood a military truck and a jeep with more Israeli soldiers, waiting nearby.

"We were dragged toward the jeep and watched as men poured gasoline and torched the house and surrounding buildings. The fire lit up the sky. Then above the roar of flames, we heard shouts coming from the hills. I knew it was the men returning home. The Israelis heard the shouts, too. All but the four soldiers who'd entered the house jumped in the truck and drove away. The soldier holding my mother pulled his gun, and before I realized what was happening, held it to her head and killed her. I managed to loosen the cord around my wrists, and when he turned toward me I charged, knocking him down. The gun spun out of his hand. I dove on it, and grasping it firmly, turned toward him. He was scrambling to his feet. Drawing a knife, he came straight for me. I leveled the gun and fired.

"I'll never forget the surprised look on his face as he fell in the dirt. Shots rang out, and I felt something strike my arm. It burned and spun me around. Lying on the ground I saw that the remaining soldiers crouched beside the jeep, their rifles leveled at me. Then, as I watched, my father and uncle came racing into the light of the fire. The soldiers were so concentrated on me they were unaware of anyone behind them. My father and uncle swung their staves at the heads of two of the soldiers. They went down before they could get off a shot. The third man fired, but his aim was spoiled by my older brother, who charged him from behind. The rifle jerked out of his grasp. He grabbed it by the barrel and swung it at my brother, hitting him in the head. He hit him several times before my father killed him."

Nassir paused.

"Nassir, I'm so sorry. That's a terrible story."

"Yes, it is, but it's only the beginning. It's the latter part of the story that can save you needless suffering."

"What do you mean?"

"After we nursed my brother back to health, he and my uncle looked after the sheep. My brother and father and I joined one of the guerrilla groups defending the land against the Israelis. We started attacking them wherever we could. For five years we raided, killing the men and destroying their property. We knew the hills and mountains far better than they, and in the beginning they were no match for us.

"One evening we attacked a convoy of industrial equipment being delivered to a new factory. We ambushed the trucks in a narrow valley and blew several of them up. Most of their men were killed in the initial ambush. Several, however, managed to escape and dug in against a low cliff. Each time we tried to overrun them, we got hit with fire from a machine gun.

"Under cover of darkness we got close enough to lob grenades. We couldn't tell whether we'd killed them all. We withdrew carefully and waited for morning. With the early light of day we moved in, only to get caught in a hail of bullets. One of our men was wounded, and we withdrew.

"Open and exposed, we were unable to attack head on. Our men took cover behind the wrecked trucks, and we devised a plan. Since I knew the terrain well, I was to work my way into the cliff behind them while the other men kept them distracted by frontal fire. I was in position by late afternoon.

"For some reason the Israelis had not contacted their base. Maybe their radios had been destroyed. Anyway we were not attacked by planes as we'd feared. As the sun sank, the shadows lengthened, and I was able to crawl to a place above the enemy position. All firing had stopped, and stillness descended with the approaching night.

"Looking down I could see the Israelis, dug into the sand behind some rocks. I counted ten of them. I watched, and there was no movement. They seemed at odd angles, and then I realized they were dead. There'd been no firing from them since mid-afternoon. Carefully, I climbed to where they were. As I got closer, I saw they were indeed dead, some of them severely dismembered from the grenades the night before.

"I climbed over the parapet for a closer look and carefully checked each one of them. I heard a sound behind me. I whirled around in time to see one of the Israelis getting to his feet. I saw something glint in his hand as he moved toward me. We were so close I couldn't get my rifle up. I felt his weight on me, and in that moment I drew my knife and drove it deep in his gut. His mouth was beside my ear, his chin on my shoulder. I could hear the agony.

"As he slid to the ground, I rolled him over. He was a young man no more than eighteen with brown hair and blue eyes. Blood oozed from a wound high on the chest, and the side of his face was badly disfigured and covered with dry blood. He looked at me and I looked at him. He tried to say something and lifted his hand. I jumped back. Then I saw in his hand a silver pen and a piece of folded paper. With his eyes he pleaded for me to take it. I reached down and opened his hand. The pen fell out and I took the paper. It was a letter that read:

Dear Mama,
We were ambushed yesterday, and most of the men were killed. Some of us were able to escape but were soon pinned down by enemy fire. In the early morning just before the sun came up, we were hit by grenades. All of us were wounded. In the heat of this awful day my comrades died. I know I'll not live long. I want to tell you how much I love you and that I thought of you and Papa at the end. Give Benjamin a hug for me. I'm sorry I'll not see him become a man. Tell my lovely Sarah I love her and I'm sorry to cause her grief. I hope she finds a good man to love her one day. May she find happiness and joy when the time comes. The sun is going down, and I know there's not much time. I see a Palestinian fighter coming. I'll try and give him this.
Love,
Your son
Josef

"I looked down at the dying soldier. His eyes pleaded, and his lips gurgled blood. I knelt beside him and gently took his head in my lap. Leaning over, I whispered a promise in his ear.

'I'll see your family gets the letter.'

I straightened up, looked in his eyes and said, 'I'm so sorry.'

In that moment I felt forgiveness flowing from him. I sat

with him, company in his dying. He gripped my arm. His body shuddered in one last breath and then lay still. I removed his identification tag and later sent it with the letter to his parents."

Shamir was crying softly. Nassir lost in thoughts of his own, let her cry. When she stopped, he continued.

"I left the group of men with whom I'd fought and went into the mountains. I thought a lot about what had happened, the events of the past five years. I saw that hatred and the thirst for revenge had poisoned my very being. The young soldier had somehow set something in motion. I saw that hatred begets hatred and in the process twists the human being into a monster. I spent forty days in the mountains, and then one day I had the distinct feeling I had to find something or someone. It was a strange feeling that stayed with me for months.

One day I climbed high into the mountains. From there I had an unobstructed view to the west. In the distance the Mediterranean stretched to the horizon. The lower slopes of hills showed green and lush, and vineyards draped the undulating hills, like patches. Small settlements, whitewashed houses with their red slate roofs, and clumps of trees dotted the landscape.

"As I wandered along a ridge I noticed a grove of cedars nestled in a small ravine below. I climbed down and walked into the grove. The smell of cedar permeated the warm air, and a breeze stirred the upper limbs of the ancient trees. It was late afternoon, and birds called back and forth in anticipation of day's end. I sat beneath a tree and, leaning against the trunk, looked up into the mountain.

"Beyond the ridge I'd just descended, the jagged sand and orange-colored peaks pushed into the blue sky. Some of the higher peaks trailed long wisps of thin cloud. I sat and watched the changing colors and lengthening shadows. As I watched, I caught a movement above me and saw an old man come into view, ascending from the other side of the ridge.

"He stood on the top for a few moments as though getting his bearings and then started down the ravine toward the cedars. He wore white cotton pants gathered below the knees. On his feet were a pair of old sandals. He wore a white, loose-fitting shirt, and around his shoulders hung a robe much like a thick, cotton blanket, in which a pale red and gray pattern had been woven. His skin showed the effects of long exposure to the sun. His hair was white and long. He had a white mustache, and on his face the stubble of several days' growth.

"I watched him as he came to the trees. He entered the glade and then stopped. He paused, waiting and listening as though expecting someone. After a few moments he approached my hiding place. I pulled back out of sight and continued to watch. He stopped ten meters in front of me. Although the light would soon fade, I saw his face clearly. There was something about him I really liked. His movements, I realized, were graceful and effortless despite his advanced years.

"In his hand he carried a stout walking staff, which he leaned against a tree. Taking the blanket from around his shoulders, he spread it on the ground and on it placed a small carrying bag. He sat down and crossed his legs and closed his eyes. His back was straight and relaxed. Dusk fell upon the mountain, and the birds became suddenly quiet. I made myself as comfortable as I could and waited to see what would happen next.

"I must have fallen asleep, for when I awoke, a shaft of moonlight came through the trees, illuminating the glade in which he sat. He was still as I'd last seen him, except that his eyes were open and he was looking in my direction.

"'Come and sit with me, Nassir.'

"I couldn't tell if I'd really heard the words, for they seemed to originate in my head. I waited.

"'Come and sit with me, Nassir. I've been waiting for you, waiting until you were ready for what I must give you.'

"Again I couldn't tell where the sound of his voice was coming from, and I remained still and hidden, or so I thought.

"'Yes, I'm speaking to you. You cannot hide from me. I know what has happened. I know of your beloved mother's cruel death, of the young Israeli soldier. Come and sit with me I've come for you.'

"I got up and stepped into the clearing. He patted the blanket in front of him.

"'Sit here,' he said.

I sat in front of him and felt a great relief then found myself crying. It was as though I'd found my way home after being lost for a long time. I cried much like you have, and when I could cry no more, I saw him still sitting there, his eyes looking into mine.

"'The light of truth is to be yours. It is latent in your heart, and it's my task to light it. Once it flames of its own accord, you will in turn pass it on to those who are ready. What I've said encompasses the beginning and the end. What lies between is yet to be awakened.'

"'What do you mean?' I asked.

"'I've come to burn that which is dead and dry. It will be consumed with a great heat and provide light for the understanding that is to come. When it's finished, the understanding of an unspeakable simplicity will be present. In due time you must kindle the same light, in those who are ready. And so it goes, generation after generation from the beginning to the end of time. The dance of life spins out and is a wonder to behold. For such a one, suffering has ended, and the heart overflows with compassion.'

"We were together for six months. I had many questions at first, and then at last they were exhausted and I felt a profound stillness within me. He sent me to find my uncle and brother, saying they had need of my help. He explained that when I was ready, I could come and see him again. My brother and uncle were glad of my help, and we worked together from that time forth.

"One day word came to us that my father and my other brother had been killed. For the next six years, I tended the flocks and went to see the master whenever I felt the need. One night I had a dream. The master came toward me, his eyes radiating a deep love, which I received and gave back. He kissed me on the cheeks, and without a word, turned and walked away. I knew I would not see him again, and I never did."

Shamir sat in the silence, thinking of the strange story Nassir had told. Tears rolled down her face.

"Who was he?" she asked eventually.

"He was a Sufi sage; I only knew him as Bokhari."

"Was he able to heal the sorrow in your heart?" Shamir asked.

"He was," Nassir answered simply.

"Will you help me too, Nassir?"

"If it is the desire of your heart."

"It is," she answered.

Tears flowed and took with them the poison that hurt her. When the moon had risen high in the sky, they returned, by its light, to the cave.

CHAPTER 8

Michael Levin and Joseph Goldstein, despite their initial trepidation, enjoyed dinner with the Tremaines. Once more they were surprised at the informality with which they were greeted. Their hosts were dressed casually and comfortably rather than in the semiformal attire they were expecting. The president wore a loose-fitting white cotton shirt open at the neck and loose-fitting light brown cotton slacks with beige loafers that appeared to be made of soft comfortable leather.

Sandra, whom they'd not met before, wore a full silk skirt with a green and blue floral design. Her sleeveless silk blouse was a solid blue that complemented the skirt. She wore pretty, low-heeled blue shoes.

Only the four of them were present, Sandra and David having elected to serve the guests themselves. At first the experience was disconcerting to the Israelis, but after a while they loosened their ties, removed their jackets, and felt more comfortable. After dinner they moved into the study.

"Would you like coffee?" David asked.

"Yes," they said.

"I'll make some," he said, then added, "I'll be back shortly." With that he left the room.

"This is quite different from our last visit," commented Michael.

"It certainly is," agreed Joseph.

"How do you mean?" asked Sandra, looking at the two men.

"It's very informal," said Michael.

"Oh," Sandra smiled. "Neither one of us like formality, and since we've taken on this job, we might as well be comfortable and do things the way we like to. Both of us enjoy cooking, which we do as often as time permits. We didn't want that to change once we moved here. It's been a fight, though, to get our way. Privacy is important to us, and it's difficult to have privacy in this position."

"I know what you mean," said Joseph.

"You know, Mrs. Tremaine, this whole day has been rather unusual and quite disconcerting."

Sandra looked at Michael Levin and saw the confusion in his face. "Please call me Sandra— I like my name!" she said with a mischievous smile.

"All right."

"How has it been disconcerting?" she asked.

"We came to your country after a most disturbing conversation with your Foreign Secretary, Doug Kersey. He had conveyed a message from your husband. We hoped in coming here to change his mind and restore support for our actions against the guerrillas in Lebanon."

"And how did you fare?" Sandra asked with a slight smile.

"He understood our position." Michael said. Joseph

nodded. "But your husband's point of view was difficult for us to accept. We find ourselves in an awkward position."

"In what way?"

There was an uncomfortable silence, and the two Israelis looked at each other.

"You may speak frankly with me," Sandra said. "What's on your minds?"

"Well, as I said, the conversation this afternoon was difficult for us to understand," said Levin, obviously uncomfortable and unwilling to go further. The two men were unaccustomed to a woman being so direct.

Sandra laughed, and her eyes twinkled, making the two men even more ill at ease. "I'll bet you wondered if he was an anti-Semite, crazy, or... ill-suited for the job as president. You wouldn't be the first to have such thoughts."

The two men looked at her, with uneasy smiles.

Sandra laughed again. "On the latter point he'd be the first to agree. He might even agree on the second point. On the first, however, he would have to disagree. I know David well, and he's one of the most sane men I've ever known. He is in no way a bigot or racist. He has for a long time been deeply concerned for the well-being of indigenous peoples all over the world. He gets upset over the unthinking and uncaring treatment they receive at the hands of government."

Just then the phone rang and Sandra picked it up. She listened for a moment and, putting it down, excused herself. She returned in a few moments with coffee. Putting the tray down, she replaced the phone in its cradle.

"David has to take this," she said. "He'll come back as soon as he can."

Sandra poured coffee for her guests and herself. She sat back comfortably and watched the two men.

"David's an unusual thinker," she continued. "He's got

a knack for seeing through what most take for granted. He says that when things are locked up, no understanding is present. In Tai Chi, he who yields, in full awareness, breaks the deadlock of force."

"He used the word *understanding,* earlier today and I had the distinct feeling he meant something quite specific," Joseph interjected.

"Do you know what he means?" Michael asked.

"What he means is, there are many points of view concerning any one thing. By definition, no two points of view can ever coincide. Understanding comes about when all points of view are seen and taken into account.

"Problems often arise because those who hold a particular point of view are attached to it, attached to what they hope to gain from it. By the same token, others, holding other points of view are equally attached. And so it is that conflict arises.

"If the idea of *point of view* is truly understood, we will see that all points of view are essential to the greater understanding of the whole. When that occurs, appropriate action naturally follows, the stalemate is broken; the resolution is at hand."

The door opened, and David entered.

"I'm sorry to be so long," he said.

Sandra poured him a cup of coffee, and Michael extended his cup for a refill.

"I know you've had a long day and the time is getting late," David addressed the Israelis. "But I want to know if you've given thought to our earlier conversation. If you've any questions, please feel free to ask."

"We've given it a lot of thought," Michael responded. "We'll take your comments back and present them to our advisors and to the Knesset. You've placed us in an awkward position."

"Yes, I can imagine the conversation must have been a

shock."

"It was," Michael admitted. Joseph nodded in agreement. Michael paused for a moment as though debating with himself.

David waited and watched the two men. Both appeared tired— tired with years and tired with war, he thought. Joseph had a reputation as a great general, usually credited with the defeat of Egypt, Syria, and Jordan in the Six Day War.

"Are you really serious?" Michael asked. "Did you mean what you said this afternoon?"

"Yes, I'm completely serious. Please understand that behind my remarks there is only a desire to see a resolution to this endless conflict. I know that if and when you move toward peace, you'll encounter opposition, and it's possible peace may not, in the end, prevail. But, for your countrymen to keep going as they have for the last forty years will, in my opinion, only perpetuate the bloodshed."

"What do you mean that we'll encounter opposition if we move toward peace?" Joseph asked.

"I mean that, no matter what position one takes on any issue, there will always be those who will oppose it. Such is the nature of the beast. The more conservative and fundamental the opposition, the more a threat of violence is present. I would anticipate such opposition in your own country, and among some of the Palestinians in the occupied territories.

"We will encounter opposition here, too. Yet, I feel strongly that reasonable men and women of goodwill can and will carry the day. There's a war weariness among all concerned. I'm convinced a resolution can be found to many of the problems before us. Don't get me wrong. I'm not naive enough to believe this will happen every time, or overnight."

"Do you think there are times when force is warranted?"

"Of course. In this case, however, I feel understanding and firmness will bring the desired results. Talk with Arafat—in secret if necessary. Find out if he's serious. Find out what he needs. Find out the needs of the people he represents. Can you help him meet those needs? Communicate your own needs, and be sure he understands them. How can he help? Find out. If you do it quietly you'll not arouse opposition, and you can work for the time being without distraction."

The Israelis sat quietly, thinking about what had been said. The only sound in the room was the ticking of the clock on the mantel.

"Don't mistake what I said today as a personal attack on you or your countrymen. It's not! If it should be misconstrued as such, that is your doing alone. I have nothing but goodwill in my heart. Of one thing you can be sure: I will always speak the truth as I see it. You'll know where I stand. However, be aware that as things change, my point of view will change too."

Michael looked puzzled. "I'm not sure I follow you."

"Sandra told me that, during one of the Canadian elections, Robert Stanfield proposed wage and price controls. Pierre Trudeau, the Prime Minister, opposed them. Stanfield lost the election, and Trudeau was returned to power. Later Trudeau implemented Stanfield's ideas. A reporter asked Trudeau why he did so. Trudeau responded that at the time it was proposed, he didn't think it was a good idea. During the next year, however, the economy had taken a turn for the worse. I thought about Mr. Stanfield's ideas he said, and came to the conclusion they were worthwhile trying. The reporter pressed him further. Trudeau's response was that good ideas were not just the province of his own party. He appreciated good and creative ideas without concern for the political persuasion of those who espoused them.

"What I'm saying is that times change. If we advocate a particular policy and that policy is good at the time, it may or may not be good a year later. In this country the founding fathers fought a revolution against the British. Under those circumstances they understood the importance of the right to bear arms. Without arms they couldn't have thrown off the British yoke. Today the right to bear arms is championed by a powerful gun lobby. It advocates the right to purchase and own guns capable of great destruction. I'm sure you know that our country suffers from violence unprecedented in a modern nation not at war. We're in a position where criminals have weapons of such power that police are outgunned and cannot do their job.

"As far as I'm concerned, the right to bear arms must come to an end in order to restore our country to a semblance of internal harmony. Do you understand my point?"

"Yes, I do," said Michael.

Joseph's face was blank, unreadable. He did not want to divulge his thoughts.

"Let's call it a night," David said.

All of them stood.

"You'll be heading back tomorrow?" David asked.

"Yes," Michael responded. "We leave in the morning."

"Thank you for joining us for dinner," Sandra said, shaking their hands warmly. "It was a pleasure to have you with us."

The Israelis smiled and thanked her. They'd enjoyed the evening and the opportunity to speak with her. David opened the door and escorted them down the hall to their car.

"I expect to hear from you," David said.

"You will."

....

The Israelis sat back in the comfortable seats, lost in thought, as the car cleared the White House checkpoints.

Finally Joseph voiced the thoughts on his mind. "The more we talk with Tremaine, the more sensible he seems."

"Yes, and it puts us in a terrible quandary."

"Yes, I think so too. What are your thoughts?"

"When we came here I had one thing in mind: to get back the support we'd lost. I was frustrated we didn't, and angry over Tremaine's comments. I took them as a personal affront. But as he took pains to point out, there was nothing personal in his remarks. Then, on the way over this evening, I realized I was tired of this constant bloodshed. The thought of peace is appealing! Until today the idea of peace was just that, an idea that would come to pass sometime in the future. Not something here and now."

"Yes, he opened a door to possibilities that may have been there all the time."

"Perhaps he's right. What kept them hidden was our own thinking and the way we interpret everything to fit our own objectives."

"Such ideas will not easily be accepted in the Knesset."

"No. Perhaps we need to take seriously his suggestion and explore privately with Arafat. As a blind we could restart the peace talks with the Palestinians while we meet quietly with Arafat somewhere else and see what he has to say."

"You know," Joseph said, thinking out loud, "Tremaine's wife is an unusual woman. Once you get used to her forthrightness, she's actually quite delightful."

Michael nodded. "They make an interesting couple, all right."

The car entered the gates of the Israeli Embassy and stopped in front. The two men left the car and entered the building.

CHAPTER 9

Travis had a busy week. Twice he met with the Joint Chiefs. At the first meeting, he conveyed the gist of the conversation he'd had with Tremaine. They agreed to enlist the support of pro-military congressmen and senators. Under Travis' guidance they determined to prevent the president from opening the military to gays.

For a week they walked the halls of congress from early morning until late evening. Travis was successful in getting the chairman of the Senate Armed Services Committee, Sam Jackson, firmly behind him. Jackson was a tough man, probably the most powerful of the southern senators, and his influence was legendary. Jackson shared Travis' distaste for the new president based on his failure to serve in the military.

The day after his meeting with Jackson, Travis met with Senator Bill Cole, who'd taken on the mantle of opposition leader. Travis figured, because of Cole's knee-jerk reaction of opposing everything Emerson or Tremaine had been in favor of, the Senator would easily support Travis in opposing gays in the military. Travis was not disappointed. But to his surprise, he found Cole disturbing to deal with. He seemed more cunning than any politician Travis had ever met. He was no doubt intelligent, yet Travis was left with the impression that the man was not completely honest. He had a way with words; he could twist them to suit his purpose and make those who opposed him look like fools.

Travis was in the Senator's office when Senator Dixon came in. Cole excused himself for a few minutes and turned his attention to Dixon, who seemed nice enough but was no match for the wily Cole. Travis felt sorry for Dixon. When Travis left the office, it was with Cole's support and an uneasy feeling.

By the weekend, when they met again, the Joint Chiefs were pleased with the support they'd marshalled. Things looked good and Travis was confident they'd hand the president his first defeat. McManus had spoken with Bill Jamieson, the Secretary of Defense, who'd listened carefully and politely but refused to support their perspective.

"We never expected his support anyway," Travis explained defensively to the Joint Chiefs. "We don't need his help."

"You may be right, but it concerns me that we've not changed anyone's mind. All those who support us on this position did so to begin with. We've been preaching to the converted."

"McManus, you worry over nothing. Tremaine wouldn't dare oppose us on this matter. What's he going to do, fire us? I doubt it."

"Don't be so sure. From what you said yourself, he gave you a warning that he expects you to follow his orders whether you agree with them or not."

"That's what he said, but he can't function without our

help, and he knows it."

"I think we need to be cautious," interjected Frank Williams. "Tremaine's no fool. Yes, he needs our help all right but, we mustn't forget—like it or not, he is the Commander in Chief."

Travis was getting angry. "How can you call him the Commander in Chief? He's that in name only. We all know that! He knows less about the military than any of the recent presidents— and none of them felt competent to tell us how to do our job."

"Of course they couldn't tell us how to do our job," said Williams, "but they did make the policy decisions. It will be the same with this president, whether he served in the military or not."

"We'll see, we'll see," Travis said, calming things down. He preferred not to pursue this further. As long as they stayed on the topic of gays in the military, they were united; but as soon as they got on to the powers of the presidency, their harmony seemed to vanish.

After the meeting, Travis went home. Entering the house he ripped off his tie, grabbed a beer from the fridge, and flung himself in a chair. Clicking through the channels he found a football game and watched for half an hour. Through the window he saw Mildred, his wife, working in the garden. The game ended and he went upstairs and took a shower. When he came down, Mildred was washing her hands at the sink. He kissed her on the neck, and she smiled.

"We have dinner this evening at the convention. We leave by five thirty, he reminded her."

"Yes," she said. "As soon as I'm done putting things away, I'll get ready."

....

They left promptly at five thirty and by six forty-five entered the hall. The convention was the largest annual gathering of veterans anywhere in the country. More than two thousand descended on the city, and Travis was the keynote speaker. Dinner was at seven thirty, preceded by cocktails. He and Mildred circulated, looking for friends and other people they knew. Travis saw McManus and his wife as well as Frank Williams and Vince Bradford, both accompanied by their wives.

In some ways Travis disliked being the speaker because he had to be careful how much he drank. He didn't want to make a fool of himself. By the time they sat down for the meal, he was already feeling the effects of the alcohol. He was glad of some food.

After dinner he was introduced with emphasis on his three tours of duty in Vietnam. The hall erupted with applause; all rose to their feet.

Travis eager to get on with it, spoke into the microphone, and the hall quickly became quiet.

"I'm glad to be here tonight, glad to be among friends and those who've served our nation in its armed services. I don't have to tell you that our military is second to none. It represents the finest fighting machine in the world and has at its disposal the most sophisticated weaponry on the face of the earth. Largely because of its might, we've been able to live in peace. Because of its power, the threat of communism was held in abeyance until it collapsed of its own accord. Most of us never dreamed we'd see the changes we have. Who'd have guessed that the Berlin Wall would be gone, and the once mighty Soviet Union would no longer exist? The world has changed, and the military must change with it.

"We must down-size and that's not easy. Because we've all served, we know how important it is to always be on guard. To show weakness is to give our enemies an invitation to exploit that weakness. This we will never do. As chairman of the Joint Chiefs, I promise we will never allow that to happen.

"Given the changing times, we cannot justify keeping two armies to fight on two fronts simultaneously. We will instead keep a large standing army capable of great mobility, and of responding to the threat of hostile forces as we did in the Gulf War. The new Army will be more mobile and more sophisticated than any the world has ever known. Combined with the Air Force, it will be capable of rapid deployment anywhere in the world, in a matter of days.

"Our Air Force has already demonstrated the unsurpassed capability of our fliers, support personnel, and the aircraft and weaponry at our disposal. With increasing technology that will continue to improve. In the Navy, as in the Air Force, we're moving more into the area of stealth technology. Modern weaponry will engender less danger for our own personnel, while inflicting higher and higher casualties on those who decide to tangle with us.

"But we are faced with a problem, one that threatens to undermine the strength of our military forces. No matter how developed our training is, or how sophisticated our weaponry, the heart of any fighting force is its morale. When morale is low, battles are lost and defeat is inevitable. Yes, we face a serious crisis, and the crisis is one of morale.

"In the last election, candidate Emerson promised gays and lesbians that he would allow them to serve. He would not allow discrimination on the basis of sexual orientation, he said. The very utterance of such words concerned many within the military organization as a whole.

"After Emerson's election, commanders reported that some young men under their command talked of refusing to re-enlist if gays were admitted. Others threatened to quit regardless of the cost. Induction centers reported a decline in enlistees.

Although I don't condone it, a gay soldier was beaten to death by another soldier in Japan. There's no doubt in my mind that such action is merely an outward expression of how disturbing a policy this can be.

"Nothing will do more to undermine the morale of our military men and women than to allow homosexuals to serve freely. Because the gays have organized themselves into pressure groups, we cannot allow them to dictate policy on such important matters as this. Under no circumstances can national security be compromised.

"Yes, that's exactly what's at risk here. What we face is a threat to our national security through the undermining of our morale."

The hall erupted in applause and a standing ovation. When finally the applause subsided, Travis continued.

"If you love your country, you must help. You must call your senators and congressmen. Let them know how you stand on this matter. Write letters, and send them, too. The President is considering issuing an executive order to implement this policy. We must do our best to stop him. If it is issued, we must be able to override the order. We of the Joint Chiefs will do our part, but it will be easier if we have your unqualified support. You must organize your fellow veterans. Under no circumstances can we allow the implementation of this policy, and you must do your part to stop it. Thank you."

Once more the hall was filled with applause. Travis made his way from the stage and back to the table. All around him veterans stood, clapping, cheering, patting him on the back and offering words of encouragement. He felt good. While he was speaking he noticed members of the press at the back of the hall and along the sides. His speech would be in the morning papers.

He and Mildred left the gathering at midnight. As they came out of the hotel, they were met by a crush of reporters, cameras, microphones, and flashbulbs. Already his speech had signaled the beginning of a war between the military and the new president, and the members of the press, smelling blood, were ready.

"What will you do if the President issues his executive order? Will you obey it?'

"I think he knows he cannot sustain it so I don't think he'll issue it," Travis responded.

"Do you speak for the Joint Chiefs? Do they feel the same way?"

"Yes, to both questions."

"Is this a clash between the military and a civilian president?"

"No, this has to do with our national security. Under no circumstances can we undermine the morale of our troops."

"Is it not the task of the President to determine national security?"

"When it comes to military matters, it's up to the military to determine national security."

"But the President is the Commander in Chief, surely he's the one with the final say."

"That would be the case if the President understood the military and was familiar with the way it works. Because of his lack of experience, this President should not be expected to function with competence in such matters. Therefore, I'm sure, he will consider carefully the advice of his military advisors."

"Is this a slap at the President because of his lack of military service?"

"You may concoct whatever ideas you want."

"What's it like to be under the direct authority of a man who never served in the military and who, in fact, was opposed to our country's involvement in Vietnam?"

Travis, realizing he was being drawn into dangerous

territory, brought things to an end.

"Goodnight, gentlemen and ladies," he said with a salute.

With the help of his military aides he made his way to the waiting car through the blinding flashes of the cameras. Nearing the bottom of the steps he tripped and, but for one of his aides, would have fallen. Quickly he helped Mildred into the car, got in himself, and closed the door. He was glad of the sudden quiet.

"Home!" he ordered.

....

David finished the movements. He found Tai Chi both restful and energizing. After going through the warm-up exercises, he felt his body slip into the effortless grace of the form. Although his body moved, his mind was still. There was something so basic about Tai Chi that he always felt connected to the earth. It was an awareness that the body was from the earth and would return to the earth. He felt a sense of oneness with the ancient Taoist monks who'd developed the art so many years ago. They'd understood the nature of the Tao and in some unfathomable way had found the means to express that knowledge through the graceful movements of the form. Over the years he'd maintained Tai Chi on a regular basis, something done as regularly as eating or drinking. Today, after an hour's workout, he was finished.

He walked slowly through the garden. It was still early, and he could hear the intensifying hum of morning traffic. Ten years ago, if he'd entered politics, he would have done so for all the wrong reasons. He could not have escaped the trap of self-importance with its incessant need for approval. Avinash had made all the difference. Never would he forget that first meeting with the master.

For as long as he could remember, he'd been interested in spiritual things. This had been the call of philosophy, which he loved so deeply. Philosophy was an inquiry into the nature of reality, an inquiry into human nature and mankind's relationship to the universe. It asked the questions: Who am I? Where do I come from? What is this "I" I call myself? What is real? What is illusion? What is good and evil, moral and immoral? He had understood intuitively that philosophy gave rise to the various psychologies. Psychology always took the form peculiar to the answers found by such questions.

He had longed to know someone who understood it all, someone who had more than an intellectual comprehension. He'd sensed that such knowledge was available but didn't know where to look, and he still had much to learn. A desire to serve had taken him into the field of psychology, which to him was an application of philosophy.

Years before he'd been engaged in social action, and that had given way to a more inward journey. At a demonstration in Boston he'd witnessed a policeman brutalize a helpless young man, breaking his spine with a vicious blow from a night stick. And he, David the pacifist, went into a blind rage, solel intent on killing. In that moment he discovered that the beast he'd so readily seen in others was resident in himself as well. At once he realized that social action was useless without a change of heart. From that time forth he sought to know and understand himself.

Thirty years ago he repudiated the church and the religion of his childhood as being too filled with dishonest men and women. He wanted no part of it. He'd rather risk hell than enter a heaven filled with such hypocrisy. He knew, even then, that he was a child of the universe and the universe was a friendly place. The fires of hell described by the preachers could no longer touch him; they were merely figments of diseased minds, and he knew it.

The ingestion of LSD and peyote broke the hold of his rational mind, his mind that had been like a steel trap. The mind, he had believed, was all-important. A rational approach, he was convinced, was the avenue to truth. At the time he had a mechanistic understanding of the world. He saw objects as objects and only intellectually understood the nature of energy.

But on those explorations with drugs he came to know first-hand what he'd taken for real— namely objects with density, size and shape, were in fact nothing more than vibrations of energy. He saw everything was made of energy. Everything vibrated at frequencies peculiar to them. Those vibrations were like signatures with specific characteristics which, in turn, gave rise to the names by which they were called. He saw that the most subtle form of energy was thought. Light took time to travel whereas thought was not subject to time.

In those altered states he recognized the truth of what had always been. He saw that what caused it to be hidden from normal awareness was the training human beings receive, the preconceived notions, the fundamental assumptions they accept as true. He saw how powerful was the agreement of consensual validation. As powerful as a black hole, from which only a few were able to escape. During those times he saw that everything was connected to everything else, that there were different energy systems with forms of life peculiar to them, that there were whole universes which, because of the sensory make-up of the human being, were largely inaccessible to him.

During those experiences he read the *Bhagavad Gita* and the *Tao Te Ching*. Those teachings directed his attention deeper and deeper. He recognized things he'd always known, and somehow forgotten. He knew and understood what Lao Tsu meant when he said: *Ever desireless, one can see the mystery. Ever desiring, one can see the manifestations. These two spring from the same source but differ in name; his appears as darkness. Darkness within darkness, the gateway to all mystery.*

His experiences under the influence of those drugs were like intimations of things to come and opened him to the intuitive understanding of life itself.

One day he came across the idea of enlightenment. Intellectually he understood it at once. It was what he'd been searching for all his life. For years he sought it through various practices and disciplines. In the end he'd repudiated them all, being firmly convinced that life was utterly simple, that life itself was the great teacher, and disciplines only served to complicate.

Then came the urge to go to India. It had always been there, like a tickle in the back of the throat. So he went. Sandra accompanied him. He was immensely glad of her guidance. Without her the shock of India would have been more disturbing.

Being a practical man he wondered whom he should see. At the time an acquaintance introduced him to the teachings and stories of Sai Baba. He read all he could and liked what he found. Here was a master with a vast following, unafraid of performing miracles. He was reputed to be an Avatar who, like Jesus and the Buddha, was of such spiritual stature that through his teachings, he could set the tone for the coming age. Millions of people from all over the world came to see him; he was well respected and deeply loved.

One day David arrived at the ashram in Puttapharti in time for the festival of Shivarati. That morning he caught a glimpse, through the vast throng, of the master with an orange robe.

Each morning and afternoon he'd gone and sat in the long lines in the dust and dirt, waiting for entrance to the courtyard of the Mandire for darshan. Once inside he found himself reading the works of Nissargadatta, and only looked up when Sai Baba came into view.

He thought it strange at the time, to be in the presence of the guru and unable to set aside the book on Nisargadatta's teachings. They were like an elixir to the soul. At last he'd found the truth he'd craved. He'd found it not in the presence of Sai Baba, but in the words of this master, now dead.

Two nights before reaching Puttapharti he'd gone to the Vedanta Bookstore in Madras. It was dark when he arrived. Leaving the taxi, he mounted the littered sidewalk and made his way toward a light coming from a doorway and two open windows. In the dark he almost bumped into a book stand upon which nine books were arranged. They had an orange cover, and in white letters the title read, *I Am That*. He felt something in his chest like a blow and wondered where he'd seen the book before. He hadn't, he eventually realized.

Later he wondered how he could have seen the books on the stand because they were lit from behind, with no light from in front. Being ornery and unwilling to see the obvious, he walked around the book stand and entered the store. An hour later he came across the book in the stacks. He opened it and knew at once he'd found what he'd been looking for. He felt his heart leap, and his whole being sang with joy.

But what of Sai Baba, the living guru present now? One morning at darshan, Sai Baba stood before him, and their eyes met. At that moment he knew this was not the teacher he'd been seeking.

He was not suited to be a disciple of a Bhakti master. It was not in his nature to submit his life to the devotion, rituals, and spiritual practices of any guru, and Sai Baba was Bhakti.

He'd heard instead an exquisite call and the peculiarities of his mind were such as to draw him to it. It was the song of wisdom, the path of Jnana Yoga, also known as Advaita Vedanta.

Colloquially the path was known as the pathless path to which access was granted through the gateless gate. It employed the mind in the all-absorbing task of self-inquiry, and ritual and spiritual practices played no part. It was utterly simple, indistinguishable from life itself.

At last he came into the presence of Avinash. Seven months after his return from India, he flew to Los Angeles with his friend Brian. Avinash had come from India and was to speak at Hermosa Beach. In a room above a restaurant, right on the strand, the meeting took place.

He and Brian climbed the stairs, entered the room, found a seat, and waited. Some twenty people had already gathered. More drifted in, some renewing old acquaintances, others sitting quietly with eyes closed. He noticed a short, elderly man enter, a man with white hair and thick-rimmed glasses through which dark brown eyes looked out. Dressed in casual slacks, shirt and windbreaker, he stood quietly watching. A few people engaged him briefly in conversation, and he was exceptionally gracious to all who greeted him. David wondered if this was Avinash.

At four o'clock the same man sat on a single chair on a low platform. Beside the chair was a bouquet of flowers. He waited for people to become quiet and then began to speak with an Anglo-Indian accent. Avinash spoke of many things that afternoon, but he said one thing in particular that became firmly rooted in David and forever changed his life.

In response to a question he'd asked, Avinash looked at him and said, "The seeker is the obstacle to that which is sought." It was as though David stepped off a cliff, for in that moment he understood Avinash completely. He knew that he who was seeking would never arrive at the destination. For entrance to be granted to this sacred place the seeker, the separate identified consciousness, must be absent.

For more than a quarter century he'd actively sought enlightenment. He'd understood that enlightenment meant a coming into oneness. At that moment he knew that he, the seeker, the one who was seeking, was the identified consciousness. The nature of that consciousness was its individuality. Being individual it could never enter the place of oneness without losing itself. Individuality was separation; enlightenment was union or oneness. With that realization the journey was over, although it took some six months before the implications made themselves known and he could articulate them.

He'd glimpsed the promised land, and like Moses of old, the named one, he could not enter; no activity on his part could ever take him there. All that was left was to wait, while the identity that waited slowly disappeared. At first he suffered a deep disappointment. His life, as he'd known it, came to an end. The search he'd engaged in all his life was over. For years the last thought before going to sleep at night and the first thought upon awakening had been of enlightenment. Everything he'd done, every aspect of his life had been involved in this all-consuming search. And in one sudden burst of understanding, it was all swept away.

He was left with a profound sense of emptiness, disturbing at first. After living with it for six months, he had occasion to speak with Dr. Klein, another Advaita master, to whom he recounted his experience. He asked him why he felt this strange kind of depression. The master looked at him and smiled. "Dispense with labels," he said. "Let go of the need to name everything and face the feelings without naming." Then lowering his head he fixed David with eyes that peered from beneath shaggy brows and in a rich French accent said, "The seeker *is* the sought!" He paused for a moment to let his words sink in. Then asked, "You know what I mean, don't you?"

David did. He underwent profound changes over the next few months. Only in recalling how he used to be, could he actually see the changes themselves. No longer was he trying to fulfill the image of a psychologist, no longer was he invested in the results of his clients, no longer did he worry what others thought of him. He accepted himself exactly as he was without concern for how he thought he should be.

One day someone suggested he invite some men he knew to an event, he had arranged. He didn't like the men. They'd been part of a mens group who had promised to let him know when they met, saying he was welcome. For six months they met privately before one of them told him the truth. He'd been deiliberately excluded from their meetings and he was angry about it. He saw within himself the pettiness of his reaction and laughed. He didn't care; this was the way he was. Then the thought crossed his mind that he might never change, and he really didn't give a damn any more. He laughed again.

Life became effortless. Nothing had changed, and it still went along as it always had and somehow, inexplicably, it was completely different. A year later Avinash delivered a stunning blow. "Give up all hope," he said. "When you finally accept that enlightenment may not happen in this body-mind organism, in this lifetime, the end is near." David thought he'd dealt with it all, but that statement brought to the surface one great gush of despair. Then came the stillness, a kind of waiting without anyone waiting. At the same time he found himself engaged in the ordinary events of daily life, no longer interested in the spiritual search with which he'd been so obsessed.

On the day of the first meeting with Avinash, David and Brian walked on a pier that jutted into the ocean across from the building where the meeting took place. The sun sank pink in the purple haze of autumn. Lovers strolled on the pier; roller skaters and roller bladers rumbled by. David looked back and saw the pink clouds reflected in the windows of the upper room where the meeting had taken place. He was struck by the thought that in that room the conduit of the eternal was present, and all around the commerce of life went on, unknowing and unaffected. He thought of another upper room some two thousand years ago. Tears of a great joy rolled down his cheeks. He looked at his friend and smiled. They both sensed something momentous had taken place that afternoon at Hermosa Beach.

．．．．．．．．．．．．．．．．．．．．

Lost in thought, David arrived at their private quarters. He nodded a good morning to the Secret Service agents outside the door. Entering, he saw Sandra sitting at the table in her gown reading the paper and drinking coffee. She got up when he came in.

"Would you like some toast?" she asked.

"That would be nice." He looked at her and smiled. He liked coming into her presence in the morning at breakfast. It was a special time for both of them, a time to touch base before going about their days. Evenings, too, were enjoyed, the time before going to bed when they sat quietly and caught each other up on their day's events.

"Travis made the front page headlines this morning," she said, bringing him coffee.

"How's that?"

"He gave a speech last night at the veterans' convention." She handed him the paper and went to butter the toast. "I don't think he likes you much."

"Could be. I think it's difficult for him to think of taking direction from me, a man who in his eyes was a traitor, a nonmilitary man."

He unfolded the paper. The headlines read, "PRESIDENT INCOMPETENT!" David read the comments of the reporter who'd written the article and the questions and answers that followed Travis' speech. On the second page he read the text of the speech itself.

Sandra watched her husband. Absorbed in reading, he

was letting his toast get cold.

"You know what I find infuriating about something like this?" he asked. "I don't mind Travis speaking his mind; he has a right to do so. But the press has an obligation to speak the truth, to report the facts, and they don't. They get carried away with a self-serving and pompous analysis. They interpret the facts according to their own petty notions. They are part of the problem. They love conflict. Such reporting is an abuse of our people.

"Though I had little respect for Spiro Agnew, he was accurate in his recognition that the press influences how things are seen in our society today. A free and responsible press is essential to a democracy. And what do we have? A press that has been manipulated in the past, a press so jaundiced by dishonesty they cannot even see the truth before them. They have, to a large extent, lost touch with their purpose, which was to report the facts and allow people to form their own opinions. They've forgotten the distinction between perception and conception."

David put the paper aside and ate his toast. Looking at Sandra, he said, "I'm glad you're in my life. You see reality clearly. Words are such a web. They create realities that don't exist. We even go to war over words. So much suffering is the result of words. And if that wasn't enough, we seek to imprison each other with the labels we attach. We're so clever in our use of language that it's become an abuse, difficult to point out, difficult to recognize, and even more difficult to put a stop to. We're suckers for words and confuse fact with fiction.

"It's something we must address if we wish to do something about the difficulties before us. The press is important because it is the vehicle of communication. To bring about change, we must talk to the people, educate and awaken them to possibilities. It's difficult to do this when the press distorts what is being said."

"Why don't you address the Press Club? Why not beard the lion in his den? Talk with the members of the press."

"That's an interesting idea."

"I think it's something you can begin at the Press Club, although I suspect it will be something that requires persistence. The press must once more see its purpose, and I doubt it will happen quickly."

"I think you're right. Anyway I like your idea. I'll ask Jonathan to look into it."

David sipped his coffee.

"I'd like to switch topics for a few minutes," Sandra said.

David nodded, "What's on your mind?"

"I want to go back to work."

"You do?"

"Yes, I miss nursing. I didn't really want to give it up in the first place."

"What do you have in mind?"

"There's a women's clinic in Anacostia that needs some help. It's a very poor section of the city, and I'd like to see what I can do."

David began to chuckle. "I think it's a great idea. I can imagine it will throw the Secret Service into cardiac arrest, though."

"Yes, I've wondered about that. Anyway, I'm going to do it, and I wanted to let you know. I want to be sure I have your support."

"Sandra, love, you have my support and my blessing. Let me know what I can do to help."

"I will."

David poured himself juice and put more toast in the toaster. "Are you going to the clinic today?"

"I thought I would. I want it to be as quiet as possible. I've no desire to make things difficult for the Secret Service or the clinic. I know the agents are interested in my safety and are doing their best."

"Yes."

"What do you have on your agenda today?"

"I meet with Travis at ten, and this afternoon Jonathan, Doug and I are going to sit down and go over the list of potential candidates for Vice President. The FBI completed the background checks yesterday."

"I'd been meaning to ask how that was going."

"Well, we're down to three candidates now, and by the end of the week I'll be sending the nomination up the Hill."

David got up, washed his dishes, and put them in the drain board.

"I think one of the most difficult things about this job is to give myself time to be alone and time to be with you. There's always so much to do and never enough time. It seems I have to rely more and more on information from others and make decisions based on it. Decision making I don't mind. The key, however, is to find those who'll give me accurate, unbiased information."

"How do you know you're getting that?"

"Most important of all is to take the time to interview thoroughly and get a feel for the advisors. Of equal importance, as far as I'm concerned, is finding the best in the land, without regard to political affiliation. Working that way has ruffled feathers, and I've been accused of creating a brain drain from the Republican ranks in order to win the next election. I'm amazed how people live with their melodramas, figments solely of their own fertile imaginations."

David walked over and held her in his arms.

"I've got to go, I'll see you this evening. Have a good day."

"I will."

Travis was on time. At precisely ten o'clock the secretary ushered him into the Oval Office. David was at the desk writing. He looked up.

"Have a seat, Travis. I'll be with you in a moment. Help yourself to coffee."

Travis walked over and sat down. He poured coffee, stirred in sugar and looked around. He noticed the newspapers on the desk. His heart gave a start and, despite himself, he began to sweat. Damn the reporters, he thought.

David finished writing and, pushing the chair back, walked around to join Travis. Travis stood and the two men shook hands. David looked at the general and felt the uneasiness in the man. Then he sat and poured himself a cup of coffee. The aroma filled the room, and the two men looked at each other and smiled.

"I like coming here, if for no other reason than for the coffee," Travis joked.

David laughed, appreciating the good humor. He hoped to keep Travis on board. Maybe the man is just testing the limits, he thought.

"What's the word from the other Joint Chiefs? Will they support a change in policy regarding gays?"

"No, they will not!"

"I trust you conveyed to them the gist of our conversation last week."

"I did, but it didn't change their minds."

"From what I've heard, you and the other Joint Chiefs have been on the hill gathering support for your position."

Travis once more felt himself off balance with Tremaine's directness.

"Yes, we have. We cannot support your proposed change,

and we intend to do all we can to stop it."

"Fair enough."

"I think we have enough strength to override an executive order."

"I think you may be right."

"So what will you do?"

"I'll issue it any way."

"Why?"

"Because I believe it's the right thing to do."

"But you can't win!"

"Well, General, you should know that a war is rarely won by the first battle."

"I get your point. But then what?"

"If the executive order is overridden, then the issue will go before the Supreme Court. I'm confident the Court will support my position. If it doesn't, then so be it. The matter will end there."

"That process will take a long time. In the meantime, gays will be excluded."

"Yes, you may be right. Emerson made a promise during the campaign, and he wanted it kept. I agree with him on this point. I also gave my word. There is too much prejudice in the world. Are we not all brothers and sisters in the great family of humanity. What divides us is the intransigence of our ideas."

"But with these people it's not just ideas. What they practice under the guise of sexual preference is immoral; it's not natural."

"I understand your opinion on the matter. It is opinions themselves that divide. If we do away with ideas of right and wrong, moral and immoral, all that remains is action taking place."

"How can you say that there's no such thing as right and wrong, moral and immoral?"

"I'm not saying that. I'm saying that right and wrong change over time and between people. The idea of morality changes too. For some people it's immoral to dance or go to movies. For others it's immoral to engage in violent acts or serve in the military. For others, the opposite is true."

"There must be some sense of morality that most people agree upon."

"I don't know what it is. Perhaps the closest thing we come to is the idea of the sacredness of life. But who wants to live ninety years if you have to spend the last fifteen in bed suffering from bed sores, with tubes down your throat, your heart monitored by a machine, unable to take care of yourself?"

" I wouldn't."

"Yet, some consider it immoral to allow people to die without taking extraordinary measures to save them. There comes a time when the quality of life is such that death is welcome."

"I understand the point you're making, but I still don't see how we can live without morality or a sense of right and wrong."

David smiled.

"Trees do, and as far as I can tell so do dogs, cows, bears, lions and tigers. So it seems obvious that it is possible to live quite well without the need to define everything in these terms."

Travis was uncertain how to take David.

"I don't follow."

"Trees make no judgment about the wind. They don't call gentle breezes good and limb-breaking winds bad. Life goes on without regard for human judgments of right or wrong, moral or immoral. Actions take place. If we see them as they are without making judgments about them, we'll find that we're drawn to act in a particular way regarding them. Such action is spontaneous and appropriate."

"But there are bound to be others who respond in different ways."

"That's true, of course, and their actions will be appropriate for them."

"Yes, but what of our differences, do they not divide us?"

"Differences have divided us, but they don't have to."

"What do you mean?"

"When our attitude is one that welcomes differences, we discover ways for those differences to work. The names of right and wrong are dispensed with, and we're left only with differences.

"When we look down from a tall building at the traffic pattern below, we see traffic flowing in an orderly manner according to certain predetermined rules. If we look down at traffic in the city of Bombay, however, we might at first think there is utter chaos in what we see. If we watch for a while, we see that there is an organicity, an intuitiveness to driving patterns, not at first apparent. To Westerners, used to their own driving rules, this kind of driving can be frightening. But once the person lets go of his preconceived notions on how it should occur, he discovers there's another way of driving that's also relatively safe.

"Driving in India is like driving without regard for right and wrong. Someone comes at you in a certain way and you spontaneously respond. Your action precipitates a chain of responses amongst other drivers, and all those responses precipitate further responses in others, and so on. Taken as a whole, these myriad responses merge, becoming one whole and beautifully orchestrated event, with no one conducting any of it."

"I'll have to think about what you say. One thing still puzzles me though."

"What's that?"

"Emerson before you, and now you want to implement

this new policy that others oppose. You think your idea is right and we think ours is. How can something like this be resolved?"

"That's a good question. First of all, I don't think my point of view is right and yours wrong. I do feel that my point of view will, in the end, prevail. Now that's my point of view. I'll do my best to argue that point of view, giving the reason I think it's better. The truth is, it might not be better. Or on the other hand the idea may be ahead of its time. New ideas are not always welcomed at first. Why? Because there are vested interests which hold the old intact. However, change begins with the introduction of ideas. Sometimes we must get used to them, live with them for a while; and then something occurs in the mind, and we're ready.

"The church for a long time resisted the idea that the earth was not the center of the universe. Openness to the idea had to occur first. Only then could the truth be perceived. If we're interested in discovering the truth, then we must be open to possibilities and become aware when fear causes us to be closed to ideas other than our own.

"In the case of gays in the military, I feel the need to articulate this position and attempt to remove all the false and unexamined assumptions upon which the former policy is based. I welcome your doing the same. I don't mind differences; I welcome them. Let there be openness and honesty even when the truth does not fit our preconceived ideas."

"I understand what you're saying. I'll have to give it some thought."

"Good."

David offered Travis more coffee, but he declined. He seemed to be thinking, and David allowed it to take place. He waited until he saw the general become wholly present and then said to him, "I'd like to change the topic."

Travis nodded.

"I read the reports on your speech last night and the comments to the press afterward. I want to talk with you about it."

Travis felt himself beginning to sweat again.

"There are certain things I find distasteful in what you said, things I find inaccurate and provocative. Your continuing as Chairman of the Joint Chiefs is contingent on your following my instructions in this matter."

Travis had trouble dealing with David. His words were potent while the tone of his voice was calm but firm. He couldn't read the man well. There was no animosity from him, and yet Travis felt great discomfort in the pit of his stomach. An unpleasant image entered his mind; he saw himself as a strutting rooster with ruffled feathers.

David watched Travis closely. He saw the general's discomfort, the small beads of perspiration collecting above his lip, and knew Travis was off balance.

"What I object to is the constant reference to the 'greatest this' and the 'greatest that.' It's your opinion that we have the greatest army, navy, and air force, isn't it?"

"Yes."

"Is it a fact?"

"I think it is."

"Whether you think it is or not doesn't make it so, does it?"

"No."

"How do you think the British, the Italians, the Russians, the French, and the Israelis feel about their military capabilities?"

"They probably feel they're very good."

"In this country we have a tendency to think of ourselves as the best in everything we do. The Japanese gave us a stiff dose of reality that contradicted that idea with regard to certain highly sophisticated technologies. We didn't like it, and to some extent

I think we resort to wild claims and bragging rather than make the necessary improvements. Do you follow?"

"Yes."

"Talk is cheap, and it alienates both our friends and our opponents. I've traveled a lot, and I know how people of other countries feel about Americans. For instance, we're considered bullies and braggarts, dishonest in our selective support of UN resolutions, uneven and unfair in our support of various policies throughout the world. We jump in and enforce our will against a weak neighbor and refuse to do so with a strong one. We have little genuine concern for others and are motivated almost entirely by self-interest. We are not well liked. Even our allies don't like us much. Why is that, do you think?"

"I don't know. I hadn't thought of it before."

"It's because we look upon ourselves as special. Our actions are governed by our 'national interest.' If a plane crashes somewhere in the world, what gets reported? Not how many people are killed, but how many *Americans* are killed. It's this kind of arrogance on our part, our lack of concern for our fellow human beings, that has contributed to our poor reputation and the hostility aimed at us. Do you follow?"

"I think so."

"Are you familiar with the Chinese sage, Lao Tsu?"

"No."

"He lived about twenty-five hundred years ago and was a contemporary of the reformer Confucius. Lao Tsu was wise. He said, *the wise ruler of a strong country does not parade his weapons in public nor make boastful comments. Why? Because he knows that whoever sets himself above others will in the end be brought low by his pride.* The history of civilizations bears out his observations."

"I don't see how we bring ourselves down by pride."

"By pride I'm referring to arrogance. When arrogance is present, there are those around who take it upon themselves to topple the arrogant in the dust. It becomes their mission in life."

"Ah, yes, I understand."

"Lao Tsu said, *there are three great treasures in life. Mercy, economy, and daring not to be ahead of others.*"

"What did he mean?"

"He said, *courage arises from mercy, generosity from economy and leadership from humility.* Lao Tsu must have lived in a time like our own, for he went on to say: *Nowadays men shun mercy, and try to be brave; they abandon economy, and try to be generous; they do not understand real humility, and always try to be first. This is certain death.*"

Travis thought about Tremaine's remarks. They had a certain unpleasant truth about them. The conversation was in some ways unsettling and at the same time exhilarating. This man is unlike any I've known, he thought. He's no fool.

David sat and watched Travis. Travis looked up to find a pair of green eyes smiling at him.

"Travis, I have no objection to you speaking your mind on anything, but I want you to learn to do so with honesty, simplicity, and humility. As the Chairman of the Joint Chiefs, you represent the government, and I want you to represent it in such a way not to alienate others deliberately. Do you have a problem with this?"

"No, I don't. I appreciate what you've had to say. It makes sense. I've thought in other ways, and I may slip back into it at times. If you can bear with me, though, I'll do my best." Travis could hardly believe the words he'd spoken. What's happening to me? he wondered.

"Good. That's what I'm asking of you."

David offered Travis a cookie and took one himself. He sat back eating, lost in thought. The call of a dove came mellow through the open doors. David looked up and saw by the sun that it was almost noon.

"I've one further thing to say to you, Travis. Last week when I spoke with you, I asked if you were prepared to serve me, to follow my orders and direction, to speak the truth as you saw fit, and in no way sabotage the orders and instructions once given. What is your answer?"

Travis thought for a moment.

"May I speak frankly, sir?"

"I expect it. Go ahead."

"I've not liked you at all. I have detested what I thought you stood for. To serve under a man who'd actively opposed a war in which I fought, and in which so many lives were lost, was in my mind some kind of poor cosmic joke. I could not support you because I felt I was betraying the young men I knew in Vietnam. I disliked you intensely and was prepared to do whatever I could to bring you down, to make visible to others what I thought you to be, a weak and traitorous man, unfit to be president. When I walked in here this morning, I felt that way. I'm ashamed to admit that much of my opposition to your policies and the support I put together to oppose them came from this perspective. I no longer feel that way. I'm surprised. What you say makes sense; I can see how petty and vindictive I've been. I still cannot say I'll support your policy regarding gays, but I will oppose it cleanly."

David felt a deep appreciation for the man before him. He liked him a lot. He watched and sensed a peacefulness he'd not noticed before in those tired eyes.

"Thank you. I appreciate your honesty," he said, smiling at Travis. "I still need to know the answer to my question, however."

"I will give you the benefit of my experience. I will advise you to the best of my ability. I will speak the truth as I see it, whether you agree or not. I will accept and respect your decisions and policies once they're made. I may oppose them forcefully when they're being formulated, but once that's done I'll support you. If I find I can no longer support you in this manner, I'll let you know and offer my resignation. Does that answer your question?"

"It does. Thank you. That's the kind of support I need!"

David stood and Travis followed suit. David extended his hand, shaking Travis' firmly.

"Welcome aboard," he said, smiling, and clapped him on the shoulder.

CHAPTER 10

Sandra stormed from the office, furious. How dare they restrict her freedom? She was not an employee of the government; her husband held the job, not her. But Phillips had been adamant. He would not let her go to the clinic. She felt completely frustrated, angrier than she could remember being in a long time. She called the Women's Clinic in Anacostia and asked to speak with the director. Briefly she explained the situation, saying she'd resolve things within the next couple of days but, until then, she'd not be able to come. The director understood and said she'd await Sandra's call.

Putting the phone down, Sandra went upstairs to the living quarters and made herself a cup of tea. She tried calling David, but his secretary said he was in a meeting and not to be disturbed. He must be with Travis, she thought.

She'd never liked formality, and especially disliked restrictions on her personal freedom. She'd lit into Phillips in no uncertain terms. Her tongue could be sharp when she was angry.

Through her rage she'd watched the blood drain from his face with the impact of her words. Thinking back on their conversation brought a smile to her face. He'd been completely taken aback by her explosion. His condescending manners had been like gasoline on a fire. He was not used to being opposed by a woman. But when he recovered, he'd stood his ground. Grudgingly, she admired him.

....

Sipping tea, she remembered another time when she'd felt such anger. It was the first fight she'd had with David. The year that followed their marriage was like a lovely dream. They lived by themselves in complete freedom and privacy. To be with him, she'd moved to Washington State, just south of the Canadian Border on the Olympic Peninsula. They lived in an old two-story country home, that David had bought the year before they met. It stood on fifteen acres of land, ten of which were wooded, the remainder consisting of gardens and lawns.

David's office was half an hour away in Port Townsend. From there they could easily catch a ferry to Victoria. So, leaving her beloved Canada was made easier by the proximity and ease with which she could visit members of her family.

Her father, protective of his eldest daughter, insisted she live with David for six months before getting married. They acceded to his request, knowing full well their union was for life. In September they were married, and six months later her younger sister came to live with them.

They'd talked a lot before deciding to invite her. Janet had gone to McGill, graduating with a degree in Byzantine history. She was an unhappy woman who thrived on crisis. She had an artistic temperament and was a strong advocate of the women's movement.

During her years in university, she'd gone from one fiery relationship to another. At times violence played a part, brought on by Janet's own arrogance and acts of physical aggression toward those she claimed to love.

Janet was depressed over the loss of her most recent relationship. Out of school, with insufficient funds to continue, she had no immediate purpose. What could she do? Her degree was of no use; there was little demand for Byzantine history majors. So, hampered by insufficient money, she bemoaned her fate and staked her salvation upon her return to the university sometime in the future.

In the meantime she had to earn a living. She'd exhausted the money her parents set aside for her education. She called Sandra late one evening, and they talked for more than an hour. Sandra had a soft spot for her sister and sought over and over again to be of assistance, even when her efforts were sometimes seen as meddling. Nevertheless, her sister's entreaties did not go unheeded.

Sandra herself had finished nursing school and had gone on to study Neuro-Linguistic Programming, a sophisticated method of effective communication used in business and psychotherapy.

Sandra's nature led her to serve in a healing capacity. In various ways she sought to alleviate the suffering and pain of her patients. Many times people came to her wanting to talk, finding in her someone with a warm heart and an open mind. They were attracted to her like moths to light, and she gave them the best she could. When Janet called, obviously distressed, she wanted to find a way to help her sister but had mixed feelings about what form the help should take.

After several conversations, she and David agreed that Janet could come and live with them for six months. They hoped this would give her time to find her feet.

The lack of privacy had been hard for everyone, and Janet proved to be moody and self-centered. Before long she interfered in Sandra and David's relationship. From her perspective, she thought David domineering and controlling of his wife.

In David she found someone upon whom she could displace her anger toward men. David had dealt with her in a straightforward and open manner. He largely stayed out of her melodramas and spoke the truth to her as he saw it. She took his unwillingness to be manipulated as further evidence of his male-chauvinist outlook.

In perpetual conflict with her brother-in-law, Janet sought to create events that forced Sandra to make choices between herself and her husband, which put pressure on her marriage. David realized what was happening quickly, but Sandra had difficulty seeing it at first.

One evening the tension erupted into a fight. In the heat of the argument she'd thrown a cup at David and threatened to walk out of the relationship. David left, and she was furious. For six months they fought on and off, far more than either of them liked. David tried several times to show her the negative effect Janet had upon them, and Sandra refused to see it. For Janet, aware of the fights, there was a smug satisfaction and the vindication of her position. Janet, a masterful manipulator, lost no time comforting and cajoling her sister in an attempt to drive a wedge between Sandra and David.

One day David and Sandra found themselves in a heated argument that escalated into a screaming match.

"My sister's right. You're so goddamned selfish you only think of yourself."

"Speak for yourself instead of parroting the complaints of your sister."

"I am speaking for myself, and right now this marriage isn't working." She pulled the ring off her finger and hurled it at

David. It missed and careened off the wall with a ringing sound.

"Sandra, can't you see what's going on? Before your sister came our relationship was good."

"Don't blame it on my sister," she interrupted. "Look at yourself; quit pointing a finger elsewhere!"

Suddenly David erupted, his anger finding full expression. Standing across the table from her he yelled, "Your sister loves melodrama, she sees things in black and white"—

"Leave my sister out of this," Sandra screamed back.

"I will not leave her out. You must listen to what I say. I love you. You not your sister, are my friend, the woman I fell in love with, the woman I married. I have no interest in making your sister into an ogre, but I will say what I see. This conflict between us was not there before she came, and it's time you see it."

The fight continued, eventually degenerating into a pushing match with escalating threats. At that moment, both of them saw the precipice upon which they teetered. Out of breath and sweating, they glared at each other. Sandra could see beads of sweat running down her husband's face, as he panted from the exertion. She was in a similar state.

Neither could do further damage short of physical violence. She'd been tempted to provoke him and see if she could get him to snap, but something told her it would be dangerous for their relationship. It was a step she was not prepared to take.

As she looked at him, an image came to mind. She saw two lions facing each other, exhausted, but so stubborn that neither would yield. From exhaustion they'd reached a stalemate. She started to laugh and cry at the same time. She saw the puzzled look on David's face. Then he smiled and took her in his arms and held her tight.

They talked for hours that evening. What Sandra saw in the image of the lions was something that affected her deeply.

She saw at once that her husband and she were well matched. Neither could dominate the other. They were equals, despite the disparity of sex, age and experience. From that time forth their relationship shifted. Fights were rare, and when they did occur, they often stemmed from tiredness. Shortly afterward, Janet left.

One cold wintery afternoon, Sandra and David went for a walk.

"You know Sandra," David said, "your sister proved helpful to us."

"In what way?"

"Like a grain of sand in an oyster, she was the instrument of discord that gave us a pearl of great value."

"How do you see that?"

"Until she came along, we rarely argued and didn't fight. I think in some way Janet picked up on some of the things that needed improvement."

"In what way?"

"As a man, I carried an unconscious assumption that I was in charge, the head of the family. In addition, I thought I had more experience and therefore more wisdom. I'd been in a marriage before and saw what didn't work. Unconsciously, I felt you should defer to me. I'm glad you didn't. If you had, it would have jeopardized the relationship. Instead I respect you as an equal. The image of the two lions was apt.

"Good partners are good friends, good companions, but must also be worthy opponents, opponents of what is petty and small in themselves and each other. We needed to learn the meaning of the phrase "worthy opponent," and Janet was the instrument through which the lesson could be learned."

He stopped and looked at her.

"Thank you," he said. "Thank you for being a ferocious fighter. I love you and have immense appreciation for you."

Sandra, looking back on that day, found herself smiling. She poured another cup of tea. It had been a long time since she'd felt as angry as she had today. David had warned her things wouldn't be easy living in Washington. She remembered the day he'd first spoken to her of that possibility.

She arrived home at eight one evening from a patient's home. David had supper ready, and they'd eaten at once. He seemed unusually quiet. She asked him if he was all right.

"I'm fine, but I need to talk with you about something. Let's go for a walk."

Wrapped in warm clothes, they'd gone outside, accompanied by Murphy, their black lab, and walked slowly through the leaves of autumn. On that rare cloudless night, the stars stretched full across an inky sky.

"I received a call from Emerson this evening. He's been persuaded to run for president."

"He has?"

"Yes. With the stranglehold the Republicans have on the White House, no Democrat wants to run against them."

"Why?"

"Well, for one thing no one wants to spend money on something that looks as though it will fail. Emerson thinks that since the odds of defeating an incumbent president are slim, those who do have aspirations for the White House don't want their names associated with a losing cause. They'd rather wait until the next election."

"Is he really going to run?"

"Yes, he's accepted already, and there are no other Democrats who wish to run against him. So, he's already the Democratic candidate for President."

"He doesn't stand a chance, does he?"

"No, I don't think he does. Anyway, we talked by phone this evening. He said it was time someone injected a sense of reality into the coming race. He said the economic, social, and political health of the country is not good. We talked about why, and what could be done. He's a good thinker with an enormous heart. Being from Maine he has that dry, down-to-earth, common-sense approach. It's unacceptable that the deficit is so high, that the elections are largely bought by mortgaging the country's future. He makes a lot of sense, and I like his ideas. As he said, 'I couldn't find a good reason not to run. I've nothing to lose, so from that perspective I can afford to speak the truth as I see it.'

"We talked for some time. He explained his thinking and posed many questions. The conversation was a lengthy exploration of how we see things. You know me, I love exercises like that, and Emerson is a good man to have that kind of discussion with. Anyway, the crux of the matter is that he wants me for his running mate."

"What?" She had stopped abruptly. "You mean he wants you for his Vice President?'

"Yes."

"What did you tell him?"

"That I had to talk with you."

They walked in silence for several minutes. Murphy rummaged through the leaves not far away. Above them, through the bare trees, Orion glittered in the cold night sky.

"What do you think, David? Is it something you want to do?"

"I'm not sure. Running would mean giving up my practice or taking a leave of absence. I've cut back so much to write that I could probably do it. Writing would go on the back burner for a while, though. What do you think?"

"I don't know. I'll have to think on it. Campaigning

would mean you'd be gone a lot, wouldn't it?"

"I'm afraid it would."

"There's not much chance you guys could really get elected, is there?"

"No, I think our chances of that are one in a million. But, Sandra, if I should accept Emerson's offer, we will both be in it to win."

"But you just said you didn't think you could win."

"I don't, but I can't enter the race from that perspective. Don't get me wrong, I'm a realist when it comes to things like this, but I would only accept Emerson's invitation if I was prepared for the possibility that you and I would live in Washington and even the possibility that we'd live, some day, in the White House."

"The White House!"

"Yes. That is one of the eventualities a vice president must consider. As I said, I'm not expecting anything, but the possibility exists. I'll not enter the race in a halfhearted manner. Am I prepared for the eventuality of winning and all that it wouldl entail? I don't want second thoughts when it's too late. That way actions become timid and ineffectual. Don't jump off the high board and regret it the moment you leave."

"I understand."

"Like Emerson, I think my countrymen deserve more than a halfhearted undertaking. That's one of the reasons I'm compelled to think seriously about running. Those who are afraid to run are more interested in themselves, the image they project, than they are in service. I care nothing for my image; I care only about service."

"When the campaign is over, will you come back here?"

"Of course. But Sandra, you must consider this for yourself. Don't assume we won't win."

"Why?"

"Because when opportunities like this present themselves, we must look at them and feel in which way we are drawn. We must honor that feeling. Life requires we make our gifts available. Such gifts were implicit in us at birth, and the only requirement is to find the fullest expression for them. If we feel drawn to follow a particular path, we must follow it. Only disturbance can result if we should choose a path thinking it cannot happen. If our choice is filled with reservations, the mind interferes with the pure impulse of the heart. The heart is master here, not the mind. The mind is always servant to the heart."

"I don't know what you mean when you say the mind is servant to the heart."

"I think you do. You know that when we feel drawn to something, the feeling is intuitive, in the heart, is it not?"

"Yes, it is."

"When asked to express what you feel, you must resort to language, which is of the mind. So in order to articulate the impulses and direction of the heart, the mind must be used. That is its true purpose. Do you follow?"

"Yes."

"What happens when you think something through, weighing the pros and cons, and come to a decision based purely upon assessments of the mind?"

"What comes to mind is I once found a job I'd been looking for. At the time the job came open, I was asked to consider another possibility. The latter job paid less and in many ways was not as good as the first one. I decided to take the first job and went down to the office for the interview. Several days later I was told I had the job if I wanted it. For some reason I didn't feel happy about it. I ended up taking the other job, and I never had regrets."

"That's what I'm talking about. So if I decide to join Emerson, it will be because I feel deeply about something that, to the mind, makes little sense. What I need to know, however, is if you can support me if I should do it?"

She realized that she, like her husband, had to consider winning. It could indeed come to pass. Murphy nuzzled her hand with his warm nose and disappeared into the woods again. Winning would mean a move to Washington and would involve curtailment of their privacy and freedom. They'd have to leave their home and she, the home-health agency for which she worked.

She liked nursing and was not willing to give it up. I'll find a way to continue, she thought. She'd be a long way from her parents and her beloved Vancouver Island, too. That would be hard. Washington was an alien place to her. She didn't like cities, and for this city, the seat of the American government, she had considerable antipathy. She was a Canadian country girl. Living across the border in the Pacific Northwest was a lot like being home, but living in a foreign city a continent away would be another thing altogether.

"You'll have to give me some time to think about it, David."

"Yes, of course."

"How long before you must let Emerson know?"

"A week."

"Okay."

"Sandra, I don't want you to feel you are making sacrifices on my behalf. Do you know what I mean?"

"Yes! You can rest assured, David, I understand. Healing is my nature; it always has been. I'm open to change. I believe we humans are like tumbleweed driven in the direction of the wind. I need a few days to let go, to reorient myself, that's all.

"I love you, David. I see the perfection of life before me. We're a team. I understood it from the start. From you I've learned much, and with you life is an incomparable adventure.

I've felt for a long time you and I shared a common destiny. I know no other words to describe it. I sensed the yearning of your heart. I knew you were in search of the secrets of life. I knew when we met at Whistler that you and I share something of great value, something for which I'm deeply grateful."

"Say what you mean."

"To be a friend, companion and lover of yours is a great joy and would have been enough by itself. But what drew me to you was something I felt more deeply. With you I found a beloved companion of the heart. With you I was able to speak of spiritual matters and know I was understood. I was happy to take you to India on the path that led to Avinash. I saw how deeply his words affected you. Through you, he reached out and touched me too. Then I was drawn to go and visit him and his words touched me directly, pointing toward the truth. I've never said this before, but I've known that you and I are companions of *the way*.

"Each day is an unknown adventure. I watch it unfold, and wonder fills my very being. Of course I'll go with you; how could I do otherwise? For now, though, there is a process going on within me, and it cannot be hurried."

They talked often over the ensuing week, and in the end David called Emerson and accepted his invitation. Without reservation, Sandra supported him. Then, for a year, she'd watched the events unfold. She'd ached inside for David when an affair he had during his first marriage became public. She hurt for him over the cruel comments of the press regarding his stand on Vietnam and questions concerning his drug experiences. She loved the honesty and openness with which he faced the crises as they came. The reporters, she felt, were like hounds who smelled blood and looked for a kill.

Early in the campaign, David was asked to speak at Brandeis University. He was a guest lecturer of the Philosophy

Department and was to give a talk and answer questions concerning the election and his role in it. It was to begin on a Friday afternoon and, after a break, continue into the evening. The university had invited members of the press. The place in which they met was a small ivy-covered hall situated beneath towering beach trees and surrounded by manicured lawns.

Emerson, as a distinguished alumnus of Brandeis, was asked to introduce David. "I chose this man as my running mate," Emerson said, "because I think he's the best for the job. I'm fully aware that, in the opinion of some, he's considered unfit to serve. I disagree. I know him well and I know what he can do. He is above all an honest man, as I know many of you are aware. He accepted my invitation to run because of a deep desire to serve. I support him, and I encourage you to listen to what he has to say with an open mind."

David stepped to the podium.

"Thank you, Emerson. It's a privilege to have this opportunity to work with you."

He turned to the audience.

"As you know, there have been rumors, accusations and allegations over my use of drugs, an extramarital affair and my stance on Vietnam. I've no desire to hide or withhold information. You may ask me whatever questions you wish, and I'll do my best to answer them honestly. As Emerson said, keep an open mind. To members of the press, several of whom are here tonight, I ask that you be honest in your reporting, do not engage in sensationalism, and above all, speak the truth."

David paused momentarily to allow the import of his words to sink in.

"I've made mistakes in my life. All human beings are subject to them and the learning to which they give rise. There's not a man or woman in this room who hasn't made mistakes and most of us will make many more before we die. I do not judge anyone for their mistakes. Mistakes are essential to life, because mistakes teach us. We do not always learn, and there's no requirement that we do. But if we don't, further suffering ensues.

"When we learn from those events, they can no longer be considered mistakes, can they? They become instead lessons in the art of living. In fact, we could argue that the only real mistake is not to learn from our mistakes. You might ask how do we fail to learn from our mistakes? The answer is obvious if we look closely. The biggest obstacle is our sense of self-importance, a kind of false pride that enables us to sidestep our own accountability while pointing fingers of blame. It is false pride that sets one man above another. Such behavior gives rise to conflict and misunderstanding and is derived from a deep and fearful insecurity.

"One thing is certain: if we strive to be better than others, we'll be brought down. Why? Because there are those around who take it upon themselves to undermine and destroy arrogance. To members of the press I say; none of you are judge and jury on any man or woman; judgment is not your task, so stick to the facts. But also report the good things in life, the accomplishments of the human spirit. As members of the press, you play an important role in a democracy. Your task is to report as honestly as possible what you see and hear. You are a vehicle of communication, not the subject of it. I think you sometimes forget that. Words and pictures are your tools, and I encourage you to be responsible in your use of them. Misinformation, innuendo, gossip, and distortion may come about solely as a result of your actions.

"In past administrations, and in the current one, there are those known as 'spin doctors,' whose job is to color our interpretation of the events and actions taking place, to make those they represent look good and others bad. We have no spin doctors in this campaign. We will do our best to say what we mean as clearly as possible. That means we may, at times, disagree with you and others; but it will be an honest disagreement. The speeches we make will be our own. Now let us have your questions."

Hands shot up all over the room. David pointed.

"You say there are no mistakes, only lessons being learned. It seems to me that such an assertion can be used as a justification for dishonesty."

" I agree, that it can be. But, as I've said, there's no interest in being dishonest with anyone. I can understand your skepticism, and yet I ask you to bear with us. See if we speak the truth. See if what we say stands the test of time. Do not mistake truth for agreement, though."

"What do you mean?"

"You may be sure we will speak the truth. However, the truth as we see it may not be in agreement with what you think. At one time, millions believed the world was flat. That agreement didn't make it true."

"I don't feel you answered my question. Doesn't the idea of learning from mistakes become a justification for deliberate, selfish, and malicious acts?"

"The way I use the word is this: A mistake arises from a limited understanding of something, and that understanding is insufficient for the circumstances at the time. So even though we make a choice based upon the knowledge we have, and follow it through to the best of our ability, it may still turn out to be a mistake. We can learn from it.

"Now, if we deliberately set out to do whatever we want without consideration for others, or for the truth, and justify our actions by saying we are subject to making mistakes, then I agree with you that mistakes become justification for dishonest acts. In such circumstances there has been no learning and no willingness to learn."

"You had an affair with another woman during your first marriage. That was dishonest on your part. How can we be sure you'll be honest in what you say to the American people or in your activities in government should you be elected?"

"You can't be sure. There's no way I can make you sure. I don't justify what I did twenty years ago. All I can say is that it was a valuable learning experience. It brought suffering for all concerned, it's true, and even that I don't regret. Those events taught all of us the things we needed to know. Do you follow?"

"No, I'm afraid I don't!"

"All right. Take yourself. You do something and it hurts someone else. You will either learn from it or you won't. If you don't, you'll repeat it in some other form at some other time. Is that not so?"

"Maybe."

"Each time suffering gets worse until it pierces the threshold of awareness. Now you can no longer ignore it or continue to blame others. Perhaps the clue lies in the fact that you are the common denominator in all such events. If you learn, all well and good. If not, and some people don't, then you'll find yourself in similar situations, repeating similar actions.

"You may be more sophisticated in your self-deception, but even that brings with it a disturbance hard to live with. Can you go through life not learning? I would say no, but you might not be learning what you need to learn. What I mean by that is, you may learn to be more deceptive, and you'll have difficulty knowing the truth for yourself. You will, however, experience a deep sense of *dis-ease* that will, in the end, bring you a miserable death...

"Just a minute, I don't think that is true." A middle-aged woman to his left shot up as though propelled. "I'm a nurse and I've seen many people die. Some of those who died were miserable, self-centered human beings who died relatively peaceful deaths."

"Let me put it another way. This is just a way of speaking. We are not who we take ourselves to be; we are not the attributes and personal history associated with the name we were given. In truth we are pure consciousness not subject to time. In order for consciousness to manifest itself in form, it takes on limitation, becomes identified with the body and develops what psychologists call an ego. It is the ego that engages in self-deception. That deception is at variance with the truth about us. As a result there is a kind of tension that exists. That tension is the tension of death. It is the illusion that must in the end die, along with the body. On the physical level, death begins at the moment of birth. Our lives are balanced between these poles, and that is normal. However, when the tension increases as it does with self-deception, life becomes increasingly miserable. Why? Because beneath it all is the truth we cannot escape. Besides, in the face of death, deception does not fare well. At the time of our death whom do we wish to fool? Whom do we wish to impress?

"On the other hand, if you learn what you need to learn, there will be an easing of suffering and life will become more enjoyable."

"I question whether all people are interested in living enjoyable or happy lives," a grey-haired man in his fifties stood in the front row. "I see people all the time who are interested in power, others in some grand ego trip, and still others who make money in ways detrimental to the environment and those around them. From what I can tell, there doesn't seem to be much enjoyment in their lives."

"You're right. But why do you think they seek to amass power or money or engage in self-aggrandizement?"

"I suppose they think it will make them happy, but it doesn't."

"That's right. So what I'm saying is that most human beings are seeking a happiness that will last. They try to achieve it in many ways, and some of those ways are through power, prestige, and the acquisition of wealth. As you've pointed out from your own observations, these methods don't make them happy. But the fact is, the impulse that gives rise to them is the desire to find lasting happiness. Do you see what I mean?"

"I think some people want security."

"Look, I'm not interested in a debate over the meaning of words. See to what I point with words. What I mean by happiness can be called by many names. You may call it security, success, peace of mind, harmony, happiness, or God, for all I care. To me it's all the same. Think about it for yourself: why have you sought power, prestige, or wealth? Has the search not been born of the idea that you would then be happy? Think about it. Don't answer me, I don't need to know the answer; you do."

Tremaine turned to take another question.

"Don't you think you set a bad example, having been divorced? After all, the president and vice president are role models in our society."

"There are many people who are divorced and live honorable, creative lives of service; there are also those who don't. There are those who stay in marriages and are very unhappy, living with sadness, loss of hope, bitterness, and sometimes violence. Still others live in marriage and find it a wonderful and enriching experience.

"We must take our attention off external things and see into the heart of a man and a woman. The heart is what matters; it is the source of inspiration. To see someone openly confess to what they have done and then to undergo a transformation is inspiring. Nothing can occur without the making of mistakes and the learning that follows."

"It's been reported that you used various forms of hallucinogenic drugs. What do you have to say about that?"

"I have used hallucinogenic drugs."

"Why? Don't you think that sets a bad example to others, particularly our young people, who are caught up in drugs like crystal meth, cocaine, and so on?"

"This is a topic that must be addressed with great care. It's a complicated one. Perhaps this is the place to break for dinner and we'll come back to your question afterwards."

It was seven o'clock before they reconvened in the hall. Tremaine stood at the podium and people became quiet.

"The question you've asked is a good one, and I trust you'll bear with me while I answer it. This is not a topic to be brushed over lightly so it may take a little time. I'll do my best to explain what happened and my thoughts on it. In the early '60s, Timothy Leary and Richard Alpert were engaged in LSD research at Harvard. At the time many believed LSD created a kind of induced psychosis. They hoped that if they studied the effects of LSD, they would find an antidote for it, and thus a cure for psychosis. Their research was based upon the work of two Swiss chemists, Stoll and Hoffman, who first discovered LSD in 1938.

"As I recall, Leary was fired from the university for using LSD himself and with students. Both Leary and Alpert reported their experiences on the drug deeply affected them. I won't go into their experiences; you can read about them for yourself. I'd gone to university with a deep desire to serve and for a while pursued medicine. I learned I was better suited to philosophy. I still had a desire to serve, and at the time was deeply involved in the Civil Rights Movement and vehemently opposed to the Vietnam War. My mind was exceptionally rational; I believed everything could be figured out, that the problems of society could be resolved when we put our minds to the task.

"I delved into the philosophers, wondered about life and the world in which we lived. While in graduate school I took LSD several times. I took it alone or with a close friend in a safe environment. What I discovered affected me deeply, and I was never able to see the world in the same manner again. The closest metaphor I can think of is this:

"Imagine you are blind from birth. You live with others who are also blind. Consequently, blindness is normal for you. No one knows what is missing. Then one day someone is able to see. No matter how he tries to tell others what has happened, they really can't comprehend, because they have no common frame of reference. If he keeps trying to tell them about it, they might think he's crazy. Why? Because he speaks of things that, from their perspective, are impossible. Now, if he should ever go blind again, he would never forget the reality he'd seen. He would also have a great desire to recover his sight. That desire would give birth to a search that might eventually lead to the permanent restoration of sight.

"Seeing as used in the metaphor represents a deep understanding. That understanding comes about naturally, sometimes through some kind of shock or the use of certain drugs. In cases where the understanding is only temporary, the search will inevitably continue because the nectar of understanding is so sweet that, once tasted, one cannot live without it. Sometimes a person will turn to drugs to help open the eyes of understanding again. However, glimpsing those realities briefly only to have them vanish as the effect of the drugs wear off, is insufficient. So the search continues and moves beyond the use of drugs.

"During the experiences I had on LSD, I came to know firsthand the interrelatedness of everything. Although I had rejected the organized aspects of Christianity as practiced by the various churches, I had studied in considerable depth the Old Testament and the teachings of Jesus. The teachings of Jesus I found simple, beautiful, and in some ways puzzling. I also studied the teachings of Lao Tzu, and read the Bhagavad Gita. I was curious; I wanted to know what they meant. At the time, the horrors of war deeply disturbed me. Under the effect of those drugs, I began to understand many things. My experiences on LSD showed me a world held together by very subtle agreements, agreements usually unquestioned. In psychological terms this phenomenon is known as 'consensual validation.' Those agreements pertain to certain basic or fundamental assumptions about life. Once those agreements are in place, which is part of the socialization process, they remain hidden, while exercising tremendous control over human perceptual processes.

"Such agreements remain unquestioned. All perceptions, the simple seeing of the reality around us, and even our perceptions of ourselves, are filtered through those beliefs in such a way that it's exceptionally difficult to see anything outside them. The Buddhists refer to this as the "endarkenment" process. The Christians refer to it as the "fall from grace." Both say that reversal of this process is possible and has existed from the beginning of time. The Buddhists and other non-Christian religions have maintained that enlightened masters have always been present to shed light on the way for those ready to see. The Buddhists refer to the process as one of awakening or enlightenment.

"During those LSD experiences, the concept of God fell away, and an intuitive understanding replaced it. I understood why the Jewish philosophers removed the vowels from Yahweh, rendering it unspeakable. The Buddhists refer to the same reality and call it the void, while in philosophical terms it is known as the noumenal."

"What does that mean, the noumenal?"

"It means that which gives rise to and sustains the phenomenal world and is not separate from it. The noumenal, the indefinable, becomes defined and is the phenomenal world with which we're all familiar. The noumenal is not susceptible to language.

"I grew up in a family in which there was emotional suffering. My family was poor, and the distress caused by my parents' valiant attempt to save their failing marriage affected me deeply. The sense of helplessness I felt over my mother's suffering was a major impetus leading me to find the cause of suffering and to alleviate it wherever I could. For years I struggled with the issue of suffering. Nowhere could I find an answer that satisfied me.

The hall was silent, then someone coughed.

"One day I had smoked marijuana. I sat alone in my study, looking out the window. I was a professor at a small college at the time. My mind turned back to the question of suffering. As I looked outside, the clouds cleared and I saw the huge ridge of a glacier caught in a shaft of sunlight. Above it a patch of blue sky contrasted with the gray mists. At that moment everything quavered as though seen through intense heat, and the normal certainty, the veneer of reality, slipped. At once I knew the answer to what I'd been seeking all those years. At the same time I remembered I had always *been,* and would always *be.* Once again, I cannot adequately explain this event in the normal language with which we're familiar. All I can say is that, from that time forth, I felt a deep sense of peacefulness. I saw clearly that all suffering comes solely from attachment— attachment to the expectations and objects of our desires. I saw distinctly and unforgettably the intrinsic harmony of all things.

"There were other times, in the mountains or in some wilderness area, when I ingested peyote. Once more it gave rise to further exploration and further understanding of the universe in which we live. I have never taken the kinds of drugs you mentioned in your latter question, nor felt a desire to do so.

"At this time certain problems arose. One was the physical effects of the drugs upon the body. I knew that I couldn't keep taking them. The other, I feel, was more dangerous. The experiences of those states of consciousness were sublime, and I wanted to repeat them. For a while this desire meant that I continued to explore with the use of drugs. Eventually it gave way to various spiritual practices and then to a teacher who could help me."

"Did you find him?"

"I did."

"Who is he?"

"I'm sorry, but I do not wish to reveal his identity."

"Why?"

"Because I wish to safeguard his privacy and not interfere in his work."

"If you told us of him, perhaps some of us could learn what you have learned."

"I understand your point, and I must honor what I feel. When men and woman come to the place of being ready for the teachings of an enlightened master, they are brought to him. No one, genuinely ready, is ever left out."

Once more a multitude of hands waved, and David pointed to a young man with close-cropped hair. He was dressed in a suit, tie undone.

"Why do you think there is such a proliferation of drugs in our society today?"

"First, we're a very drug-oriented society. Everywhere you look, drugs are advertised. They're offered as a panacea, a healing potion for all kinds of ills. Modern medicine relies on drugs to cover the symptoms of disease. The art of healing itself has been lost. But that's another topic we can discuss another time.

"The use of drugs is so pervasive and so acceptable that it has become, in many ways, one of the unseen fundamental assumptions we take for granted. Perhaps the only way to see how deeply imbedded drugs are in our society is to travel in other countries where the use of drugs is not so all-consuming. Since we live in a drug culture, though we may be unaware of our bias, we have a tendency to look to drugs for answers, or to escape pain and suffering. My sense is that in all human beings there is a desire to find a certain peace of mind, which includes absence of pain and suffering. In more traditional societies, religion and various spiritual practices sought to provide that peace of mind. In our society the role of religion has been largely discredited by the hypocrisy of its members, and the impact of science upon the simplistic beliefs it advocated. Christianity has cut itself off by setting itself up as the pinnacle of spiritual achievement..."

"What do you mean?"

"What I mean is Christianity has asserted that only those who accept the teachings of Christ will enter paradise. The question then arises, what about those who don't know of the Christ? What about the Buddhists, the Taoists, and so on? Christianity has answered that question by sending missionaries all over the world in order to convert, in order to save. That kind of thinking has been the height of arrogance. Why? It presumed Christ was the ultimate savior of mankind. Christ is considered either the most enlightened or the only enlightened being of all time. All other enlightened masters are not seen or recognized.

"Christianity looks back to the time when Christ walked the earth and forward to the time of his return. Most Christians don't understand the teachings of their founder. Jesus tells a lovely story of a man who met God. God told him to prepare for his return. The man went home and prepared a room with a bed, made sure he had plenty of food, and then waited. One day an old beggar came and asked for a place to rest. The man shooed him away, saying he was waiting for a special guest.

"Months later a young woman came by and asked for

food because she was hungry. She was refused. Later a young girl with her brother came by. He was sick, and she was hungry. Once more the man refused help.

"Years passed, and one day God returned to speak to the man. 'Where have you been?' the man asked. 'I've been waiting for a long time!'

God responded. 'I came to see you three times, and each time you turned me away.'

"There's an exclusivity to Christianity that renders it largely incapable of understanding the teachings of its master. The Greeks have a word to describe that state of mind. It's called *hubris*, which loosely translates as "overweening pride." Since Christianity has, because of its beliefs, cut itself off, many have looked elsewhere.

"At the turn of the century, there was a belief that science would replace religion. It didn't. With the discoveries of modern physics, the universe became less certain again. The microcosm and the macrocosm resembled each other and were considered as different aspects of the same indivisible whole, made up of energy vibrating at different frequencies.

"At the same time in our society there arose the belief that material possessions would bring about a level of security and happiness. As we know the race for possessions has failed to yield what we hoped for. Happiness, by and large, has eluded us. Yet, within the human heart there is a longing to find something of lasting value. It cannot be found in society, its social structures, sciences, technologies, affluence, or even in its religion.

"We've tried to escape an ever deepening despair. This hunger, this unrequited longing will not let us go; there is a divine restlessness that draws us onward. How many dead-end roads must we travel before we find one road that takes us home?

"Many have turned to drugs as an escape from poverty,

violence, suffering, and despair. Some have intuitively understood that death is an aspect of life and that our preoccupation with the denial of death is foolish. For some, the suffering in life makes death more enticing. So what's the big deal with death? Why be so uptight over it?

"Some drugs ease pain and suffering and give a brief interlude of relief. The relief, not the drugs is sought. For some, the exploration of altered states is a genuine exploration born of curiosity and a certain intuitiveness. For others, drugs, like alcohol, ease social tensions and enable social interactions to be more relaxed. For others, the drugs and alcohol aggravate fear and paranoia, giving an intensity to thoughts that precipitate emotional states and accompanying physical acts such as violence.

"During the sixties many young people took LSD and other hallucinogenic drugs. It was sufficiently widespread as to create a cultural upheaval. The accepted norms and values of society were questioned, and racism and war were explored from internal states. From those internal states the social norms were seen. Racism and war were expressions of a misunderstanding. Love was glimpsed at the heart of life, though sometimes it was confused with sexuality.

"There was a stridency and arrogance among the young people of the time. Pointing fingers of blame at others, at the failure of institutions, was easy; creating solutions was much more difficult.

The glimpse afforded by these peculiar drugs was sometimes written off as being drug-induced, and the reality the drugs revealed succumbed to the label of unreality. Fortunately, there were some who didn't give up, but instead pursued the exploration until they found the pearl of great price."

"You point a harsh finger at Christianity. I'm not sure other religions are any better."

"I agree with you. All religions practice rituals and rites that have no bearing on anything. They've become mindless repetitions of things that have long since lost all meaning. These practices and the beliefs that accompany them are simplistic. Other than as acts of social cohesion and agreement, they are useless.

"When we explore the spiritual understanding of life itself, we find all belief is, in the end, useless. It may or may not be true. To believe in God or to believe in no God is the same. The atheist and the theist are just at different ends of the continuum. To know the reality, the word God seeks to represent, is the only thing of value. It is the basis for the spiritual search. The spiritual path arrives at the destination, and when it does so there is no longer a desire to speak of it, for the understanding is that it really cannot be shared, cannot be adequately spoken of.

"Too many in Christianity believe their religion to be the only one that is true. They believe it is the ultimate and final revelation of God. Because of this conviction, most Christians have no awareness of other enlightened masters besides Christ. In this way, Muslims and Christians are alike.

"Adherents of Buddhism and Hinduism, however, generally accept that other enlightened masters exist, many of whom walk the earth today. Therefore, because of a lack of exclusivity they have an ongoing awareness and acceptance of these masters and are able to seek them out. Don't get me wrong. I'm not judging Christianity; I'm merely attempting to point out the implications of what I see. I'm sure there will be some who will disagree."

A reporter in his early thirties interrupted.

"You engage us in conversations which, for want of a better word, might be called philosophical. We're used to getting the runaround, hearing ambiguous and deceptive statements from politicians. Sometimes your answers are not straightforward; they seem deliberately ambiguous. Why is that?"

"I'm sorry you think my answers are not straightforward. I think they are. I do realize they may be lengthy and tend to be philosophical. I know no other way to get across what I want to say. If we wish to understand what's going on, we must be willing to move beyond appearances to the truth that lies behind it. To do so requires responding to your questions in such a way as to penetrate to the heart of the matter. As I've said, human beings tend to operate from basic fundamental assumptions about life that are so imbedded in us, we rarely consider them as anything but fact. Consequently, we're incapable of questioning that of which we're unaware.

"Sometimes I may not answer questions to your satisfaction because they're rooted in assumptions I do not share. At times, to answer your question, I may need to search out the assumptions upon which it is based; and sometimes I dispute them.

"I understand what you mean when you say that many politicians are deliberately vague and ambiguous. I can assure you that is not my purpose. My sole interest1 is to bring about understanding. If you don't grasp something I've said, you're welcome to let me know, and I'll try again. Don't go away unsatisfied."

"I don't understand what you mean by fundamental assumptions."

David looked over to see a young woman standing with her hands resting on the back of the chair before her.

"Fundamental assumptions are assumptions we hold to be true without question. By that I mean we never think to examine them because we don't even see them. Over the course of time some of those assumptions *are* questioned; they lose their hold on us and fall away. I'll give you some examples with which we're all familiar.

"The earth is the center of the universe, the earth is flat. Then on a more mundane level: man is head of the household, human beings are by nature sinful, Jews are the 'chosen of God', Christianity and the teachings of Jesus are the highest pinnacle of spiritual understanding, the United States is the greatest civilization the world has ever known. I could go on but I think you can understand what I'm saying.

"There's a Zen story that addresses the same point. A man was fishing one day when he caught a fish. Because it was too small, he threw it back in the water. For the first time the fish realized he'd been swimming in something." David smiled. "There may be times when I will attempt to pull you out of the water of your assumptions where, like the fish, you swim wholly unaware of what you take for granted. I'll take one more question, and then we'll call it a day."

"Do you think you and Emerson can be elected?"

"Can we be elected? Yes. Will we? Probably not."

....

David's conversation with the students at Brandeis was an important watershed in the campaign. For a while the repercussions of it rocked the population as a whole. It became the subject of radio talk shows and TV news pundits. The religious right was incensed by his remarks, while for many who took the time to think about what he said, he had made sense.

The Republicans subjected David and Emerson to scathing attacks. They attempted to portray them as men bent on undermining family and religious values, which they themselves claimed to represent. The press for its part became less hostile, more open, and in a sense more curious. More and more they enjoyed the engagements with the Democratic contenders. There was something refreshing about them. Although they seemed to have little hope of being elected, their campaign addressed many things other politicians were afraid to touch. They spoke to the concerns of a large segment of the population. But the general consensus was they couldn't be elected, so why throw away votes?

Ten months later the Republicans lost the election, and the unlikely became reality. Most unlikely of all, here she was, a Canadian in the White House. She chuckled at the humor of it.

Sandra finished her tea, washed the cup and put it away. Living with David, she thought, had never been dull. And, as a healer in her own right, she had a need to be of service. She would not be limited by her husband's position. She could be just as forceful as she'd been with Phillips, and she could be patient too. Before long she would be working in Anacostia.

CHAPTER 11

Eight o'clock the next morning, Phillips walked into the Oval Office. David extended his hand, offering a warm greeting and friendly smile. He and Phillips had, over the months, come to know each other well. The Director of the Secret Service was a veteran of the agency; he'd worked his way to his current position. Gray-haired and distinguished, he was widely considered the best in his field.

In twenty-five years he'd served a variety of presidents, some he liked and some he didn't. This president he found difficult to deal with, but he didn't dislike him. No, in fact he respected him. Tremaine wasn't driven by the same things that drove his predecessors. He didn't appear to fear death for one thing, and he had assumed control over the agency right from the start. He did what he saw fit and expected the agency to do its job. He didn't allow the agency to dictate his movements based on what was best for security. Phillips disagreed with Tremaine on some things, yet found his ideas and his observations quite interesting. He made a lot of sense.

"Phillips, I know you're doing the best to make sure my wife and I are safe. We greatly appreciate your efforts. I'm sure you understand, that we cannot allow you to determine what we can and cannot do. I will not prevent Sandra from going to Anacostia if that's what she wants. Nor will you."

"But this is an unusual request," Phillips protested. "Anacostia is not a safe place at the best of times, not even for those who live there, let alone a white woman and the president's wife. We can't guarantee her safety."

"You can't guarantee our safety here, can you?"

"Well... no, I can't, but protecting you is a lot easier here than in Anacostia."

"Granted, but we've gone over this before. My job description requires I govern myself in ways appropriate to the job entrusted me. Your job is to safeguard me and my family, to the best of your ability, *while* I do that job. Your job is made more difficult because you must afford us a certain level of privacy. For that reason, we've asked for less intrusive protection. My hope is that we can lessen the need for protection still further as time goes on. We cannot safeguard against everything, which is what we've been trying to do, in our society as a whole. By trying too hard to protect ourselves, life becomes more and more circumscribed; we buy more and more insurance; we safeguard against this and safeguard against that. We're so busy safeguarding ourselves that we don't have time left to live. The fear of what might happen contaminates the enjoyment of each moment. That doesn't make for good living. I believe that process can be reversed, and one way is by living life fully, despite threats and fears. We can, of course, take reasonable and appropriate steps. I realize Sandra and I don't make your job easy, but that's the way it is. I'm open to your input and suggestions on how to do things, not on whether we can or cannot do them. As I've said before, that decision is mine."

"But Mr. President, this is dangerous for all concerned. She could be exposed to threats against her life, the threat of kidnapping and international terrorism."

"I understand your point, but the presidency cannot be a prison. Neither Sandra nor I find this acceptable. We'll not live our lives out of fear. We will all die sooner or later, and none of us know when. "

"You have to consider the potential threat to the country should either of you be kidnapped," Phillips insisted.

"Look, Phillips, I appreciate your concern and your persistence. I've left instructions that are to be carried out if such an eventuality should occur."

"I don't follow you."

"I will not go into the details, but suffice to say that Sandra and I have talked about this. If something should happen, there will be no extraordinary measures made to save us. I keep saying to you that we're not afraid to die. Don't get me wrong— there's no seeking of death. And by the same token, there's no desire to create unnecessary worry or difficulties for those like you, who have a particularly difficult job to do.

David looked at Phillips. He could see the man was not happy.

"Look, Phillips, life is dangerous. If we allow fear to run our lives, this freedom we value so highly will vanish. Fear has brought about much of the sorry state we as a nation find ourselves in today."

"I get what you're saying, but you have a responsibility to the people who elected you. You must not put yourself or your family at undue risk. Going to Anacostia is, in my opinion, undue risk."

"Let's look at the problem another way. Clearly you put yourself at risk on our behalf, and I imagine neither your wife nor your family is particularly thrilled over what you do. Their attitude doesn't stop you from doing your job, does it?"

"No, it doesn't."

"Like you, we must all take risks in life, and one day we will die. Some even suffer illness and injury. We can never safeguard against everything. Even when we attempt to safeguard ourselves, we really can't.

"I heard of a man who went to unusual lengths to preserve his life. He hired guards, put in the most sophisticated security system possible. He had a doctor and surgeon on call twenty-four hours a day. His home and his vehicles were bullet proof. He never married for fear of blackmail. He lived life out of fear. In his early forties he had minor surgery that proved successful, and he recovered well.

"Then one day, he slipped getting out of the bath, struck his head and died. Such is life. It was his destiny to die that way. He could not have escaped it."

"I think I understand what you're saying."

Tremaine smiled. "Then Sandra will be going to work in Anacostia as soon as you've made the best arrangements possible. Let us know when you're ready."

"I will."

David and Phillips stood and shook hands.

"I'll expect to hear from you soon."

....

Five days later David, Doug, and Jonathan met with Joseph Goldstein, the Israeli Foreign Minister.

"We felt it was important to apprise you in person of what is happening," Goldstein said.

"Thank you."

"We've had indirect talks with the Syrians and Lebanese.

If we stop attacking inside their border and withdraw our troops, they'll do their best to rein in the guerrillas. They say they cannot promise anything, but they're willing to try, and I think they mean what they say. Normally such assurances are insufficient, but we're willing to try, too. In fact we're willing to explore a wide range of options, and we want your support."

"I've already told you how we feel about this perpetual conflict. We'll be happy to play a part if we can. But the truth of the matter is this must be a genuine undertaking on your part."

"We understand. There's been a lot of discussion between the Prime Minister and the Cabinet concerning the conversations we had with your Administration. Needless to say, there's been some stiff opposition. I doubt whether we'll get far in the Knesset at the moment. The Prime Minister and I have given a lot of thought to the matter. As I've said before, we're in a very difficult position. In the past we've felt the need to respond with considerable force when attacked.

"In the areas we conquered, settlements have developed and the land has become productive; this has been accomplished by the sweat of our people. Our enemies want the land returned. We might even consider returning it; but if we do, we'll meet fierce opposition from those who've settled there. They have the support of the past administrations who saw the settlements as a way of conveying to our enemies that, if they provoke us, we'll respond quickly, and that any land we take we keep.

"Perhaps that strategy has painted us into a corner. Syria wants the return of the Golan, Jordan wants the return of the West Bank, and we've serious problems in Gaza. Opposition to the return of these lands is also very strong. We find ourselves locked in a position from which it's difficult to extricate ourselves. We have our share of fundamentalist hard-liners, who are unwilling to negotiate with the "enemy," unwilling to swap captured land for peace. They see only a continued escalation of force until the countries along our borders are willing to sue for peace on our terms."

"Very unrealistic."

"Yes, unrealistic, we agree. But what to do? As you know, going against the will of a large minority is difficult, and against a majority, almost impossible."

"Surely your people must be tired of war," Tremaine said.

"They are, but there's no consensus on how to end it."

"Then that's what you must work with. Offer hope to honorable men and women. Discuss what's required for peace to take hold. Offer them a way out from this perilous policy of war."

"That's what we intend to do: begin a national discussion on peace and war."

"The people must face the facts of human nature. They must be realistic, not idealistic. In a situation such as this, where so much human life is at risk, to distort reality with desire is not wise ."

"We agree. A year ago we won election with a promise to explore ways to bring about peace. But the negotiations have not been fruitful, and many are skeptical. The "Intifada" continues unabated, and our people are still subject to terrorist attacks wherever they go. We sense a softening in the stance of the PLO, but there's also been a proliferation in radical fundamentalists, not accountable to any central authority. This is why Syria and Lebanon tell us they cannot guarantee the control of such groups.

"Our concern is that the PLO will lose power because of so little progress in the peace process. These radical groups will increase in strength and become more intransigent, more difficult to deal with."

"There's no doubt you've a difficult task ahead," David agreed.

"To bring about peace, the social and political problems must be resolved, particularly in such places as Gaza. We will grant Palestinian self-rule, but there can be no effective self-rule in an area where there are few jobs, no social structures such as schools, sewage treatment plants, housing, medical facilities, banks, and so on.

"This will be a large financial undertaking. I'm not sure anything like this has been done before. However, until we deal with these issues, Israel's safety will remain at risk, and peace will not be possible. Like it or not, we and the Palestinians are inextricably bound to each other. No matter how distasteful, the fact is we need each other to survive reasonably well. Perhaps, by working together, we may yet resolve these difficulties."

"I agree, and I'm glad to hear you say it."

"We need your help."

"What do you have in mind?" David asked.

"We're extending an invitation to you and your wife to visit Israel in the near future. We want you to see firsthand the country and the kind of situations we're faced with. We want you to address the Knesset. Although the Prime Minister and I found your remarks provocative during our last meeting, upon further consideration we realized they made a great deal of sense. To say some of these things to our countrymen would be to invite political suicide. Then where is peace? For you to say such things could help us, and this process, with no risk to you."

David smiled. "You want us to break tough ground."

"I'm not sure what you mean."

"In the autumn after the harvest, the plow breaks up the tightly packed earth. Later the disc harrow is brought in for the finer work of preparing the soil."

Joseph smiled and nodded.

"You offered your assistance, and this is one of the ways we felt you could help. You have the ability to help people see from different perspectives. We've given it a lot of thought, and we'd like you to come."

"How soon do you need to know?"

"I fly back tomorrow. If you know by then, fine; if not, you can let us know through normal channels. There's no deadline, but the sooner the better."

"I'll let you know before you return; the details can be worked out later. If we have any questions, where can we reach you?"

"I'll be at the embassy; you can reach me there."

"Great," said David, standing. The four men shook hands, and David saw Joseph to the door.

"I'll be in touch," David said, shaking hands again.

Joseph smiled, then turned and walked away.

David closed the door behind him.

"Jonathan, get my schedule and go over it with Elsie."

"Are you going?" Jonathan asked, trying to hide a smile.

"Of course. I'll visit Jordan, Lebanon, and Syria while I'm there. I want you to set up the trip and coordinate it with Jonathan."

For two hours they discussed the options, objectives, dangers and opportunities of such an undertaking.

....

Late in the afternoon, word came that Tremaine's nominee for Vice President had been approved. Fifty-year-old Senator William G. Morgan of Maine was to be sworn in early next week.

CHAPTER 12

Nassir sat quietly waiting, back against an old cedar. He had a clear view across the undulating hills that fell away to the Mediterranean in the west. To the east, the hills gave way to the steep sides of the mountains with their rocky peaks. Two months had passed since he took Shamir into the mountains. They'd walked and talked and many tears had fallen down the dark pretty face.

Shamir took it upon herself to prepare meals that Nassir and his brother enjoyed. It was good to have the presence and skills of a woman in his life again. He'd forgotten the different perspective a woman brings, and he appreciated her input. She was good with animals and soon learned to work with sheep. His brother had accepted her readily and in his own simple way showed his appreciation for her.

With the recent conflict between the guerrillas and the Israelis, Nassir moved further north away from the border. Under his guidance they'd been careful not to draw attention to themselves. Some of the guerrillas that operated in Lebanon were men from outside the country and could be dangerous if encountered. He preferred caution to possible conflict.

Two days ago he learned Kahlil wanted to see him. They'd meet at the old cedar grove. Shamir wanted to know where he was going, but he preferred not to involve her. She'd packed his skins with nuts, dried fruits and meat, and then he'd left, telling her he'd return in two days. She was afraid; he could see it in her face. She was brave, too, and he knew she'd be fine.

....

More than twenty years had passed since he first began to meet the men and women who sought him out. The train of events began innocently enough one evening in Tyre. He'd gone to pick up supplies, several years after the death of his father and brother. That evening he walked beside the ocean, watching the activities of the fishermen around their boats. Suddenly he saw his friend Hafaz coming toward him. Nassir hadn't seen him since they'd ambushed the Israeli convoy twenty years earlier. Hafaz had aged; he looked worn-out. Nassir watched his old friend approaching and sensed the bitterness and sorrow that seemed to ooze from him. When Hafaz was close, Nassir spoke.

"Hello, old friend."

Hafaz stopped and looked sharply at Nassir, who stood just a few feet away. Recognition lit up his face with the long lost joy of friendship regained. He flung his arms around Nassir, dancing and kissing him on the cheeks.

"Nassir, Nassir, I'm so glad to see you. I've thought about you often and wondered if you were still alive. I was with your father and brother until they died. They told me you'd gone into the mountains."

"Yes, since the attack on the convoy I've lived in the

mountains. I've been tending sheep with my younger brother. I had enough of fighting. It seemed endless and futile. I wanted no more of it."

"Nassir, do you have time, can we eat together? I want to talk with you."

Nassir agreed, and they found a little place where they could sit and eat quietly, and drink the strong coffee. Hafaz poured out the sorrow of his soul.

"Sometimes I think war is the ultimate futility. It costs so much, and when it ends you have to settle for less than when you started. In the meantime you can't really live, In some ways, you become a brute bent on destruction. There's no room for enjoyment and love. To raise a family is an impossibility. Most of those I've known are dead. And after all these years, the Israelis seem more firmly entrenched than ever. The harder we fight, the more powerful they seem to become. For so long I've hated them and everything they represent. I've killed, mutilated and maimed hundreds of them. They still continue to exist despite my hatred.

"When I was younger that hatred gave me strength, a burning fire in a righteous cause. Now I feel hatred has gutted my being and eats away at my soul. Gone is joy; death is a familiar companion and I find myself welcoming it, for life is increasingly futile."

"Hafaz, my friend, I know of what you speak. I hear the longing of your soul, I'm glad your heart is still open after all these years. In time of despair the certainty of so-called righteous causes are more likely to fall away, and questions arise as to what lies behind them. Until then there is no hope, just more suffering and more pain. Sometimes it's easier to destroy than create. When I went into the mountains the thoughts you've expressed filled my mind and nearly drove me crazy. I needed to get away from the madness and see if I could find myself. I'd been the child of loving parents and beloved brothers. I'd become a vicious and capricious killer, taking insult at the slightest thing, a danger to myself and to all I met."

"What happened? How did you get away from it?"

"Growing up and tending the sheep with members of my family gave me familiarity with the mountains. Though I didn't realize at the time, the mountains were a place of solace for me, a place where I could feel their stillness and their age. At night I looked at the stars and wondered at my role in this vast unfathomable universe. For months I wandered alone, except for occasional meetings with my brother and uncle who tended the sheep. I felt the poison and the horrors of war slowly seeping out of me as though absorbed by the mountains themselves. I had not, for a long time, thought of the God of our forefathers, yet one day I found myself pondering this mystery again. I didn't want these thoughts because the idea of God created problems I didn't want to face."

"What do you mean?"

"With the idea of God comes the idea of some kind of justice, and when I looked around there seemed to be very little of it, from my perspective. Then came the obvious questions: if there really is a God, how can there be so much suffering, so much hatred, so much death? What about right and wrong? Why does my enemy prosper after stealing our land, the land of our forefathers passed down for generations? Why must an innocent young Israeli die for something he's too young to understand? Why are my enemy and I so alike, creatures of flesh and blood, love and hate, living on the same planet, a tiny speck of dust in the vast expanse of space?"

"What did you discover? What were the answers you found, if there were any?"

"Those questions tormented my mind, while at the same time a subtle feeling grew deep within me. Somehow I felt at home on this planet, in these mountains beneath the stars. I couldn't explain it; I just felt it. I sensed there was something I didn't understand and that this lack of understanding created the disturbance. I was tormented with doubt as to the existence of God and eventually came to the realization that what I believed meant nothing at all."

"I don't understand. Why did it mean nothing?"

"I saw that it really didn't matter what I believed."

"But why?"

"Because what I believed didn't seem to have any bearing on the truth or falsity of anything."

"I still don't understand."

"I saw that my belief or lack of belief in God made absolutely no difference. The truth was that I really didn't know whether God existed or not. At first I saw that my rejection of the idea of God came from anger and frustration over what I considered to be the injustices of life. Later I felt I should believe in God, that believing was the right thing to do. I was even afraid not to believe. I lived with these thoughts for some time until I came to see what was the most important of all was to know the truth for myself."

"What was the truth?"

"That I didn't know whether God existed or not. That admission was just a beginning. Until then I'd either believed that God existed or that he didn't. As long as I believed, one or the other, I was incapable of finding the truth."

"I still don't see why believing has no bearing on the truth."

"I'm sorry, Hafaz, I've not really tried to explain this before."

Nassir sipped his coffee and thought for a moment. Hafaz looked at his friend and felt a sense of calmness that hadn't been there in the old days when they'd fought together. His black hair had begun to turn white; dark, imperturbable eyes were set in a dark face. His body seemed lean and strong. Not a trace of bitterness or pain of any kind seemed present in the tranquil expression or the kind eyes. Hafaz wanted to know more about his friend. What had he found? Patiently he waited.

"We believed that by fighting the Israelis, we could force them to leave the land and go back where they came from. That was our belief. It hasn't worked, and so, even here, our belief had no bearing upon reality. They believed they could destroy us by wiping out our villages, by the sheer destruction they could bring upon us. That belief proved false as well. When people give up their beliefs, reality lies before them. Neither we nor the Israelis are going to go away. As long as we're locked in our stubborn and self-righteous beliefs, we'll continue to kill each other. That's the futility that you spoke of."

"Yes, I see. So what can be done? We can't convince others of the futility of their actions. We can't stop them, can we?"

"No, we can't. They must realize for themselves, like you and I."

"So what can be done?"

"I don't know."

They'd talked many times following that meeting. Hafaz wanted to leave the guerrillas, but he was under tremendous pressure to keep the group intact. He was an experienced fighter and knew the terrain well. For him to leave would be a great loss.

Nassir remembered the last meeting they had. Hafaz had come into the mountains, and they met at a prearranged spot. Nassir had waited, as he did now for Kahlil. As the sun slipped toward the sea shadows, highlighted the contours of the hills below. Then he saw Hafaz threading his way along a ridge below him. Nassir stood and made his way toward his friend.

As usual they'd talked late into the evening, sharing bread and cheese Nassir had brought with him. They sat silently for a time, not saying a word. The moon lifted above the mountain to their backs, bathing all around them in its unearthly light. Nassir heard Hafaz's voice beside him as they gazed at the hills below.

"My brother, you've helped me find a measure of peace. I don't know whether I can leave the group of men I'm with or not. At first I wanted to, and yet I feel a responsibility to those younger and less experienced than myself. I've tried to speak to them of my deepest thoughts. They don't want to hear—they think I'm crazy. In their veins still beats fresh the thrill of war, of living on the edge. As you know, my friend, that edge brings exquisite appreciation to life because we cannot know how long it will last. I've outlived all those my own age but you. I feel my time is near. I look out over these hills that I've loved for so long, and feel their beauty as never before. I'm thankful for one more time with you— to sit beneath the moon and feel somehow, despite the suffering, that I'm part of the earth, and part of the stars. My beliefs in God have vanished, and in my heart something stirs that I've not wished to speak of before. I mention it now only to let you know, for I feel that you'll understand and be pleased."

Nassir put his arm around his friend's shoulders.

"I understand," he said softly, smiling to himself.

"The thought has crossed my mind," Hafaz continued, "that I'll not live much longer. Perhaps my destiny is to die doing what I've been doing. If that happens, I want you to know there's peace in my heart. I feel the events that play across this planet are far beyond the comprehension of one such as I. I no longer feel I have much choice, if any, in these matters. I feel like an actor playing a part in some great drama, the end of which I cannot know from here."

Nassir sat silently beside Hafaz, a deep compassion welling up inside him. He saw clearly what his friend meant to convey.

Nassir had sensed for some time now that separation was in reality illusion. Though he couldn't explain his understanding, he felt one with his friend and with all human beings and all forms of life. He knew that the illusion of separation was somehow essential to the functioning of life in the world in which they lived. It was an effect of something he had no name for, something he knew like a memory he couldn't quite recover or words he couldn't quite capture.

When the time came for Hafaz to depart, Nassir had walked with him for several miles. They embraced, kissed and parted. Nassir never saw Hafaz again.

....

Months later a young man called Idries found his way to Nassir's camp. He was tired and hungry when he arrived. Nassir fed him, and over coffee learned that Hafaz was dead, mortally wounded in an Israeli ambush. Some were able to escape. Hafaz had spoken to Idries of Nassir many times, and before he died asked Idries to find him.

"Tell my friend I died well because I learned to live well," he said. "I'm tired of the bloodshed and glad to leave at last. Tell him I've cherished our talks and felt the silent stirring in my heart even in the most terrible of times."

"Then he said to tell you, 'the heart of the messenger is open, the fruit is ripe. Many more will come.' He said, you'd know what he means."

From that time forth many had sought out Nassir. Some found him, some did not. His reputation spread like a quiet whisper on a gentle breeze. He'd been known as a fierce fighter, a man who, one day, turned his back on fighting to find peace in the silent mountains tending his family's sheep. For many years those who tired of the bloodshed and hoped for another way came to see him. He talked with them in ones and twos, and sometimes more. He met them in the hills and mountains and from time to time in villages and towns and occasionally in Beirut.

....

Nassir stood and stretched. The sinking sun cast elongated shadows, and the rocky peaks of the mountains took on a peach hue. He turned and looking down over the hills, caught sight of a movement directly below him, a mile and a half away. As he watched, two men detached themselves from some trees and turned east, following the ridge, and began the long ascent to the grove in which Nassir stood. Kahlil and one of his friends, he thought.

He'd first met Kahlil two years ago. At the time Kahlil was not in good shape. He'd lost his family. Two younger brothers had been killed fighting the Israelis. His parents were killed by an Israeli commando unit, and his eldest brother was shot in the head in front of him. The killing of his eldest brother had particularly unsettled him.

He and his brother had been recalled to Beirut following an attack on a northern Israeli settlement on the western Golan. There he'd received a bullet wound. His brother had helped him escape. Once across the border of Lebanon they were instructed to return to Beirut. Two days later they met their cell leaders. Kahlil's wound was still fresh, and his brother was concerned for him since it hadn't been properly tended.

The family had been staunch Muslims, and from an early age the children were indoctrinated. Their duty as Muslims required them to do everything in their power to destroy the infidel. Jews and the great Satan across the sea were the enemies.

Kahlil and Habish had seen the brutality of the Israeli soldiers and the destruction their war planes brought. Eagerly they awaited the opportunity to slip away from their families and join with other patriots who sought to drive the infidel into the sea. Perhaps if they were lucky they'd find and kill some of the Americans who were known to work with the Israelis.

Habish and Kahlil wondered why they'd been recalled. It was late afternoon when the old van carrying them pulled in front of a bombed-out building. They were led through the rubble and past several crumbling walls to the back of another building. Entering a doorway, they climbed a set of narrow stairs and found themselves in a dark hall. The guide knocked on a door. It opened, and they were quickly whisked inside. With the heavy sound of a dead bolt, the door closed behind them. There was little light in the room, and Kahlil suddenly felt afraid. He'd never felt afraid around his own people before.

A candle burned on an old crate directly in front of them; looking around the room, he saw men sitting on chairs and old sagging couches. The smell of stale sweat and tobacco filled the room. A bearded man with short-cropped hair and hard, flat eyes sat directly in front of them. For two hours they'd been forced to sit side by side and answer questions about the raid led by Habish. As the questioning went on, Kahlil found himself more and more afraid. Something was terribly wrong. Why were they being questioned so harshly? Who were these men who presumed to question them?

For six years Habish and Kahlil had fought together, even after the loss of their young brothers. No one had ever questioned their patriotism and allegiance to Hizballah before, but now their allegiance seemed to be in doubt. Habish must have felt the same way. He was getting angry. Suddenly he tried to stand and was immediately forced back into the chair. Kahlil saw the glint of a 9mm pistol placed at the back of Habish's head.

The man in front suddenly moved. As though in a dream, Kahlil heard the muffled report and saw his brother jerk forward and fall. Blood oozed from a dark spot at the back of his skull, and formed a small, sinister pool on the floor. The candle guttered in the putrid air. He couldn't believe what had happened. Before he could move, he was yanked from his chair and taken from the room.

For weeks Kahlil had been locked in a nearby room. He was informed that his brother was a traitor who'd questioned the orders he'd received from Beirut and could no longer be trusted. Kahlil knew his brother had been unhappy. Habish had talked to him for months about the killing, the raids, and how he thought they were counterproductive. Kahlil hadn't taken him seriously, just listened. Now he thought back to his brother's conversations and realized that perhaps he'd been serious after all.

A week after his brother's death, he was questioned for several days. In the end he was told to return to his unit in the south. Kahlil, still in a state of shock, found himself wondering who these men were, and why, in their eyes, his brother was a traitor? He'd been told that to fight the enemy was his duty and to question the orders of his superiors, an act of treachery. Habish, he was told, had questioned his superiors, and that could no longer be tolerated. He was told, "Anyone who so forgets his duty as to question the sacred work in which we're engaged, cannot be allowed to continue. If he keeps questioning, he must be eliminated. We cannot risk a man like your brother leading others in this frame of mind. He puts men's lives at risk; that must not be allowed to happen."

Three days later Kahlil returned to Tyre where he rejoined his unit. While his shoulder healed, he remained in town. One evening, while walking slowly along the road fronting the sea, he saw a white-haired shepherd sitting on worn stone steps that led to the beach and the fishing boats. Fishermen sat hunched at their nets, sewing and swapping tales. Old men had come to talk and listen too. The shepherd drew his attention. There was nothing unusual about him, but Kahlil felt compelled in the old man's direction. As he approached, the old man turned and fixed his eyes on the young soldier. Kahlil realized the shepherd was not as old as he'd first thought. The shepherd suddenly got to his feet and extended a hand in greeting.

"My name's Nassir," he said. "I've been waiting for you."

Kahlil found his heart beating fast.

"I'm sorry," he said, "you must have the wrong person."

"No, you're the one."

"But you don't know me."

"That's what you think."

With a jolt Kahlil wondered if this was a spy, sent from the Beirut cell.

"You need not concern yourself. I'm not a spy," Nassir said with a humorous smile.

Kahlil felt disoriented. How could this man know what he was thinking? he wondered.

He looked at Nassir and immediately felt at ease. He was surprised; he didn't know how he knew, but he realized he had nothing to fear from this man.

"Would you join me for coffee?" Nassir asked.

Kahlil agreed, and within a few minutes they were seated at a small table sipping the dark coffee. They were in the very same place Nassir and Hafaz had first sat so many years ago. Nassir put his cup down and looked directly at Kahlil.

"Kahlil, there's a heaviness in your heart, and disturbance in your mind. In such a state a great opportunity awaits."

"How do you know my name?"

"I don't know, I just do."

Kahlil's mind was swamped with questions. "I don't understand," he said, shaking his head.

"You don't have to."

Kahlil thought for a moment. "What makes you think I have a heavy heart and my mind is disturbed?."

"I see it, that's all."

"See what?"

"The violent death of your brother, a death brought about because he questioned what he was doing, as you have now begun to do."

Kahlil found himself shaking.

"Who are you?"

"I've told you, I'm Nassir."

"You know what I mean."

"You're right." Nassir paused for a moment and looked at Kahlil, assessing him.

"For as long as I can remember, I've known things about people. At first I thought everyone had the same ability. Only as I grew older did I learn this was not the case. From time to time I find myself drawn to places where I meet certain people. When I see them, I know things about them. All of them are hungry for the truth, and desperately tired of the false—People like yourself. I live and work as a shepherd in the mountains with my brother. For years, I fought the Israelis, and then one day, sickened by the violence and bloodshed, I turned my back on it and went into the mountains to be alone to think and to find the truth I needed to find."

"You just walked away from it?"

"Yes."

"And you never went back?"

"No."

"Didn't anyone try to track you down and bring you back?"

"No. Our unit was small and made up of Lebanese who'd

suffered at the hands of the Israelis. We were like a family."

"It's not that way anymore," Kahlil said. "Now we have Iranians with us. They speak the truth for Muslims who're engaged in the struggle against the ungodly. They direct us, and they'll tolerate no doubt in the word of God. My brother's misgivings led them to kill him."

"What makes you think it's the word of God?"

"They say God doesn't compromise with evil and that it should be destroyed by whatever means necessary. If the destruction of evil means dying in the process, then it's better to die than to live in such an unholy world."

"What do you think?"

Kahlil looked around, suddenly nervous.

"You're safe here," Nassir assured him.

"My brother was a good man. He had a warm and loving heart. I think he'd begun to question whether the killing was accomplishing anything. He could see it was destroying the young men of our country, while the Israelis seemed to grow in strength and numbers. He also began questioning what he was taught by the Iranians. He asked me once if I had any idea how some men seemed to know so clearly what God wanted when he didn't. I couldn't answer his question. I'd never really thought about such things."

"What do you think now?"

"I'm not sure. I certainly began to think about it after he raised it, but we never spoke of it again. What they did to my brother is no better than what the Israelis have done to the other members of my family. My brother fought and killed for what he believed in. How could anyone doubt him? And yet, these men held a gun to his head and shot him in front of me. That I cannot accept. These last days have been a time of great turmoil. I used to be glad of the guidance of those who told me what to do, who quoted the holy Koran and explained its meaning to me. I was glad I didn't have to think and make up my own mind. Life was easier when I only had to follow instructions."

"And now?"

"Now I'm not sure anymore. Could it be that the enemy we face is not really the enemy of nations and race, but the enemy of hatred, of power and unquestioned allegiance to our religion? Perhaps the enemy lies within us."

Nassir looked at Kahlil and smiled softly.

"You have said it."

"What do you mean?"

"I mean that your mind has begun to voice the questions that arise in your heart. Your doubt is the stirring of a desire for freedom. When that occurs, there's a turning inward, and the true meaning of religion may at last be known."

"I want nothing else to do with religion!"

"I understand your feelings, but don't allocate the meaning of religion to the narrow-minded and bigoted. As you realized for yourself, these people appear to be the most pious of men. Such piety is anathema to the teachings of the masters. These men are in the very hell they speak of, the hell they claim to avoid. They've no idea what they're doing. They're the blind who lead the blind, and as such can be dangerous."

"Why dangerous?"

"Somewhere deep within them is the knowledge that they're asleep, that they don't understand. That knowledge is the beginning of freedom. But those who're afraid cannot tolerate even the hint of such a thing. So, like sleepwalkers, who give the appearance of being awake, they hurt themselves and others. Among them walk the masters who truly see. From time to time the masters feel the stirring of the sleeper and are drawn to shake him into wakefulness."

"Are you saying that those involved in religion are all asleep?"

"No, but the fact is, most are."

"How could that be? What about the ministers, the holy ones, the wise teachers, those who are there to guide us and interpret the sacred words to us?"

"None are the true masters! There are exceptions, but so rare as to be almost nonexistent."

"And yet religion is supposed to be where truth is."

"Why should it be?"

"I don't know. It's what I've been told."

"Do you not know from your own experience?"

"Only recently have I begun to suspect that these men do not know what they profess; their hearts are cold while their words are on fire. But, growing up, my brother and I knew some good men who were our teachers."

"I'm sure there are many good religous men but they aren't awake; they're not the masters I'm speaking of."

"I still don't see why."

"When you look carefully you'll discover the religion of your forefathers is made from beliefs, some of which condone killing, torture and destruction. Regardless of what they are and how long they've been held, they are merely beliefs. What master would be interested in living and working within the constraints of an institution which professes to know, when in fact it does not? For this reason the masters go largely unnoticed. They're found in all walks of life by those who're ready to awaken, while they remain unknown to the sleepers."

"Wasn't Jesus a master?"

"Probably."

"And Mohammed?'

"Maybe, maybe not."

"How can you tell?"

"It's impossible to tell for sure. We have to go by the feeling of what they had to say. The teachings of Jesus were simple, the teachings of the Prophet complex. Truth is simple, not complex."

"But these were the founders of our Muslim faith; were they not Muslim?"

"At the time there was no such thing as the Muslim religion. Those who took the teachings of Jesus, for instance, turned them into beliefs to be adhered to and followed. Mohammed tried to codify the teachings of Jesus, as did Jesus' followers in the Christian religion. To believe and to know are not the same.

"Those who are asleep turn the knowledge of a master into beliefs. The beliefs are handed down through the generations and undergo changes that take them further and further away from the original intent. It could be said, that the masters know, while the sleepwalkers wander lost in the dreams of their beliefs. There's sometimes danger in being a great teacher such as Jesus."

"What do you mean?"

"When a teacher becomes well known, there are many who seek him out. Amongst the sleepwalkers, some are destined to awaken; others are not. Those who aren't become afraid of him, afraid of his power, afraid that his light will expose the pettiness they feel in themselves. Sometimes the fear becomes so strong that the most fearful will seek to destroy him. Most masters are not well known. They function best in obscurity, and the teachings are handed down in secret."

"Why in secret?"

"By secret I mean there's an understanding on the part of the master that life has an intrinsic harmony, that it's a great dance, perfect in every way. But the harmony is not readily apparent to most people. The masters know that when the time is right, there'll be those who seek them out. In those interactions, the open heart is rewarded with the guidance it seeks. Awakening like everything else is a matter of destiny. Like the blossom that bursts forth, gives way to the fruit, which in due time ripens and is ready to be plucked. These teachings are not teachings to be subscribed to or practiced. They're merely descriptions of an inner process, understood by those who are ready and not noticed by those who aren't."

"I get the feeling you think beliefs are not useful."

"True. When a master speaks the truth, his words are merely a description of a process. But all too often the words are misinterpreted as instructions to be followed. These instructions become codified into beliefs, and the world is divided between those who believe and those who don't. Belief is a source of conflict and bloodshed. Some of the worst atrocities the world has ever known were perpetrated by those who claim to follow the teachings of a master."

They sat quietly for a few minutes sipping coffee.

"I don't know what to do," he said finally.

"Say more."

"My brother's dead, and he was the last of my family. I believed in what I did, now I'm not sure anymore. It's hard to keep focused on what's to be done, and I feel hatred for those who killed him. For days I've thought of how I could kill them. At the same time, I feel a strong bond with those in my cell. We've fought together, and learned to depend on each other. I feel an allegiance to them, I can't let them down."

Nassir listened quietly, knowing there was nothing he could say. Kahlil would discover for himself what to do.

In the years that passed since that first meeting, they'd met twice in Tyre, and several times Kahlil had sought Nassir in the hills. The young man always came when he had questions. They'd sit and talk for hours, and then he'd leave. Once in a while he brought friends with him. Nassir watched now as the two men made their way toward him.

Kahlil introduced his friend Tariq. Nassir greeted them then passed them a water skin. With practiced ease they aimed streams of water into their mouths and slaked their thirst. For a while they sat quietly, the two younger men catching their breath while Nassir sat enveloped in the silence and the approaching darkness. The branches above stirred in the freshening breeze, and stars glittered overhead. Kahlil spoke.

"Our unit is moving from Tyre to Bent Jebail. Iranians and Syrians are joining the cells, and we're being divided. With the added numbers, we can launch concerted attacks from many locations at once. They've equipped us with more hand-launched rockets. There's talk of taking hostages and killing those of our own people who favor peace with the Israelis."

"Sounds like an escalation of hostilities."

"Yes. there's fear that peace negotiations are going on, and they intend to make them unsuccessful."

"What makes them think negotiations are going on?"

"The Israelis suddenly stopped their attacks a week ago. They didn't get what they wanted, which was for us to stop the rocket attacks across the border. For them to stop their attacks under these circumstances is unheard of. There's also a lot of pressure on the political cells of South Beirut."

"Where did it come from?"

"We don't know for sure, but some think it's from the Syrian government."

"Why?"

"There's a rumor our rocket attacks have upset something that's under way. What could that be but peace?"

"Why are the Syrians and Iranians getting involved in the local cells?"

"The Iranians are hard-liners; they don't want any compromise with Israel or any of its allies. They're afraid we're getting soft, like my brother. By working with us directly, in the field, they can keep an eye on us, keep us on track. They're fanatics!"

"It makes us nervous," Tariq said quietly. "They constantly quote the Koran, and we must study with a mullah who travels between the cells on a regular basis."

"I see."

"The Syrians who've joined our cells are also hard-liners; they want nothing but the annihilation of Israel. Hizballah, the Party of God, is dependent on Syria for supplies and arms. So, it must listen to the Syrian government, which is sometimes more moderate in its approach. Hizballah will not, however, always follow instructions."

"Syria does not have complete control over us," Kahlil added.

"What else?" Nassir asked.

"As I understand it, we've been told to let up, to reorganize, reconnoiter, and get in position to launch hit-and-run rocket attacks. We know very little beyond the activities of our own cell, but we've heard we'll be working more closely with Hamas. They'll work from inside Israel while we work from outside.

"This gives us time to re-provision with rockets and other supplies. But if there's any truth to the rumors, there may be something else behind Syria's instructions to lay off for a while. There's talk the American President may come to Israel to address the Knesset."

"I see."

"We've heard he'll visit Syria and Jordan. None of this is confirmed, but it wouldn't surprise me, given what's happening on the cell level."

Once more they were quiet, each man thinking.

"You've been wondering how much longer you'll stay." Nassir said, voicing the question in Kahlil's mind.

"I don't know what to do. You are my teacher and what you teach makes a lot of sense to me. But I'm not quite ready to give up what I've lived for for so long."

"If you're meant to leave you will; if not, you won't. No anxiety on your part can change what is to come. The grass does not resist the wind. And, on the other matter, I am not a teacher, Kahlil."

"You are to me!"

"No, I merely direct your attention to that which you already know. A teacher is someone who helps others learn something. Knowledge is acquired. Look closely at our interactions. Nothing new is learned, nothing is acquired."

"I don't follow."

"You've come here when you felt the need to do so. Usually a question was present. A question arises in the mind and seeks resolution. Look carefully, there's no resolution when you believe. The tension of the question still exists, while doubt remains at the heart of belief. The question is answered only when understanding dawns. That understanding is the recognition of something that has always been. And that which has always been is truth.

"We've spoken of belief before. When you believe, you mistake words for reality. Truth, which always is, remains forever obscured by the beliefs we hold so firmly. Therefore, the understanding that is truth comes when beliefs fall away. This is the reverse of most learning and teaching."

"So when you talk with us, you already know what we don't?" Tariq asked.

"From here, there is no knowing, because the object that knows is absent."

"So, in the case of a *true* teacher," Tariq continued, "if I understand you correctly, you're saying he draws the student to the edge of understanding, then somehow tickles the awareness into existence."

Nassir chuckled quietly. "As I said, I don't like the term *teacher* because it has connotations not applicable to what we've been engaged in. Nevertheless, Tariq, you've put it well. We must be careful with words, for they are merely vehicles to convey what lies beyond them, the reality itself. There's no interest in arguing about words, only in understanding that to which they point. What you've said is accurate."

They talked for a while longer then shared the meal Shamir had prepared. Before leaving, Nassir gave instructions on how to find him from Bent Jebail.

CHAPTER 13

"I want a copy right away," he said into the phone. "No, I don't give a damn how you get it, just get it. Have it in my office by tomorrow morning.... What do you mean you can't get it by then?.... By when? Okay, have it on my desk by Tuesday morning at nine.... Yes... Yes, I know. No, you don't need to be concerned, no one will know. No, we'll keep you out of it.... If your name comes up, we'll just deny it. No, you don't have anything to worry about.... Okay, Thanks! Good-bye."

As Senator Cole put the phone down, a cynical smile spread over his face. He picked up a cigar. Biting the end off, he spit it into his wastebasket, a skill he gained over years of practice. Flicking a lighter, he puffed until a cloud of smoke billowed above him. He pulled out the writing tray at his desk, put his feet up and leaned back in his expensive old leather chair, and puffed contentedly. Life was undoubtedly good, and he was at the pinnacle of his power.

A man in his fifties, Cole had thinning hair, always a little greasy, which gave him a seedy look. He was five ten and weighed a hundred and seventy pounds. A hard drinker, he had a sallow complexion and the cold gray of his eyes was ameliorated by a wateriness that sometimes gave the unsetling sense that he was crying. He had a reputation for getting his way, was known to be savvy, and, some felt, unscrupulous. He was not easily swayed by the opinions of others. With the defeat of the Republican administration, he assumed the mantle of spokesman for his party's policies.

With the fall of the previous administration, Cole had somehow remained clear of scandal himself. There was talk that he'd been involved in the whole Japan affair, but no one could substantiate anything. As minority leader he kept a tight rein on his fellow Republicans; most had stayed in line. Legislation that passed did so only because the Democrats had a majority, and then only with numerous riders attached, and after bitter and prolonged struggles.

He'd hated Emerson with a passion and made it his mission to disrupt the new president in every way possible. When Tremaine came to power, he continued the same policy with one additional proviso. Tremaine didn't even possess the saving grace of having served in the military. And, he thought, Tremaine is a maverick, a free thinker, more difficult to handle than Emerson.

It was Cole who ordered his henchmen to dig into Tremaine's past. What he found he leaked to the press. Several times he was sure his revelations would ruin Tremaine, forcing his resignation; but time after time, the President slipped away unscathed. The press has gone soft, Cole thought. Never mind, he was a patient man; and sooner or later Tremaine would slip up. No one could be that smart. Besides, he had a lead on something, and if it proved out, Tremaine would have to step down.

The phone rang, and Cole picked it up.

"Yes, Midge, put him through. Hello, Cole here.... Who? .... Congressman Smythe, good, thanks for getting back to me. I understand you want to look at the budget that's coming down?.... I know it's not down yet.... Yes, I know, but I don't want any surprises.... You know what I mean. We vote as a block, no breaking ranks.... I know how Emerson thinks, and it was his budget until he died. Tremaine will follow his lead in this matter.... No, it's not a Republican budget.... I don't give a damn. If you break ranks with us, you'll not get your grain subsidy bill into committee.... No, Smythe, don't give me any of that liberal crap, we already know how this administration works.... Listen, son, I've been around the Hill for a long time. I know how things work, I'm telling you that Tremaine's no different from any other Democratic president.... No, he doesn't make more sense; he's a con-artist, a shrink; he's good with words, that's all.... I'm not going to argue with you.... Just keep in mind who your friends are, those who can help you, that's all.... Right, Right.... As soon as I get a copy of the budget I'll let you know.... Good.... Yes.... next week.... Good ... Good.... Okay.... Yes, there's still an opening on that committee.... Good.... Then we understand each other.... Yes, I'll be in touch.... Bye."

Cole put the phone down and, leaning back, lit his cigar and puffed hard. Through the clouds of smoke, a low shaft of sunlight struck a wilted bouquet of flowers and fallen petals on the corner of his desk. It had been another full day. Four days it had taken him. He'd been on the phone with each Republican on the Hill. He was satisfied, certain he had them in line. They'd follow his lead now. There'll be no surprises, he thought. My troops are well disciplined. Pressing a button, he spoke into the intercom.

"Midge, did that memo get sent out to McLelland's?"
"Yes, it went out yesterday."

"Anonymously?"

"Yes."

"Good. I'm finished for the day, I'm going home. I'll be back in the morning at nine. Have a nice evening."

"I will. You too," came the disembodied voice.

....

Three days later Mark Turner, the president of McLellands, sat at his desk. He finished reading the letter and was angry. He buzzed for his secretary. An elderly woman with white hair and a pleasing smile pushed the door open.

"Mary, where's Angus?" he demanded.

Her smile vanished from her face. "He went out to lunch with the Canadians. He said he'd be back by three. He should be here any moment." She looked at her watch.

"As soon as he gets back, send him in; I need to talk with him. Tell him if he's got something on, he'll have to put it on hold."

Mary nodded and left. She'd known he'd be upset, but she'd not expected such a strong reaction. Turner was not by nature an angry man. He tended to be quiet and self-contained. Fifteen minutes later Angus walked breezily into the office. Mary gave him the message.

"What's it about?" he asked.

"He had a letter saying the president is about to issue an order that all paper used by the government must be recycled."

The news was a jolt to Angus, too. He knocked on the door and pushed it open.

"Come in, come in," Turner muttered impatiently.

Angus walked to the desk, and Turner indicated the letter.

"Read it," he said.

Angus picked up the letter and sat down. Quickly he glanced it over then tossed it on the desk.

"If it's true, it's bad news," he said.

"You're damned right it's bad news," Turner sputtered. "We've got to find out, and quick. Who would know?"

"There are several people."

"Get on it right away. Find out all you can and get back to me. If it's true, then we've got to put a stop to it."

"Right, I'll get on it at once. I'll have to fly to Washington. I can't do it from here."

"I don't care how you do it—just get it done."

Angus knew by Turner's voice that he was dismissed. Outside, he talked briefly with Mary, giving her instructions.

"Call me at home when you've booked the flight. I'm going to pack and let Julie know."

....

Turner swiveled in his chair and looked out over the city. In the distance, above the haze, he could see the mountains of the Olympic Peninsula. Damn, he thought, this couldn't come at a worse time. The Canadian company, Crown McLelland, had just settled a contract dispute following a lengthy strike. On top of that, the Canadian government had increased the stump rate for Crown Lands. The advantage American companies had enjoyed, because of the difference in currencies, had almost been eroded by the increased prices. Only the steadily increasing purchase of paper by the government bureaucracies in Washington had enabled them to feel they could afford such a high settlement in the Canadian operations.

If the government was going to use recycled paper, McLelland's mills were just not equipped for it. With existing contracts to be renegotiated in January, they could lose business to the smaller companies, some of which had developed the capacity to use the recycled paper by mixing it with their existing pulp. Turner shook his head. We can't let this happen, he thought; Angus is good; his group is powerful. Damn it, we'll have to invest more money in the PAC. This is not something we expected. Our budget is set. Shit, this could mean a lot of work and money, and still we could lose it all.

Turner gazed through the window. The Olympic mountains had assumed the purple haze of late afternoon. All his life he'd sought out the mountains when he was troubled. They calmed him, and at this time of day there was a marvelous beauty to them. A niggling thought insinuated itself in his mind. Perhaps we've been greedy and shortsighted. Perhaps we've taken the land and the trees for granted. Fifty years ago, when he was first starting out in the forestry industry, no one had ever thought that the vast wilderness of Canada would someday be unable to meet the demand for trees?

The same thing was happening now to the tropical rain forests. Have we abused the land, taken it for granted and now the time has come to pay the piper? He wondered. He didn't want to think about it. The problem was beyond him; he was too old to deal with it. Soon it would be in the hands of a new generation. He couldn't afford to think of such things. He had a job to do. He was a businessman, entrusted with running a company, and his stockholders expected him to make money for them, in the shortest possbile time. Besides how many of them would still be alive fifty years from now? It was not up to him to set policy or resolve the world's difficulties. Business is business, he thought.

Turning around, he reached for the desk lamp and switched on the light. Its opaque green glass shielded his eyes while its warm glow revealed papers scattered across a highly polished wooden desk. Slowly he sorted and put them away.

Standing, he pushed his chair neatly in place, took his coat from the rack, and walked out of the office, muttering "good evening." Mary watched him go, the door swinging shut behind him.

....

Senator William G. Morgan strolled leisurely through the grounds of his new home. It was the first time he'd done so since he and his wife Marriane had moved into the new residence only the week before. Until today he'd been busy finding his way around and learning what was expected of him.

Marriane, he knew, found Washington a big adjustment. Thirty years in Camden, Maine, was a long time, and she had good friends there. She'd gone to Washington with him on many occasions, but was always happy to return to the old seaport she loved. He also would miss the "down east" practicality he loved about New Englanders. They'd be less accessible to him for several years now. A realist, he knew that as Vice President, newly appointed, his time would be less his own than he was used to. He shook his head, still disbelieving. The sudden change from Senator to Vice President took some getting used to. Almost four months had passed since Emerson's death.

He'd not known Emerson well, but many years ago he'd taken political science courses from him, at the University of Maine. He'd been impressed with the man then, and was impressed again when Emerson ran for and became president.

Tyler liked Tremaine, unknown to him until the campaign. Morgan liked him. He sensed that Tremaine was an honest man, and Morgan had followed carefully what he had to say during the presidential race. Tremaine and Emerson had made a good team. Morgan's initial antipathy for those who'd opposed the Vietnam War had given way to a grudging respect for the man. He'd read the press reports and the speech Tremaine had given at Boston University the week after Emerson's death. Morgan found himself agreeing with most of what the new President said. Tremaine articulated his views in such a way that it was difficult not to see what he was driving at, while the clarity of his observations couldn't be avoided.

The interviews Morgan had with Tremaine were lengthy and substantial, lasting more than a week. Overall, they'd been a delightful surprise. Morgan found Tremaine a relaxed and attentive person, with a mind free of preconceptions. Tremaine's questions had been probing and far-reaching. He wanted to know Morgan's thoughts on foreign affairs and dug deeply into his views on the Middle East, asking the basis for his observations and conclusions. For four days they explored the issues of crime, the courts, guns, violence, drugs, poverty, unemployment, and the effects of the demilitarization of American industry.

Tremaine wanted to know why Morgan thought the way he did, what he saw as key issues, what ideas he had concerning the resolution of the difficulties facing the country. At one point he said, "Some accuse me of being a philosopher and not a practical man. My response is that philosophy sets the tone, expresses a fundamental way of seeing life and our role in it as human beings. Philosophical understanding is imbedded in all cultures and all ages. It is from this context that behavior springs forth. To understand behavior, I find it helps to understand the philosophical background from which it emerges."

Morgan found himself coming back to that statement over and over again. The more he thought about it, the more he sensed it was true. Under Tremaine's probing, Morgan had once more been reminded that public service was a high calling when it expressed the sincere desire to serve. He knew by the end of the interviews that he and the president were in complete accord in their understanding of service. Morgan found himself smiling. If the truth be known, he thought, 'I'm excited to be in this position. It'll be challenging, I'm sure, but what an opportunity.'

Morgan climbed carefully onto a large rock, left by glaciers, thousands of years ago. Carefully he made himself comfortable, sitting some twenty feet above the ground. The rock was still warm from the sun. Pleasant in the cooling air of evening. Birds gathered high in the trees, anticipating the end of day. All about him the cacophony of their cries was a pleasing welcome.

It was already dark when he saw the lights through the trees, warm and welcoming. As he approached the house he could see Marriane through the window working in the kitchen. He chuckled to himself. He could still see the pained look on the cook's face when Marriane had patiently explained that she enjoyed cooking and was not about to give up control of "her" kitchen, no matter where she lived, no matter the position her husband held.

For twenty-seven years they'd been married. Twenty-seven years of joys and sorrows, hopes, and disappointments. Life had been rich and rewarding. He and Marriane had three children, two boys and a girl. Mary, the youngest, married a fisherman, and together they worked their business off the rugged cost of northern Maine. Ross, the eldest, was an accountant for a firm in Cambridge. Ted, their middle boy, had entered medical school four years ago at the University of California, San Francisco.

The thought of his son brought a rush of emotion. During a mid-semester break his son had gone with his friend Damien to his home in Los Angeles. One evening the two of them had played basketball in a park near Damien's home. By all accounts it was an enjoyable reunion with some of Damien's high school buddies. They'd played for two hours. With slaps on the back and firm handshakes they parted. Fully expecting to meet again, they went their separate ways with light hearts and tired bodies.

Ted and Damien walked five of the seven blocks home when they rounded a corner and found themselves suddenly caught in the cross-fire from two rival gangs. Ted, mortally wounded, died before they could get him to hospital. Damien received a gunshot wound to his thigh.

Ted's death hit the family hard. It had been devastating to Marriane. She'd gone through a depression difficult to shake. Morgan cut back his duties in the Senate, took himself off several committees, and reached out to his wife. The death of their son brought them closer together, further solidifying their friendship. 'Death makes one realize what is really important, the intangibles such as love and appreciation,' he thought.

His son's death gave rise to a fierce desire to bring an end to what he saw as the needless violence that plagued so much of the nation. Somehow he wanted to help. He loved this country: the vast diversity of its land, the apirations of its founding fathers, and the spirit of its people. This democracy, founded with so much hope and boundless enthusiasm, was in trouble. Far too many of its citizens had abrogated their responsibility, and now saw themselves as helpless victims. The price of being taken care of, he thought, is the loss of a sense of autonomy. We've asked our government to take over, step in where we have stepped out, and now we feel powerless.

In the years since Ted's death, he and Marriane had found nothing that offered them the hope they sought. However, when Morgan described his conversations with David, he was pleased to see the excitement and hope suddenly in his wife's face. Her expression served to confirm what he sensed for himself. He had the feeling the country was on the verge of great change. This change would not be heralded with great fanfare and then vanish. No, it would be quiet and profound, somehow linked to the philosophical understanding of the new president. David had rekindled in Morgan his own sense of inspiration, freedom of thought, and the wondrous sense of possibilities.

....

It was Friday evening when Angus left the Hill and caught a taxi back to his hotel. He sat back and relaxed, thinking of the events since his arrival two weeks before. Quickly he'd mobilized the PAC and invaded the Hill. Not a congressman, not a senator had been missed. He was satisfied that the company was safe. No president would dare go against the opposition he'd mobilized. He looked out the window, watching the people pass by, not really seeing them. Tomorrow he'd catch a plane and by evening be home. Sunday he'd go fishing. He smiled in anticipation. He was glad to leave Washington.

....

Cole sat back in his favorite recliner. He was alone in the den, engrossed in a baseball game on TV. The bases were loaded and the Red Sox up to bat in the last inning. He swished the ice and whisky in his glass and took a long swallow. The phone rang in the hall, and his wife picked it up. A line drive to center-field held his attention, and the announcer's excited voice filled the room. He didn't hear his wife enter.

"It's for you," she said, tapping him on the shoulder.

"Just a minute, dear." The throw to home plate was fumbled and a run scored. The fans erupted, and the announcer went wild.

"Take a message, dear, I'll call back later."

"They insisted on speaking with you now."

"Iris, I told you I'm not available to take calls."

"I know, dear, but he was insistent. He said to tell you it was James."

Cole flicked the mute button, got up, and crossed the

room to his desk. "I'll take it here," he said. "Close the door when you go." He waited for his wife to leave and picked up the phone. He said nothing until he heard the click of the phone in the hall.

"Cole here." He listened intently. "Are you sure?" he asked at last. "What's the girl's name?.... Jennifer Ramirez.... and she has a daughter, you say? How old?.... fifteen. And Tremaine's the father? .... You're sure?.... She's prepared to go public with this?.... Can she take the pressure?.... Good. Look, meet me at the Toledo tonight at ten? Bring everything you've got..... Yes, I'll see you at ten."

Cole hung up the phone and smiled. "Gotcha! Now you bastard, let's see you slip out of this."

CHAPTER 14

"Jennifer Ramirez?" David was incredulous.
"Yes," Jonathan said
"Are you sure?"
"Yes, I'm afraid so. She held a press conference in San Francisco an hour ago; it's all over the news. The press is clamoring to hear from you; the switchboard is jammed with calls."

David slowly spun the chair around and, leaning back, sat looking through the window. The signs of autumn were everywhere. The leaves had begun to turn, their colors already brilliant. Two weeks ago roses had flourished in the warmth of Indian summer. Now they were gone, replaced by rose hips reflecting orange in the late-afternoon sun.

His mind drifted back in time, to the day he first met Jennifer Ramirez some seventeen years ago. He was on holiday in San Francisco at the time, and they'd carried on an affair for close to two years. It was one of the contributing factors in the demise of his marriage. He'd broken it off in the hope of working out his differences with his wife, but it hadn't helped. He'd never seen Jennifer again. He'd tried to get in touch with her but had been unsuccessful. He'd reached her mother once and she told him Jennifer had gone away and requested her whereabouts be kept private. He'd respected her wishes. He had no idea that she'd had a child—his child.

"What are you going to do?" asked Jonathan.

David swung around and faced his friend. "I'll talk to the people through the press," he said quietly. "Let them know. Schedule it for seven this evening." He wanted to talk with Sandra before then. "See if you can get in touch with Jennifer for me, will you? I'd like to speak with her. Let me know what you find."

Jonathan nodded and left the office, closing the door quietly behind him. David turned back and gazed into the colored world beyond the window, wondering about the daughter he'd never seen.

....

An hour later David and Sandra sat across from each other in the kitchen, drinking tea.

"Jonathan couldn't get through to her. All communication is being routed through her lawyer."

"What if it's not your child?" Sandra asked.

"There's really no way of knowing," he responded.

"There are blood tests that can determine if the child is not yours."

"I know, but I don't want to put her through that. I would dearly like to talk with her to find out what happened. One way or another, I'd like to help her and the child, not make it more difficult for them. The press is reporting that she left after our affair because she was pregnant, and deeply hurt at the sudden end to our relationship. I know how painful it was for me, and I'm sure it was painful for her."

"What are you going to do?"

"I'm not sure. We'll have to see what happens."

"I love you, dear, and I trust you. Know that my heart is always with you."

"Thank you," he said, taking her hand and kissing it. "Before I go, I want to know your feelings and thoughts on the matter."

Sandra thought for a moment. "It happened a long time ago," she said, "before we met. It occurred at a time in your life when there was great turmoil. I know that all those things, painful as they were, were necessary. Without them you wouldn't be here today. If we'd met before these things had softened you, I doubt we'd be able to get along. Freedom rarely comes without some suffering."

....

Jennifer sat on the edge of her seat watching the television. Her heart was beating fast and she felt a lump of fear in her throat. What had she done? she wondered. She watched as David stepped up to the podium and listened as he spoke.

"Seventeen years ago I had an affair with Jennifer Ramirez. For two years we were lovers and friends. I cared for her deeply, but I was married at the time, and by the conventions of our society, my behavior was immoral. I know my actions hurt my wife deeply and in the end brought suffering to Jennifer and members of her family. At the time we parted, I didn't know she was pregnant. I didn't know until today. I don't really have anything else to say, but perhaps you've some questions."

"By your own admission, your behavior was immoral.

From this, the following question must be asked. Are you still fit to lead the country in the capacity of its president? Are you not a bad example to our young people, and are you not an embarrassment to the people of this country?"

"Good question. Yes, there are things I've done in the past that might be considered immoral or unacceptable in our society, things which in and of themselves, might set a poor example of how to live. We all make mistakes. When we learn from them and show evidence of having done so in our actions, that's what is important; that's what constitutes growth and sets a healthy example. To pretend that we've made no mistakes, to lie about the ones we refuse to admit to, is not a healthy way to live. Our ability to speak the truth, to admit our mistakes, and live life beyond the fear of what others might think of us, that is a worthy example."

"That argument seems self-serving," yelled a reporter.

"It may seem that way to you, but be assured, to be self-serving was not my intention. It was merely a thought in your mind, which you mistook for reality. What happened, happened. I cannot undo what is done. All I can do is speak the truth as I see it and move on."

Members of the press strained forward, microphones thrust toward the podium, flash bulbs popping. A barrage of questions and shouts filled the press room. "Yes," David pointed to a woman reporter on his left.

"It seems to me that you're avoiding the issue. You got this girl pregnant, and as far as we can tell, failed to provide for your daughter. What makes you any different from any other deadbeat father who's refused to take care of his kids?"

"You may call me what you will. The fact is that until today, I was unaware that Jennifer had a child. Happily will I contribute to this family for the expense and care involved in the raising of my daughter. I'm sorry I didn't know sooner."

"Your offer comes a little late, don't you think?" the woman continued above the shouts around her. "With all due respect to the office you hold and on behalf of single mothers everywhere, I have to say you're a flake, just another man trying to cover his sorry ass."

"I'm sorry you feel that way, and I understand your point. I cannot change your mind, nor do I have any desire to do so. What you've exhibited by your questions, comments and tone of voice is that you're not open to what I have to say. Instead you've drawn your own conclusions, made your own judgments. In so doing, you've imprisoned not me, but yourself

"You look at the world through your own conceptualizations, and don't see what you've done. You've filtered your perceptions and twisted your reality into something angry and ugly. I don't know who hurt you, but I would urge you to think about what I've said."

David pointed to the back of the room. "Yes."

"You seem to use your abilities as a psychologist and professor to avoid answering our questions. You're clever, able to shift the focus back onto us, the members of the press. You seem to avoid the consequences of your actions. Will you remain in office, or will you step down as some are urging?"

"No matter what my position is, if your mind is made up, if you, like the young lady before you, have drawn conclusions about these events, there's really nothing I can say to you. But for those who ask the same questions with an open mind and a sincere desire to know the truth, I'll do my best to answer.

"I do not accept your conclusion that I've avoided questions. I've answered them to the best of my ability and in complete honesty. They may not be what you want to hear from me. I know there are many who want me to step down. I'll not do so. I pledged myself to do the best I could to serve this country through the office of the presidency. That's what I'm doing, and it's what I'll continue to do.

"At the next election you can render your opinion on how I've done. If we as a people do not allow for the fact that we learn from mistakes, then we're lost. There's not one of you here, nor in the entire country for that matter, who has lived an exemplary life, without mistakes and with nothing left to learn."

Through the clamor David noticed a woman at the back of the room. She appeared to be in her late fifties, neatly dressed and unassuming. He pointed to her.

"I wonder, sir, what you mean by an exemplary life?"

"An exemplary life is a life in which honesty, integrity and accountability exist side by side."

"How can we know whether you live an exemplary life and what you speak is the truth?" she pursued.

"First, I would ask you to think about what I say and weigh my words with an open mind and an open heart. Perhaps this openness will help you to have a clearer understanding of what is going on. Second, put yourself in my place. Would you stand in public and admit to the things that you've done, things deemed by your fellow citizens as immoral or wrong? And, if you did, what words would you use? And to those who don't believe what you say, how would you respond? And then, ask yourself why they don't believe you."

"Your affair with Miss Ramirez seems to have brought an end to your marriage. It would appear that learning did not take place."

"My relationship did indeed contribute to the demise of my marriage. There were other things, too. What was learned cannot be judged from outer appearances."

....

Jennifer found herself remembering the last meeting

she'd had with David. He'd flown down to San Francisco for the weekend. Saturday they wandered along the beaches looking for shells. It was autumn, and there was frost in the air. They'd stopped for lunch, their faces burning in the warm air of the little restaurant still open on the strand.

Afterwards they'd walked in the park, stopped for tea, then headed back to the apartment. It was evening when they arrived. They'd showered, and then made love. It had been wonderful. Afterwards she'd slept, and when she awoke, supper was almost ready. Just enough time for a glass of wine. Over dinner, he'd told her.

"Jennifer, I find what I'm about to say very difficult. I don't even know how to say it."

Her heart had sunk. She knew what was coming.

"I care about you a great deal," he continued. "I've come to love you. You're a good woman, and I have no desire to cause you suffering. I would love to see you again, enjoy the pleasure of your company, for you've been a good friend and a wonderful lover. Now I know I must leave. I've hurt my wife Nance, and she's asked me to give the marriage another chance. I've agreed. To do so I must end the relationship between you and me. I cannot give my all to this marriage as long as my attention is divided, and the desire to be with you is fed by our good times together. I must try to work it out with Nance and I know I cannot entertain any expectations that we might someday be together."

That night had been their last in each other's company. In the morning after breakfast, she'd driven him to the airport. She'd wished him well and meant it, even though she was so miserable she wanted to die.

That evening she'd gone to the bar and gotten drunk. She woke up the following morning in a young man's bed, and as she lay there, the memory of the preceding night came back to her. She'd made love to a stranger. He asked if it was safe, if she wouldn't get pregnant, and she'd lied. He'd taken her at her word. Nine months later Susan was born. Jennifer had wished the child was David's, and when her mother and friends jumped to that conclusion, she'd not dissuaded them. In fact she'd almost come to believe it herself. Good God, she thought, what have I done?

....

After the press conference David returned to the Oval Office. He sat looking through the window, listening to the ever-present sound of distant traffic. For fifteen minutes he sat quietly, then he turned, picked up the phone, and asked for Jonathan. Jonathan entered quietly, and the two men sat across from each other in front of the big desk.

"When you spoke with Jennifer's lawyer, what did he say?"

"He said that she didn't wish to speak with anyone from the White House. All communication was to go through him."

"What else?"

"She wants to be reimbursed for the raising of the child."

"Good, work it out and let me know what happens.

"Now, switching topics, there's a meeting scheduled with Doug Kersey and Bill Morgan for tomorrow afternoon. See if you can move it back to Friday morning. I must talk with the senators from the Pacific Northwest over the use of recycled paper."

"Ah, yes," said Jonathan, with a knowing look, "I heard the Hill was swamped with lobbyists. They've twisted a lot of arms and marshalled some strong opposition."

"That's the way it sounds, all right; anyway, we'll see what they have to say. I'll see you in the morning."

CHAPTER 15

Miguel and four top men sat around the table. Armed guards were posted at the doors. The only light in the room came from a hurricane lamp suspended over the table and two others hanging on either side of a large map on the wall. Red, green, blue, and yellow pins marked specific areas of the map in such a way as to provide a semicircle inland from the lakefront in an area where abandoned warehouses now stood. For four hours they'd gone over the plans in minute detail. Everything was in place, everything ready. Six months of planning was now at an end. Miguel looked at his watch. It was eleven thirty. Pushing his chair away from the table, he stood up. The other men did the same.

"Good luck," he said, extending his hand. In a matter of seconds the room was empty. Miguel lit a cigarette. The light from the match showed the hard face of a man in his mid-fifties. His black, close-cropped hair was streaked with gray; his eyes, unusually dark, had a flat quality about them. He was short and stocky and in excellent physical condition, something he still took pride in. Going to a metal closet, he opened the door and removed an M16. He placed it on the table and broke it apart with practiced ease. Checking each part carefully, he reassembled it with precision and speed. When he was finished, he put it away and, picking up his jacket, slipped out the door and up the stairs to the empty room of a gutted house. Rubble and bricks were strewn haphazardly, and the cold smell of concrete assailed the nostrils. Winter was not far away. Miguel pulled his collar up and stuffed his hands in his pockets.

....

Later, if anyone had noticed, they'd have seen him walking, alert and watchful toward an abandoned pier of shambled warehouses, barely visible in the darkness. Stars glittered above, and a stiff wind came sweeping off the lake, numbing his fingers. Turning his back to it, he hunched over and lit a cigarette before continuing on his way. In a few moments he came to an old shed at the edge of the pier. A door hung crookedly on one remaining hinge. He stepped inside, into the quiet, where the wind could no longer reach him. Sitting on coils of old rope, he looked out at the dark and restless lake. He was tense, anticipating the events about to take place. He always felt this way before this kind of action, even in Vietnam.

His mind slipped back to the year of 1966 when he'd first gone to Southeast Asia as part of a unit of Green Berets. He was known as Jack Vincent then. He operated for a year behind enemy lines. At the end of his tour, he was recruited by the CIA and joined an elite unit that operated beyond the conventions of war. Its actions were top secret, and, he learned later, funded completely by opium grown in the highlands of the Iron Triangle.

Their tasks included the assassination of South Vietnamese political and military figures. The purpose? To justify actions of the American military against certain targets in Laos, Cambodia, and North Vietnam. *Reprisals* they were called. The unit was the toughest he'd ever known. These men loved killing, and most, he was sure, were psychopaths.

He knew why they wanted him. He was a tactician, with an uncanny sense of the enemy and an ability to lead men as well as plan an operation. He was completely unpredictable in his actions, and he never asked of his men what he wouldn't do himself. For that reason he was both respected and feared. He was a warrior. Even after all these years, except to a few, his unit, Medusa, was virtually unknown.

He'd been in charge of one of the most lethal rogue units ever assembled, one that meted out death with dispassionate efficiency. Why had he agreed to join, he wondered? The pay was good and that was important, but he knew his decision had more to do with something else: a license to kill. And killing had gotten into his blood; it was an addiction, one he couldn't escape. But that was only one side. The other was the risk to his life. That combination gave him a richness and intensity of experience he'd not known in civilian life. He liked living on the edge.

By the late seventies he left Vietnam and went to Iraq, where he'd been hired to train commando units of the Republican Guard in the techniques learned in Vietnam. For four years he trained and led small efficient killing-units across the border into Iran, where they'd struck with relative impunity. Through it all, his origins remained completely unknown. For all intents and purposes, he was a mercenary from Southeast Asia.

Later he traveled in Syria, where he worked with the Muslim guerrillas operating from Lebanon across the border into Israel. He had no love for the Israelis, but had a grudging respect for their toughness.

Somewhere behind him he heard the sound of a car moving along the deserted street. 'Drug dealers' the thought flashed through his mind. He listened until the car was gone. Drugs, he thought, a poison eating at the heart of the country he once called home. He found himself reflecting on the events that had led him from super patriot to implacable enemy of the country of his birth.

He despised hypocrisy. His involvement in Medusa and later in the Middle East and even, for a time, in South America, had given him a new perspective. Now he understood, from behind the scenes as it were, the effects of his nation's policies in her dealings with third world countries. He had no respect for American leadership. It had betrayed one of the principles upon which the nation had been founded; the right to self-determination. Wasn't that the reason they'd kicked out the British and 'formed a more perfect union'?

After raids into northern Israel, he'd formulated an plan for a new form of guerrilla warfare. This kind of warfare would take place inside the belly of the beast, what the Muslims called "the great Satan." Convincing those in power had taken some time.

"You want to use drugs as a weapon of war?"

"Yes."

"How do you propose to do that?"

"The country is corrupt; it's lost its way; and the people no longer have purpose. In this empty state, more and more are turning to drugs, particularly the Blacks and Chicanos."

"Explain it."

"These people are second-class citizens. They're not able to find good employment; opportunities have been scarce, working conditions hard, and pay poor. To get away from their suffering, they've turned to drugs."

"I still don't see how you wage war with drugs."

"It's easy. When you attack someone head-on, he resists; it's true of individuals and countries alike. To bring down the great Satan, you must not attack head-on. Feed the corruption that rots in its belly. Spread drugs into every corner of the nation. Make them cheap and available, to Whites most of all. This is effective warfare; it's how David brought down Goliath."

One of those present had objected. Turning from Miguel he had spoken with his brethren. "How can we provide Miguel with drugs? Surely, like alcohol, they are forbidden by the prophet in the Holy Koran!"

"The great Satan is a monstrous evil, beyond anything the world has ever known. We must not shirk from any method necessary to bring about its destruction. We must act quickly, and if this strategy saves the lives of our people, so much the better."

The arrangements were made, and one day he quietly slipped into the United States via the Canadian border. He'd been in the country now for three years.

Miguel found himself smiling. The process had been easier than he expected. Jack Vincent merely applied for a job as a waiter in one of the better restaurants of Boston. All he needed was his Social Security number. He wondered if the use of the Social Security card might activate inquiries from the authorities, but nothing happened. Later he'd moved to Chicago. He didn't need to work; he had enough money. He worked mainly because he enjoyed the work and believed in what he'd come here to do.

For more than a year, as Miguel Lopes, he'd devoted himself to the recruitment and training of a small elite corps drawn from a gang called the Scarlatis. From his connections in Southeast Asia he was able to bring in large quantities of high-grade heroin. None of it he saw, and no link with him could ever be traced.

Miguel looked at his watch; it was time to get under way. Returning to the basement, he prepared for the night's activities. Quickly he dressed in dark and warm clothing. With the colors added, he would easily be mistaken for one of the Capones, a rival gang. His men had prepared in a similar manner.

At two o'clock he left and made his way in the direction of the waterfront. He slipped through the darkness, following back alleys and threading his way through the rubble of abandoned cars and garbage. He knew that, at this precise moment, three units of seven well-armed men were moving into prearranged positions.

He'd ordered all street lights within six blocks of their destination taken out. It was three in the morning when he joined the men of his own unit, the one of which he was directly in charge. Silently, they took up positions between the houses across from the warehouse. No dogs barked; they'd been poisoned earlier in the week. A small window high in the wall of an old warehouse gave off the only light. Two men leaned against posts that propped a sloping tin roof above the door that marked one of two entrances. The rear entrance, he knew, was covered by the second unit, and the third one lay in wait for the police who would arrive.

Lying propped on his elbows behind a low concrete wall, he caught his breath. When he was ready he slid the M16 into place. With the strap wound tightly around his arm, the weapon became an extension of deadly intent. Sighting carefully and compensating for the wind, he took aim. The scope, fitted for night vision, brought the targets into easy focus. At precisely three fifteen the rifle cracked and one of the guards went down. The other followed with a bullet through his heart.

With the first shots, pandemonium erupted. Two of Miguel's men laid down a withering fire from automatic weapons, raking the lower three feet of the warehouse along its length.

As expected, men burst out of the door; most died, but some made it outside and lay hidden behind the parked cars. During a brief pause, the sound of gunfire came from the other side of the warehouse. Within minutes Miguel saw shadowy figures on the roof, but his snipers took them out before they could do any damage. Miguel watched, a grim smile on his face. The Capones will be gone this time tomorrow. Most of them in the morgue, he thought. The Scarlatis would then be hounded and rendered useless by the authorities. The attack would look like another war between rival gangs. And, twenty-one well-trained men would slip away and move to another city, and there, start all over again.

....

It was six in the morning when David arrived at the office. The news from Chicago was on every radio and television station. Lurid pictures and ugly headlines bannered the morning papers. Twenty-nine gang members dead, four wounded. Six civilians dead, including two children. So far there was no accurate count of the wounded. Three police officers had also died, with seven more wounded.

The police who'd tried to intervene had been pinned down and out-gunned. Fire had broken out and, fanned by strong winds, burned out of control. It had already consumed four large warehouses and a block of two-story tenements. Firefighters trying to reach the area were driven back by sniper fire. The cost was five men dead. Only the fireboats along the waterfront approached, and they'd soon backed off when one was hit by rocket fire and set ablaze, killing two more men. Governor Mendoza mobilized the Illinois National Guard, which was ordered to cordon off the area.

David picked up the phone and called Jonathan. "Postpone the meeting with Brock. I'll meet him at four this afternoon. In the meantime, get Travis and the FBI director over here. Yes, nine o'clock in the Oval Office."

Putting the phone down, he walked across the room and pushed open the French doors. Stepping outside, he made his way through the garden. The early morning sunlight cast long shadows, and a white frost covered the lawns. He found a chair beneath the arbor still dry. Pulling it out, he sat down and closed his eyes. The air was chilly and the sun warm. He heard the sound of a robin in a nearby tree and listened for a while to an exquisite song welcoming the new day.

Sitting quietly, his mind became empty. The time for action had not yet come. Suddenly before him, the smiling face of Avinash filled his mind. The eyes were dark and still and the familiar smile graced the master's face.

He felt a deep sense of gratitude for this man. He recalled a morning several years ago in Bombay.

He'd arrived at the end of the road near the master's home, and stepping from the taxi, bought a bouquet of red roses from a vendor on the sidewalk. Afterwards he walked slowly down the hill for his meeting. The doorman had smiled a greeting as David climbed the stairs and closed the gate to the elevator. Avinash had come to the door and ushered him in. They sat quietly in the empty living room high above the noisy street. David had watched the kites through the window as they turned slowly in the hot air rising from the streets below.

"I know that for a long time you've been seeking your guru. That search is over, is it not?"

The words had come unexpectedly. David's heart jumped. He'd always wanted to know if Avinash was the one he'd been seeking. For some reason he'd felt constrained from asking, and in time the question had become irrelevant, fading from his mind. The implication of Avinash's words struck him, and he looked at the master through moistened eyes. "How long have you known?" he asked.

"Since our first meeting."

"You knew then?"

"Yes."

"And you never said a word."

"No."

"Why? you must have known how much I wanted to know"

"I did, but you needed to know for yourself. My words have only confirmed this awareness."

It had been true. How long had David known? He couldn't remember. "What's to be done?" he asked.

Avinash chuckled. "You know better than to ask such questions, David."

"What will happen now?"

"Life will continue as it has; nothing will change. The desire for enlightenment that has been so long with you will slowly fade as the identified consciousness becomes less and less prominent. Difficulties will continue to arise, the conditioning of your upbringing will still function, and the whole drama of life will be played out upon the screen of awareness.

"The difference is that you'll see yourself now as merely one of the characters in the drama, your thoughts and reactions just items amongst others that play out on the screen of awareness. As you already know, you're not what you have thought yourself to be. You are what you have always been, the same consciousness without which life, of any kind, would not exist."

"What is life?" David had asked.

"Life is a divine novel created by consciousness and played out in consciousness. And you, David Tremaine? Merely a character in the novel, destined like all others to play a part."

"Life, as I've said, is a great novel, with many twists and

turns. It would be boring indeed, would it not, if everything worked out and the conflict engendered by good and evil was absent? How many would read a novel in which there were no problems, no difficulties to overcome, no challenges to be met, and everything always worked out just the way we hoped?"

"Will enlightenment come?" he asked suddenly.

"If enlightenment occurs in the body-mind organism known as David, it cannot be until the author of the question, the ego, has vanished and with it the question with which it was so concerned. When the fruit is ripe, it falls. Not before. Who can say when that is? It is all in the hands of destiny. This is a living dream. Enlightenment, after all, is merely awakening from the dream.

"Consciousness is whole, everpresent, untouched by the the identity assumed at birth, or carried over from lifetime to lifetime. You will respond to the name you're called, and the body will continue to play out its allotted part; and when the time comes, it, too, will simply drop off."

David had thought of the master's words over the years. He found them strangely comforting.

Then one day, it happened. Quietly, and unobtrusively; like a footfal in the night .

David heard footsteps and, opening his eyes, looked up to see Jonathan coming toward him.

"Everything is arranged," he said. "Travis and Jackson will meet you at eight."

Nodding, David got up and walked with his friend to the office. "See if you can get Morgan in here by eight. I want to talk with all of you before we start."

....

"Come in, gentleman, come in." Tremaine walked across the room to meet them, shaking their hands. "I think you both know Morgan and Jonathan Makarios," he said, introducing his vice president and chief of staff. "Have a seat." As the men seated themselves, Tremaine poured a cup of tea and handed it to Mike Jackson, the director of the FBI, who was a tea drinker. Jackson smiled and nodded appreciation as he took the cup. Tremaine poured coffee for the rest of them while Morgan passed it around. "Help yourselves to what you need," he said, indicating milk and sugar with a gesture.

Tremaine looked at the men in the circle. Travis was dressed in civilian clothes. He looked alert, his face bearing a ruddy complexion, freshly scrubbed. Jackson had on a blue suit, well tailored. He was a lanky man well over six feet, with steel gray eyes and hair to match. He was in his sixties, married and had three grandchildren. He'd been an agent in the field for thirty years before his appointment by the previous administration. Emerson, impressed with him, had asked him to stay. Jackson agreed.

"Well, gentlemen," Tremaine began, "we've a fine mess on our hands. I want an up-to-date report on what's happening and your suggestions on how best to handle it. Jackson, you can start."

"It's difficult to say what is really going on at this point, but I can tell you what we know as of half an hour ago."

"Go ahead."

"At three fifteen this morning, an attack was launched on a gang called the Capones, at their headquarters located in an old warehouse along the lakefront. It was a well-executed attack led by someone who appears to have considerable training"...

"What makes you think that?" Tremaine asked, interrupting the director.

"The attack was well thought-out, well coordinated, and seems to have anticipated the moves the police and the guard would make."

"How so?"

"When the police arrived, they walked into a trap. They were allowed to get close to the warehouse and then found themselves surrounded, pinned down by sniper fire. When they tried to break out, they were hit with rounds from automatic weapons."

"Automatic weapons?"

"Yes. When the firing let up, the police tried once more to withdraw but were unable to do so. As I said, the operation was well planned.

"Later, when the National Guard arrived and were deployed to cordon off the area, it became quiet; all gunfire ceased. By six, Chicago time, the Guard was in place and considered the area secured. At six thirty the guard came under sniper fire from behind their positions. Fifteen were killed, and we don't know how many wounded. Police and other guardsmen sent to help were met with sniper fire on all approaches to the area. Then, as suddenly as it began, the firing stopped. No one seems to know what's going on."

"We've reports that nine police officers were killed and seventeen wounded," interjected Travis.

"What about civilians?" Tremaine asked.

"There are civilian casualties," said Jackson, "but, again, we don't know how many."

"And the fires?"

"There are fierce winds fanning the flames, which now threaten a large industrial area not far away," Jackson answered. "The fire department hasn't been able to do much because of sniper fire."

"Someone wants this to keep burning," Jonathan said, thinking out loud.

"It would seem so." Jackson responded. "Two men on the fireboat that was attacked were killed as well."

"Do any of you know what this is about?" Tremaine asked

"No, not really," said Jackson. "It may have something to do with rival gangs. We thought maybe the Scarlati gang was behind the attack on the warehouse, but right now that's speculation on our part."

"What can be done?" Tremaine asked, turning to Travis.

"It's a very bad situation from the standpoint of civilians trapped in the area. We must find whoever this is and neutralize them."

"How many men do you think are involved in this action?" Tremaine interjected.

"Our best estimate is that there may be as many as sixty armed and well-trained men," said Jackson.

Travis nodded. "What we suggest is to send in small, highly mobile well-trained forces, such as two augmented units of Green Berets by land, and a unit of Navy SEALS by water. In each of these units there will be six snipers and their spotters. We'll try to pick these guys off. This should minimize the possibility of further civilian casualties, and do the least damage. We'll have to see how things develop."

"How soon can they go in?" Tremaine asked.

"They'll be in Chicago by evening, and as soon as it's dark, they'll go in."

"Anything else?" Tremaine looked at Jackson.

"The agency is working closely with local police; we've set up a joint command center from which we're coordinating the operation, including the guard and, when the time comes, the units that will go in at dark."

"Who's in charge?" Tremaine wanted to know.

Travis responded. "Brigadier General Clint Duval was chosen. He should be at the command center by now. He's experienced in urban warfare, having spent time in Saigon and later in Beirut."

"All right," said Tremaine, "we seem to be in good hands. Keep me informed."

Both men nodded. Tremaine stood, shook their hands, and saw them to the door.

CHAPTER 16

It was a few minutes to four when two men strode purposefully along the corridor leading to the Oval Office. Brock was a senator from Oregon and Prescott a congressman from Washington. For years they'd been staunch supporters of the logging industries. Today was no exception.

Cleared for entrance, they were ushered into the room. Tremaine stepped from behind the desk to greet them, hand outstretched.

"Thank you for changing your schedules," he said. "With this crisis in Chicago, it was impossible for us to meet this morning."

Both men nodded. Tremaine pointed to seats in front of the fireplace.

"What can I do for you, gentlemen?" Tremaine asked when the two men were seated.

From the moment they entered the office, they felt ill at ease. They'd expected to see the president attired in the usual suit. Instead he was dressed casually in baggy brown pants and a dark green sweatshirt with "Boston University" across the front. They, in contrast, were dressed in suits, the uniform dictated by custom for men of their station.

"In the Pacific Northwest, there are many who think that recycling paper is not a good idea," Senator Brock said, coming to the point at once.

"Yes, I'm aware of that."

"We agree with them; not personally, you understand," Brock explained, his voice oily. "It's our job to represent our constituents."

"Are you not interested in conserving resources?"

"Of course we are," interjected Congressmen Prescott. But we're more interested, right now, in conserving the jobs threatened by this policy."

Tremaine looked at the two men and waited for them to continue. They shifted uneasily.

Prescott continued. "Do you realize that if you implement your policy of using recycled paper, the pulp and paper companies such as McLelland will have to downsize, and a large number of employees will be laid off?"

"Look," said Tremaine, "I *am* aware of the situation, and the changes that will take place."

"We don't think you realize how bad the situation will be or we wouldn't be here talking with you," responded Brock. "The effect it would have on the primary and secondary industries would be catastrophic. The lumber industry has been hit hard the last ten years due to such environmental issues as the preservation of the spotted owl."

"You don't approve?" Tremaine asked quietly.

"It's not a matter of approving or not approving," blustered Prescott, "It's a matter of the preservation of human livelihood."

"Let's cut to the real issue, gentlemen, the issue of change. I've no interest in a lengthy conversation about irrelevancies."

"How can you say that the preservation of jobs is irrelevant?" Brock demanded.

"I didn't say that." Tremaine's voice was steady. "I don't buy your basic premise, that's all. Your view is limited. From where you operate, the problems we face cannot be resolved. They'll just keep getting worse."

"How can you say our views are limited?" demanded Brock. "We live in the area we represent, and know firisthand, the problems of the lumber industries."

"I know you do, and what I'm saying to you is that your views are limited. They don't address the full scope of the problem."

"But..." Prescott began.

"If you give me a few minutes I'll explain what I'm driving at," Tremaine said. Something in his tone let the two men know it was time to shut up.

"Change is inevitable. It cannot be halted, but for some reason most human beings have a built-in resistance to it. As people, we suffer when we resist change. So instead of fighting it, perhaps we'd do better to embrace it."

"Not all change is for the better," Brock interjected, unable to control himself.

"Let's just say that change is necessary and inevitable. It cannot be stopped. The logging practices in this country have been a sad commentary of greed, waste, and destruction of one of our great resources. We've been poor stewards of these great forests."

"I disagree," Brock protested. "We're the most advanced nation in the world, and our logging practices are far superior to those of Latin American countries. One only has to look at what's going on in the Amazon to know that we would never do something like that."

"It seems to me, gentlemen, that you're more interested in hearing yourselves talk than in understanding. I'm not interested, as I said, in being drawn into a conversation that has no real relevance to what must be done." Tremaine paused and looked steadily at the two men before him. They lowered their eyes. He waited until they looked up before directing a question to Prescott. "Do you have an open mind, or is your mind made up?"

Prescott squirmed. If there was one thing he prided himself on, it was his open mind. "I'm open," he said.

"Good. Now how about you, Senator?" he asked, turning to Brock.

Brock leaned forward. His heart was pounding, and he was angry. His face flushed, and beads of sweat covered his forehead. He disliked being talked to in this way, but he had a lot of people depending on him. He couldn't allow his personal feelings to override his purpose.

"I'll hear you out," he said.

"Thank you. Going back to your comment comparing our logging practices with those practiced in the Amazon, we cannot justify our failures and mistakes by the mistakes and failures of others. What's happening in the Amazon rain forest is a terrible problem, and one that concerns me a great deal, but I'm afraid at the moment it's one I can do little about. What's happening in *our* forests is my jurisdiction, and I intend to do something about that."

"What do you have in mind?" Prescott asked.

"To begin with, I'm sending a signal to the country and the logging industry that we'll no longer squander our resources. We'll become more efficient, less wasteful, better stewards. We can begin that in government itself."

"But if recycling puts men out of work, we create another

problem, which the government ends up paying for through workman's compensation or welfare. I, for one, am opposed to the expansion of the welfare state," Brock argued.

"On that point you'll get no argument from me," Tremaine responded. "Everything is interrelated; everything is connected. As much as possible, we must take into account all those interdependent aspects, or we will never move ahead."

"If you continue with the idea of using recycled paper in government offices, do you have any idea of the effect that single step will have on the pulp and paper business?" Prescott asked.

"I think so," said Tremaine. "But go ahead and tell me what you think."

"Big companies like McLelland employ thousands of workers. If they cannot maintain their current production levels of pulp, many will be laid off. In addition, Crown McLelland's in Canada has made financial concessions to end a lengthy strike. They've obligated themselves and would not have done so had they been aware of your policies at the time. The loss of revenue would cripple them. They might not survive."

"Those things I'm aware of. One of the problems we face here and in Canada comes from our attitude toward what we've traditionally considered one of our greatest assets, namely the immensity of our natural resources."

"I don't follow," said Prescott.

"Because of the vast resources, in this case trees, we've been careless and exceptionally wasteful. Millions of acres of land have been stripped. The problems of erosion and the destruction of animal habitat have been largely ignored. And, in addition, even with clear-cut logging, the amount of wood left behind is beyond imagination.

"Only in the last ten or fifteen years have we started to pay attention to these problems. In Norway and Sweden, the lumber resources are considerably less. For that reason these countries are generally more efficient in their logging practices and take better care of the land. In areas where they've cut, you'll not find wood lying around. All of it is used."

"I don't mean to be presumptuous," Prescott interjected, "but what makes you an authority on such matters?"

"I don't consider myself an authority, but I do know something about it. Have you ever planted trees, or traveled in Scandinavian countries and looked closely at their logging practices?"

"No."

"I didn't think so. One danger of being a member of Congress is that you may only see what logging companies show you, what they want you to see. Unless you're willing to get off the main roads, you'll not see the devastation. I planted trees for three years as part of the reforestation programs of Washington and Idaho. I traveled in Sweden and saw first-hand the difference in logging practices between their country and ours. In Europe, wood is scarce and thus highly valued.

"Getting back to the main issue, you still haven't dealt with the problem of unemployment your proposal would cause," Brock interjected.

Tremaine ignored him. "Not long ago I had a conversation with the chairman of Honda Motors concerning the building of more fuel-efficient cars. What he said to me was, 'Tell us what you want, how many miles per gallon, and by when. We'll do it.' That attitude I like. All the other companies, including our own 'Big Three,' kept telling me it was too costly and therefore not practical. My grandfather said we'd never put men on the moon. He never lived to see it, but it happened."

"Get to the point; be specific," growled Brock.

Tremaine went on without acknowledging Brock's irritation. "Requiring the government to use recycled paper creates a demand; and that demand, like any other, will be met by industry. It may not be met by the giants because it's more difficult for them to make adjustments. But there's no doubt the demand will be met by someone willing to change.

"Those companies more flexible and capable of adapting will rise to the occasion. One of the hallmarks of success in industry is the ability to adapt. For years industry has believed 'bigger is better.' Industry, made up of people like ourselves, is not always receptive to change. If they choose to ignore the need for change, they will fall by the wayside. The idea that bigger is better was always questionable. Although it has its advantages, we've been slow to recognize its drawbacks. Change will correct that."

"But what about the big companies?" Prescott persisted.

"Yes, what about them? If they try to hold on to the old ways, they'll go down. When creative minds get to work, they'll find ways of diversifying, of being more responsive to the needs that arise. Perhaps they'll have to get smaller or break into independent subsystems. The point isn't how they'll do it; the point is that they will do it.

"We are not businessmen; we are not scientists. It's the task of business and science to figure these things out. I've faith that they'll do so. Our task is to keep in mind the public good. To do that, we can't afford to be shortsighted, can't afford to allow segments of our constituency to dictate short-term goals that are not in the best interests of the nation as a whole or of the planet upon which we live."

"We're supposed to represent our constituency, and if a large segment of it feels a particular policy is no good, then we must represent that perspective when necessary," said Brock.

"Of course, I have no problem with that. You must, however, keep in mind that your states do not always represent the interests of the nation as a whole. My task is to keep that in mind. All points of view are taken into consideration. That means they'll be considered from the perspective of the whole. No one point of view can be allowed to dictate to others. Now, the fact is, it's time to develop long-term goals. We must be willing to embrace change, willing to adapt; and above all we must have confidence in our greatest asset."

"And what the hell is that?" snapped Brock.

"The creativity of the human mind," Tremaine said with a smile. "And we as politicians must be creative, too. I don't mean clever; I mean intelligent. I don't know about you, but it's obvious to me that one task of political leaders in a democracy is to educate their constituents. If we fail in this task, then we'll find ourselves reverting to a kind of crisis management. Once that starts, it's difficult to stop."

"How can we hope to educate our constituents when their livelihood is threatened?" demanded Brock.

"We must enable them to see the limits of personal self-interest. We must help them see that their interest is really tied to the whole. AsI see it, human beings like challenge. We're bored without it. We have for too long depended upon the welfare state. There have been some obvious benefits. Its liabilities, however, have been less readily visible, something political leaders are loath to face."

"And what are the liabilities?" Brock asked.

"We've become dependent on government agencies rather than on the creativity of our minds. In times of crisis, such as war or natural disaster we pull together; the creative power of our bodies and our minds comes into play. The desire to feel useful, to contribute to something larger than our own small needs, is precisely what has caused so many people to enter the Peace Corps. This is the meaning of true service.

"When we lose ourselves in work that we consider worthy, it makes us feel useful and life becomes worthwhile once more. Of course, service is not for everyone, but it is for many."

"This is getting off the point," Brock interrupted rudely.

"No," snapped Tremaine, "this *is* the point. The practical problems will be worked out; but for that to happen, we must have open minds. We must look at things in new ways without being tied to the past, to our traditions. We cannot secure the world by making change stop. Change is inevitable, and the only security that exists is in accepting this fact. To refuse to do so is the height of stupidity."

"Are you calling me stupid?" Brock exploded.

"Can you embrace change?" countered Tremaine patiently, not wanting to get into conflict with the senator.

Before Brock could respond, Prescott interjected, "Coming back to the problem raised by the government's intention to recycle paper, what can the government do to help ease the transition that you point to?" Prescott hoped to steer the senator from the abyss.

"We have some ideas, but nothing definite at this point. You can be sure, however, that we will sit down with anyone who is open to new ideas. I have faith in the human being's ability to find solutions to the difficulties he faces. Your ideas and the Senator's are welcome. But don't make the mistake of telling me 'it can't be done.' That is unacceptable."

Brock was boiling. Who does this young upstart think he is? he wondered. "Some things *are* impossible to do," he argued, "so don't tell me that it's unacceptable to talk about them."

Brock had clearly reached the limit of his self-control, and Tremaine wanted to end the argument. "Look, gentlemen," he said, an edge to his voice, "I don't have much time to spend with you at the moment. Think about what I've said. I welcome honest ideas and suggestions, but I'll not waste time discussing issues with men who've already made up their minds, men unwilling to explore options openly."

The room was silent except for the crackling of the fire. In the distance a horn blared above the hum of traffic. Tremaine stood and the two men followed. He walked to the door ahead of them, opened it, turned and waited. Prescott extended his hand. Tremaine shook it, his eyes looking into the man. "I appreciate your willingness to be open," he said. "We'll talk further. I'm sorry, but with what's going on in Chicago, I don't have time for lengthy discussion." Prescott nodded and stepped into the hall.

Brock extended a hand, eyes averted. He wanted to escape before he completely lost control. Tremaine shook the hand and held the grip, refusing to let go, stopping the older man. Surprised, the senator looked up.

"I hope you'll think about what I've said. I'm open to honest exploration, but I'll not be bullied." Tremaine released the hand, and Brock strode through the door. The back of his puffy neck was red.

....

The two men walked brusquely down the hall, the sound of their shoes echoing off the marble floor. Neither had spoken since arriving at the Capitol. Congressman John Prescott had sat silently in the car on the way from the White House, his mind going over the events that had transpired. He'd been shaken by Tremaine; his usual sense of certainty was in disarray.

Rarely had Prescott seen the old man so steaming mad. Most of Brock's colleagues deferred to the senator, whose white hair and dignified bearing had created an aura of wisdom and respectability that he'd carefully cultivated. Prescott knew the senior senator felt exposed and vulnerable, and he could be a dangerous man to cross.

"Who the hell does that goddamned asshole think he is?"

Brock fumed.

Prescott turned and looked at his friend. He'd known him for many years and couldn't remember seeing him as rattled as he was now. "He's the president," Prescott found himself saying.

"Don't give me that crap." Brock turned on Prescott, his voice carrying loudly down the hall. People in the corridor turned to see what was going on.

"We were rude to him..." Prescott stopped, cut off by the glare of his angry friend.

Brock turned on his heel and headed for his office.

"We'll talk about this later," he said as he disappeared through the door.

Prescott shook his head and walked slowly down the hall.

CHAPTER 17

Boston Globe
November 1, 1993

FANCY FOOTWORK
President seeks to restore tarnished reputation

Presidential aide Jonathan Makarios tried unsuccessfully to arrange for the president to address the National Press Club in New York on November 15 This move was seen by conference organizers as a blatant attempt by the president to restore his tarnished image following disclosure of the Jennifer Ramirez affair. Public opinion polls showed a decline in the president's approval rating of thirty points, down to 21%. This equaled the rating he received following the revelation of his use of drugs during the election campaign.

Senator Cole, the leading Republican spokesman, was quoted as saying, 'The president has betrayed the trust of the American people. A man who has admitted to such indiscretions cannot be trusted with the governance of the country. He is an admitted drug user who avoided the draft during the Vietnam War and counseled other young men to do the same. He is a womanizer, the father of an illegitimate child, for whom he cared nothing. Only with the recent revelation was he compelled to assume the financial obligation for his daughter. His interest in addressing the National Press Club in New York can be seen as nothing more than a blatant attempt by a clever man to buy votes.

Cole hinted there'd been talk amongst ranking Republicans concerning impeachment proceedings. Not since the Nixon presidency has government been so badly shaken by the scandalous behavior of one who holds the highest office of the land.

On a related matter, Harvard University president Dr. James Channing confirmed that President Tremaine would address the faculty and students of the university on November 10. When asked if the press would be invited, Dr. Channing responded, 'Of course.' When pressed as to why he had agreed to host the president, Dr. Channing stated emphatically, 'I did not agree to have the president address the university. I requested he do so, and he accepted.' In light of the refusal by organizers of the National Press Club, Dr. Channing's invitation can only be seen as a slap in the face of ordinary Americans. It should have been anticipated that the academics would stick together.

Sandra crumpled the newspaper and threw it across the room. "Those bastards, those deceitful, hypocritical bastards!" she muttered.

....

Cole returned to his office following a late breakfast. The

day's newspapers lay on his desk. Lighting a cigar, he leaned back and slowly leafed through them. A smile of satisfaction spread across his face when he came to the *Boston Globe* article.

The phone rang. Tossing the paper on the desk, he leaned forward and picked up the phone. He sat back and made himself comfortable before putting it to his ear.

"Yes ...Who? ... Sandra Tremaine! ... Here, right now? ..... At your desk? ... And she wants to see me? ... Yes, I'll see her but stall her for a few minutes. I'll let you know when I'm ready."

Cole bolted out of his chair, and in one sweep, grabbed the newspapers and stuffed them into a drawer. Taking a used handkerchief from his pocket, he dusted off the desktop, being careful to sweep the ashes into the garbage pail and empty the ashtray. From the bookshelf, he selected three books and placed them strategically on the desk, titles visible: *Political Theory for the 20th Century*, *The Role of Contemporary Women in the Modern World*, and *Enlightened Self-Government, Its Theory & Application*. He placed a pad of paper directly in front of himself. He tore the notes off the pad and placed them beside the books, next to which he placed a pencil.

From the shelf beside the door, he took photos of his wife and children and placed them prominently on the desk. Quickly he surveyed the room, making sure everything was in place. On the coffee table he spotted the most recent *Penthouse*. Sifting quickly through the magazines on the table, he found two more and stuffed them in the drawer along with the newspapers. He opened a cupboard and looked in the mirror, straightened his tie and dragged a greasy comb through his thinning hair. Then, opening his mouth, he rubbed his fingers over his teeth, and practiced a smile. What could she want he wondered as he closed the cupboard door.

He sat down, and spoke into the intercom: "Send her in."

Cole pored over his notes, pencil in hand, and pretended

not to hear the door open.

"Senator Cole, Sandra Tremaine is here to see you," his secretary announced.

With that, the senator glanced up with a contrived expression of surprise. He walked around the desk and extended a soiled hand.

"Mrs. Tremaine, Mrs. Tremaine, what a pleasant surprise," came the obsequious voice as the office door clicked shut. "Have a seat, my dear." He pulled up a large, overstuffed, black leather chair and Sandra sat down.

As Cole walked around the desk to his seat, Sandra's eyes swept the office, taking everything in, including the books on the desk.

"What can I do for you?" Cole asked as he took his seat.

Sandra sat in the high-backed chair and steepled her fingers, pondering how to begin. Deliberately and with care she crossed her legs, all the while keeping her eyes fixed firmly on Cole. She saw the flicker of his eyes, but he had caught himself, conscious that she was watching him.

"I see you've been reading," she said quietly.

"I beg your pardon, what did you say?"

"I see you've been reading," she indicated the books.

"Yes, I like to keep abreast of things." Cole was pleased with his clever choice of words. He'd never met Sandra before, and at least part of his surprised look was genuine. She wore a white blouse under a navy blue V-necked sweater and a red tartan kilt. She's a attractive woman, he thought, well built and shapely.

Sandra chose to ignore his covert language. "I take it you believe in the equality of human beings?"

"Of course, of course."

"Then why do you hide behind your desk?"

"What do you mean?" Cole was beginning to feel uncertain, like a man in quicksand. What was she talking about? The dark eyes seemed to bore into him. He wanted to turn away, but she wouldn't let him. He was beginning to sweat.

"Hide behind my desk? What do you mean?" he spluttered.

"Look, Mr. Cole, I've come to speak with you. I'd appreciate it if you'd demonstrate your belief in the equality of human beings by sitting over here across from me. That wouldn't be too much to ask, would it?"

"No, no, of course not." He walked from behind the desk and, pulling a chair into place, sat in front of her.

"Thank you. I want to deal directly with you." She let the statement hang for a moment.

Cole sat back in the chair and tried to recover his balance. Sweat dripped under his arms, giving off a sour pungent odor. He felt self-conscious. "How can I help you?" He had to get something going; the silence was unnerving.

"I read the quote from you in the *Boston Globe*. I was so angry afterwards I had to see you in person. I had to know what kind of a man would make such statements."

Cole was struck by the power of Sandra's words. Her eyes never wavered. They seemed to see inside him, which made him even more uneasy. "What do you mean?"

"You know what I mean, Senator. You've violated your public trust. By your words, you are doing your best to discredit my husband. You lie; you make him out to be something he is not. In doing so, you make it difficult and maybe impossible for him to give to the people of this country what they need and what he's capable of."

"And what might that be?" Cole couldn't keep the sarcasm from his voice.

"There was a time when holding public office was a way in which gifted leaders and legislators provided service to their countrymen. It was a high calling, a calling which no longer receives the respect it once did."

"And what's that got to do with me?"

"It's people like you who give politicians a bad name. You manipulate facts and distort reality, making it appear as something it's not."

"What makes you think I distort reality and misuse facts?" Cole demanded.

"I know my husband, and when I read your comments, I knew they couldn't be further from the truth."

"You can't prove that!"

"I don't need to. You and I both know the truth.

Cole relaxed, dropping all pretense. "It is men like your husband who do not belong in politics." Cole leaned forward. "I will drive him out if I can."

"What is it about him that fills you with so much animosity? What has he done to make you so angry? This is more than politics, isn't it?"

"Mrs. Tremaine, I don't know what you're talking about," came the syrupy response.

"Oh yes, you do. You know exactly what I'm talking about." Sandra paused, collecting her thoughts. "I had to see you in person. I had to be sure about you."

"Sure of what?" Cole snapped.

"I had to see you for myself," she continued, ignoring his question. "I knew that in person you would not be able to hide from me." Sandra saw the flicker in Cole's eyes. "You're afraid of Tremaine, afraid that if he's as good as you think he is, there'll be no room in government for you or others of your ilk. From what I've seen, there will be no meeting of minds here."

Cole shifted uneasily. "Mrs. Tremaine, you speak in riddles. You don't know anything about me."

"I know more than you think. I know you're afraid,

although I doubt you'll admit that even to yourself. Now that I know what I do, you'll be much easier to deal with."

Before Cole could respond, Sandra stood and looked down at him. "I'm sorry for you, Senator; dishonesty and fear are cruel taskmasters." Turning on her heel, she left the office, closing the door quietly behind her.

....

With a bump, Air Force One touched down at Logan International Airport. An hour later, David and Sandra entered the packed hall at Harvard University, accompanied by Dr. Channing. As they walked onto the stage, the hall became quiet. The two men wore the traditional gowns of academia, while Sandra wore a long flowing cotton dress with a floral print of burnished orange. Channing showed the Tremaines to their seats, then stepped to the podium.

David looked at the sea of young, eager faces that stretching into the darkness at the back of the hall. A section at the front, below the stage, had been reserved for members of the press. It was full.

Dr. Channing began to speak. "I'm pleased to welcome David and Sandra Tremaine to Harvard. When I called Dr. Tremaine and invited him to speak, the telephone line was filled with static, and I had to call back on another line. I thought it an interesting coincidence, considering the topic of the lecture this evening.

"It was my intention to provide Dr. Tremaine with a stage from which to address the nation concerning the role of the press in a free society.

"It's my observation that the role of the media has changed since Watergate. In my opinion, that change has not been for the better. It's as if the press is gun-shy, having been taken in by the lies of highly placed government officials. This has produced a pervasive skepticism among many journalists and prevents them from reporting the truth when it is spoken. Instead, their reporting has been biased, prejudicial, and at times, inflammatory. Controversy, not accuracy, has become the watchword. It's difficult for citizens not to be affected by this change in emphasis, this all-pervasive negativity that offers no hope and fosters a kind of national despair, rendering us almost incapable of extricating ourselves from the morass we're in.

"In my opinion, this is a serious problem. It is to this issue that I've asked Dr. Tremaine to address his remarks this evening. Please welcome Dr. David Tremaine, President of the United States."

The applause was deafening. Everyone in the hall, including a reluctant press, stood in welcome. David shook hands with Dr. Channing then took his place behind the podium. When the applause quieted, he began.

"Thank you, Dr. Channing. Both Sandra and I are pleased to be here tonight. A number of months ago, Sandra suggested I speak to the National Press Club in New York. She believed it better to deal directly with members of the press concerning matters relating to them. She thought that such a gathering would provide an ideal opportunity to speak with a representative cross-section of the national press corps. Since the Press Club declined our offer, Dr. Channing invited us here instead, and issued an invitation for members of the press to join us.

"It's my hope that this will be an informative evening, one that will provide a better understanding of the role of the press in a democracy such as ours. I would warn you, however, that when a mechanic makes repairs, he must pay attention to what has failed, what is no longer working. I will do the same concerning the press. Attention will be focused on those things which, in my opinion, do not work well anymore. Until we are aware of the problem, the necessary corrections cannot take place.

"When the wind blows across the hill, trees bend. They do not complain that the wind is too strong or the wind is too weak. The tree does not have an opinion. It simply responds to life the way that it is, in the way that it does.

"A dog gets up one morning and it's raining. One day it snows. Sometimes it's hot and sometimes it's cold. Other than the basic survival of the organism, the dog is really not concerned with what he experiences. He doesn't formulate the idea that something is good or something is bad; he simply takes things as they come.

"What's the difference between the dog's behavior and a human being's? The dog accepts things as they are and doesn't take anything personally. By and large, human beings are not like that.

"Human beings tend to interpret things. They attach a meaning, and that meaning is self-referencing. By self-referencing, I mean the tendency to perceive events and circumstances from the perspective of the *me*, even when this particular *me* is not the focus of attention. This self-referencing can be seen in the identification one has with particular groups, such as *my* family, *my* party, *my* religion, *my* country, and so on. In this way, the *me* adds personal meaning to what transpires in the world around the human organism. This personal meaning enables him to feel involved, while in reality there's no connection other than the one projected by himself. When the self-referencing of events does not occur, a great deal of misery is absent.

"It's important that you understand me clearly. So before we go further, let's deal with your questions. "Yes, in the front row."

"First of all, I don't understand the connection between what you've been saying and the role of the press."

"If you bear with me, I think it will become obvious as we go along."

Suddenly several members of the press were on their feet, their questions loud, insistent and rude.

"I will get to your questions in good time," David addressed them. "Keep in mind that you are not the only ones here. Let us make this evening one of exploration, and let us do so in a civilized manner." David waited as, one by one, those who'd stood up sat down again.

"Yes, over there," he said pointing to a student several rows behind the area cordoned off for the press.

"What you've been describing with the dog, I have seen myself. Are you suggesting there would be greater peace of mind for human beings if we functioned more like the dog by not getting bummed out when things don't go our way and like the dog, not carrying a grudge?"

"Yes, that's the idea."

"Well, it does make sense, but I wonder if it makes us less human, less emotional, and less caring to others. If we face facts as you've so often told us, we will at times see things that seem unfair to those we love, things like accidents or illnesses. I can see we've no choice but to accept these things, and at the same time I find myself wondering if the acceptance you speak of will make us callous and uncaring."

"What's your name?"

"Michael."

"It's a good question, Michael, one which goes to the heart of a prevalent misconception. When we face facts, is there not an acceptance of things as they are?"

"There is."

"Might that be called detachment?"

"Yes, that's a good word for it."

"When we don't accept facts as they are, what does it

mean? It means that we want things to be different from the way they are? Is that not so?"

"Yes, it is."

"When there's no acceptance of things as they are, are we more likely to take offense, take things personally?"

"More likely to take things personally."

"When this happens what happens to anxiety and tension?"

"They go up."

"When anxiety and tension are present, how compassionate and loving are you?"

"Not very," Michael said with a laugh.

"When detachment is present, there's no disturbance in the mind. When there's no disturbance in the mind, are love and compassion more likely to be present?"

"I would think so, but I'm not sure. What about a truly uncaring person who has no concern for the misfortune of another? It seems unlikely he would have compassion."

"I would say that the uncaring person you describe already has a disturbed mind. That mind would be almost completely self-referencing. But to more directly deal with your point: you have equated detachment with not caring; my point is, that the opposite is true. The really caring person is detached; he has compassion for those who suffer in learning the lessons of life. His very presence is uplifting, whereas when sympathy is present, there's a sense of hopeless commiseration. My mother used to say 'misery loves company.' Sympathy thrives in the presence of the miserable."

"I'll think about what you've said. Thank you, Dr. Tremaine."

"You're welcome. More questions on this point?"

"Yes, over here."

David turned to look at a white-haired man with neatly

cropped beard, and tortoise-shell glasses perched on the end of a long nose.

"It seems to me," the man began, "that this detachment about which you speak is devoid of emotion, and as Michael mentioned, it could make one less caring, less human. This is still my question, so perhaps I've not understood you completely."

"I'll see if I can make it clearer. When detachment occurs, there's a certain equilibrium present, which in turn allows compassion and understanding to appear— just as the moon appears in the pond when the wind dies away."

"Are you suggesting that we should be detached in order to achieve compassion and understanding?"

"No, I'm not. I'm simply suggesting that when detachment is present, compassion and understanding are more likely to occur. And when this happens, the responses of the human being are spontaneous and appropriate. Why? Because they derive from a greater understanding of the circumstances at hand. This is an overall intuitive understanding, not to be mistaken for the understanding of the mind. When this occurs, the responses are compassionate. Obviously, the human being is not devoid of emotion at these times, as you suggest, but is instead not distracted by anxiety and tension. Does that make sense?"

"It does. Like Michael, I'm going to think it over. Thank you, Dr. Tremaine."

"Perhaps we can move on."

Hands continued to wave in the air. David responded, saying "If you can wait a little, I think your questions will be answered. I'll take more questions later, and if at the end of the evening they aren't answered, please write to me, and I'll respond to you.

"As a student, my understanding was that one role of the press consisted of reporting facts. Today, however, I think many members of the press have drifted away from that function. Instead, we find ourselves more and more subjected, not to facts, but to the interpretations of the reporter. And, of course, such interpretations are usually self-referencing.

"And what form does that interpretation take? It is the pitting of one point of view against another, coupled with the idea that one point of view deserves to win, the other to lose. And what point of view do you think deserves to win? Of course, *your* point of view.

"The problem with interpretative reporting is that it does not foster understanding. Let me explain what I mean. If ten human beings witness a single event, there will be ten different points of view concerning that event. Now, if we were absent when the event took place, and wanted to get a comprehensive sense of what happened, we would have to accept all points of view as perfectly valid. No single point of view by itself would be right; no single point of view would be wrong. In fact, right and wrong wouldn't enter in. The concept of right and wrong is something *we* superimpose upon the situation. This superimposition is the very thing a dog does not do."

A member of the press jumped to his feet, constrained anger in his face.

"Yes?"

"Are you suggesting that all points of view are equally valid?"

"That is precisely what I'm saying."

"I'm sorry, but I can't accept that."

"And why not?"

"Not all points of view are of equal importance."

"What does importance have to do with anything? Points of view are precisely what the words imply; different perspectives on particular events. The idea of importance is a subjective judgment."

"But don't you accept that some things are good and some things are bad?"

"Even that is a point of view."

"Why is that?"

"When I was in India, the very same question came up. I had the same difficulty you're having. An elderly man I was visiting at the time responded by saying that from the perspective of the human being, the eradication of the smallpox virus was a good thing, but not from the perspective of the virus itself. Everything is relative. If we're open, if we've not made up our minds ahead of time, understanding can occur. When that happens, our responses will be appropriate to the situation. In this way we'll be less likely to repeat the same mistakes."

"Are not some things truly evil and need to be stopped? It seems to me Hitler is a good example."

"I would say that our tendency to interpret things in black and white gives rise to the likes of Hitler in the first place. At the end of the First World War, the penalties to which Germany was subjected for having lost the conflict were crippling."

"Just a minute. Do you mean that the reason Germany was subjected to such stiff terms was because she lost?"

"Yes. The allies would say it was because Germany started the war, but we all know that the crimes of the victors go largely overlooked. Anyway, to answer your question: The Treaty of Versailles created considerable hardship for the German people. It was in many ways punitive. As I said, the kind of economic and social hardship experienced by Germany gave rise to a climate that made it easier for the likes of Hitler to come to power.

"His dislike of the Jews was not completely baseless. During these difficult times, many in Jewish communities prospered. They did this through hard work and shrewd financial dealings. The tightfisted monetary policies of some made them easy targets for the frustrations of the German people.

"If in the first place we'd been more understanding of the dynamics that led to the First World War, instead of casting it in terms of right and wrong, the climate that brought forth Hitler might have been absent.

"Our biased perspective is the cause of much of the conflict and suffering we face. Because of our biases, we blame others and absolve ourselves of responsibility. Since we refuse to face the facts, we cannot resolve our problems because we cannot correctly identify them."

"What do you mean?"

"What I mean is quite simple. A mechanic must correctly identify the problem when he repairs a car. If the problem is with the carburetor and he removes the transmission, it will not solve the problem, but will instead create an additional one. The same idea holds true in medicine. If there's a problem with your heart but the doctor diagnoses appendicitis, removing your appendix does not resolve the problem of the heart. Busy blaming others, how can we correctly identify the problem? If you can't identify the problem, how can you solve it. You cannot solve what you do not see.

"Still, the great drama of life goes on; life is the way it is. And when a Hitler comes to power, there will be those called upon to destroy him. Maggots appear when there's food for them. So to answer your question: Yes, certain things will arise that many agree are terrible, and these things will have to be stopped. There'll be those, like Churchill, whose task is to wage war; and when it's done they'll step from the world stage."

"But what about this problem of good and evil? Surely you agree we must do everything in our power to destroy evil and elevate good?"

"How can you? Have you never wondered why revolutions to overthrow despots end up with despotic revolutionaries at the helm? Is it not obvious that so-called good and bad arise together, like the head and tail of a coin? Can you have up without down, the outside of a cup without the inside? The Taoist sage Lao Tzu said, *What is a good man, but a teacher of a bad man? What is a bad man, but a good man's charge?* If we really understood this point, then social workers and psychologists would be less arrogant, more appreciative of the service they're able to provide; for without the poor and the suffering, the psychologist and social worker would be unemployed. Anyway, that's another point. Does that answer your question?"

"No, I don't think it does. It's not really an answer at all."

"It may not be what you're looking for, but it's the best I can do. Perhaps you might think about it, see what you come up with. Yes, over there, the gentleman with the mustache." David pointed to the back of the press section. A dignified elderly man stood up.

"If I understand you correctly, sir, what you're saying is that we should go back to the ideal of reporting the facts. Is that correct?"

"Yes. I don't like to use such words as *should* because they smack of some kind of moral superiority. I'm not speaking from that perspective, but from the perspective of what actually happens. When facts are reported, people will make up their own minds. If the reporter attempts to persuade by the way he reports the facts, he interferes in that process. One of the basic premises of a democracy is that citizens exercise their own minds on issues presented to them. They may well argue and dispute with each other, but the facts will be the facts because the reporter has done his job.

"Additionally, when facts are presented to us concerning our own behavior, it's easier for us to listen when they're not twisted to serve someone's idea of what should or should not be."

"I agree with you. I've been disturbed with the direction of televised journalism. The facts are too often shaded to support the hypothesis of the journalist involved. I don't think this is helpful. It relegates this powerful medium, television, to the level of the tabloids at the checkout stations. Despite this fact, the polls show there's more interest in this kind of drama than in knowing the facts. And for those employed in our industry, such as myself, there is pressure to produce what sells."

"Yes, I understand your point. My feeling about this is that we think the reporting of facts is dull and dry. This is not necessarily the case. Perhaps it is time to look at the meaning of entertainment. That which is entertaining captures one's attention. Confrontation, conflict, and rudeness certainly get our attention, too, but they do not enliven the spirit. Such things appeal to the baser side of human nature."

"Thank you, Dr. Tremaine. I hope my colleagues will think about your comments, and that we may all take an honest look at what we in this industry are doing."

"It is my hope, too. Thank you for your remarks." David pointed to a young woman waving in the student section. "Yes."

"Sometimes I think the press would be better off if it saw itself as an instrument of perception rather than an instrument of persuasion."

"Is that how you see it?"

"Yes. To me the press is an instrument whose function is no different from a microscope."

"Please say more."

"To me the function of reporting is to make clearly visible what is there. If the microscope is defective or the lens dirty, it cannot do its job. When the press attempts to persuade, the lens becomes distorted."

"I think it's a useful analogy, and I happen to agree with your point."

Dan Forester, the anchor for IBC stood up. "There are some who'll argue that the press and the legal profession are based on the adversarial principle.

The press has always been an agent of persuasion, at times an adversary, if you will, of government and big business and nations."

"Did not the adversarial role of the legal profession have its origin in the chivalry of medieval Europe? As I recall, it was believed that those aligned with God would win. It assumed that since God's will would prevail, only good would happen. This, it turns out, was not true, as victims of this process were quick to report."

"That may be true, but it is also a fact that the adversarial principle is alive and well, still practiced by journalists and members of the legal profession alike."

"Then do it honestly; let people know what you are doing."

"What about the negativity of the reporting, and the topics focused on? I find it depressing. There's no good news to be heard. "A blond woman in her mid-twenties had posed the question.

"Good observation. It is depressing, isn't it?

"It is... So that brings up another question."

"Go ahead."

"Should we not pass a law that balances the negative and the positive?"

"No direct action is required. To see things as they are is all that's needed. From another perspective comes a Sufi story that speaks to the issue of passing laws. Students came to a sage to learn the secrets of life. Having attempted to teach them how the mind works, the sage could see they did not understand one important point. To make his point clear, he issued the following instructions: 'Follow what I say with care. From this moment forth, you are forbidden to think of monkeys.' Of course, at that moment, the students failed."

Unexpectedly, a young man in the press leaped to his feet, his face flushed with anger. The man's sudden movement interrupted David's train of thought.

"It sounds to me as if you're afraid reporters will ask questions. That's our job. The more I listen to you, the more I hear press censorship. I think you want us to stop asking questions because you're afraid of where they might lead and of the embarrassment they might cause your administration."

"What you've done is a good illustration of my point. The fear you mention is yours, not mine; the dishonesty you allude to is likewise yours. The fact is, I have no fear concerning questions you or anyone else may ask. I have nothing to hide so why would I be afraid? As I've said before, the answers I give may not fit your preconceived notions, but they are nevertheless truthful. In speaking here tonight, fear was not present until you introduced it to the minds of those within hearing of your voice."

The young man realized he had drawn glances from those around him and, embarrassed over his outburst, sat down.

David continued. "When a reporter poses questions, he selects that aspect of reality to which our attention is drawn. In this instance, you introduced the idea of fear and dishonesty. I remember another incident after the last election.

"Emerson held his first press conference, and one of the reporters posed the following question: 'Your political party has been denied the White House for twelve years. We know the Republican party exercised power through questionable means. Now that your party is in power, will you resist the temptation to get even?' By the question posed, the reporter revealed his own thinking and introduced to public awareness something that was not in Emerson's mind at all, the idea of revenge.

"If you wish to tarnish a man's image, it's easy to do.

Arrange a press conference, then ask him if he's beaten his wife lately. No matter what he answers, you've managed to sully his name.

"When I was a graduate student, I took a course in the philosophy of history. Until then, I always thought of history as the recording of particular events occurring in time. It suddenly dawned on me that history was not a factual reality but rather a complex reflection of the historian's point of view on events taking place around him. It also became clear that through the manipulation of the news, it was possible to create the illusion of events that actually did not occur. I first saw this happen in the sixties; it was a tactic exploited by both anti-war activists and government agencies alike. You might remember a recent example whereby illusion was created by the clever use of words. In the *Boston Globe* two weeks ago, an article appeared under the heading "FANCY FOOTWORK." The reporter mentioned in his article that Senator Cole had hinted that key members of the Republican party are considering impeachment proceedings against the president. For several days following this statement, newspapers all over the country carried articles concerning impeachment, the historical antecedents, the more recent events stemming from Watergate, and the current situation raised by the Senator.

"Now what was it all about? Nothing. Was there really any talk of impeachment amongst Republicans? As far as I can tell, other than the senator, the answer is *no*. Senator Cole introduced the idea, knowing it would be picked up by the media and made into something that really didn't exist.

"Today, the language and images of television weave a reality that is largely unreal. This happens in the reporting of the news, the advertising and the programs produced. We've become masters in the art of prefabricated reality, a reality too often divorced from events taking place. By reporting in the fashion of the article in the *Globe*, reporters contribute to the problem they're meant to safeguard against. They become purveyors of illusion, making it increasingly difficult for the average person to distinguish between fact and fiction.

"It's this kind of thing the courts go to such pains to avoid in legal cases. They know how easily the truth can be distorted, and they do everything in their power to safeguard those brought before them. In the arena of politics, such safeguards do not exist."

"Yes." David pointed to a young woman in the front row to his left.

"There seems to be an inordinate preoccupation with death and suffering in both the press and society at large. It seems unbalanced and oppressive. Often I'm left with a feeling of hopelessness. It seems to me that this kind of preoccupation is really not healthy. It also seems, as you've pointed out, to be a distortion of what is really going on. Would you please comment on this?"

"I think you said it well. You used the term *unbalanced*. It's true. What we're subjected to through the media tends to deal, as you said, with death and suffering. It's another example of what I mean when I talk of illusion. As you said, the press tends to focus on the negative aspects of human nature. There's nothing wrong in reporting such things, but the lack of balance creates a negative sense of reality which, taken as a whole, is inaccurate. By drawing attention to one side of human nature, the side that is destructive, vicious, and cruel, and failing to report the creative, loving, and caring aspects of human nature, we've created a sense of despair, cynicism, and hopelessness. When this is coupled with the kind of death-dealing programs so prevalent on television, we shouldn't be surprised when our children are drawn to violence and death.

"When a child grows up in the streets of Belfast or

Mostar, or in Gaza, his psychological climate is permeated with death, violence, and suffering. Psychologists have known for a long time the effect this kind of environment has upon children.

"Too many of our children are subject to a similar reality in the ghettos of our cities. Meanwhile, all of our children, the middle and upper-class children as well, are subject to the virtual *reality*, of television and movies. The reality portrayed consists of an inordinate level of violent and destructive behavior. In time, as our children grow, what they've witnessed on television becomes actualized in the society at large. The finality of death is obscured by actors whose deaths we've witnessed so many times. Most parents would not leave their children alone in dangerous circumstances or in the presence of psychopathic killers; yet that is precisely what we've done by leaving our children alone with our television sets. Young minds and emotions are being shaped by ugliness, and charged with a destructive energy.

"The effect of television on the young was understood very well by the Apple computer company. They donated their computers to schools. They knew that once children had experienced the versatility of those computers, they'd tend to use them when they became adults and entered the work environment. As it turns out, the donation was a farsighted investment.

"Anyway, the effects of actual reality and virtual reality upon children show many similarities. A major difference, however, is that we evidence more concern for children caught in actual combat than we do for those children caught in the combat of virtual reality, portrayed on screens in our homes and theaters.

"When our young murder one another, as well as adults, we are shocked and dismayed, at a loss to know how such tragedy came about. 'What is wrong with our children?' we ask, wringing our hands. Where did these monsters come from? The answer is simple. They came from us; they cut their teeth on the television and videos we created."

"Are you saying that the press is responsible for this?" asked a young man in the wheelchair.

"I'm saying that the press drinks at the same trough. The emphasis of reporting is, as the young lady pointed out, on the negative and violent aspects of human nature. This unbalanced perspective is shared to a large extent by the entertainment industry as a whole. The press, however, is responsible for reporting the events that take place throughout the world. The questions they pose determines the reality upon which we focus. How easy it is for one group of people to dislike another group, based solely on the misinformation and bias of the reporting. Perhaps this is why so many of our countrymen condone the violence of the Israelis, for instance, and have no comprehension of what it's like for the Arabs living in the squalor of Gaza or the West Bank.

"There is often little difference between the news and the so-called entertainment that follows. What results is a blurring of reality. The big broadcasting companies have recognized the public's fascination with the negative aspects of reporting and so have spawned a series of so-called news programs in which reporters are often rude to those they interview. This brash confrontational style does not foster understanding and compassion, but instead further divides one group of people from another."

"Violence and negativity sell. People watch it with fascination," responded the man in the wheelchair. "That's why the broadcasting companies program what they do."

"In a circle there's no beginning and no end. We must start somewhere. Tonight, the point of entry is with the press itself. The press must take responsibility in matters that pertain to it. Of course, that doesn't mean that we, the population as a whole, are not responsible. We are. We, as well as the media are responsible for the psychological climate we've created for our children through the medium of television. It's important that we understand what we're doing to ourselves and our young.

"Television, perhaps more than any other medium in the history of the world, determines the outlook we have on the world and each other. We must come to terms with it; we must see how it affects our perception of reality. If we fail to see this clearly, we may well lose two important freedoms: the freedom to think and the freedom of direct perception. These are subtle freedoms, not readily apparent. If we lose them, we'll be unaware we've done so."

A man in his forties, his face unshaven, stood in the front row. "Dr. Tremaine, one of the functions of the press, as I see it, is to be a watchdog on behalf of the people. Our job is to ferret out and bring to public awareness corruption, wherever it is found. The press has done a reasonably good job of this when it comes to such things as politics, business, and religion. But what of corruption in the press itself? The question I would ask is, can the press monitor itself? What happens when the lens of communication becomes distorted, as the young lady mentioned? Who is left to draw attention to this distortion? Politicians and educators may attempt to do it, but when they, through their own actions and the misrepresentation of the press, are seen as dishonest, how can they be heard or believed when pointing to the dishonesty of the press itself?"

"A very good question. I'm glad you raised it. It's a concern I have and one for which I don't have an answer. I think it's something we must think about.

"In many ways the press is like the telephone line Dr. Channing mentioned earlier. What purpose does it serve when its ability to accurately transmit what is being said is impaired? The press must not be like the messenger who lacked integrity.

Carrying a letter for delivery to a distant place, he opens it and, not finding the content to his liking, decides not to make delivery. Instead he interprets and summarizes to us what he's read. This is a serious problem. It presumes we, the public, are less intelligent than the messenger, that we do not have the ability to face facts and take appropriate action. Deprive people of this responsibility for long enough, and they'll come to believe that they are, indeed, incapable of making decisions and taking action.

"Many years ago during the Vietnam war, sanctuary was granted a young soldier by five students. This occurred at Boston University. I was one of the students involved. I was asked to come to the phone to talk to a reporter from the soldier's hometown in Oregon. I spoke briefly with the reporter before being cut off by an operator. When I tried to get the operator to reconnect us, she refused. I asked to speak to the supervisor. She came on the line and also refused. The operators were from the same community as the soldier. They knew the reporter and were convinced he would give a sympathetic reporting of the soldier's views. They did not want me to talk to the reporter. To them, the young soldier was a traitor. No matter how hard I tried, they would not put me through. I never forgot that experience. I found it frightening. The operators controlled the means of communication and were in a position to prevent it when they so desired. Freedom of the press is of the utmost importance in a society like ours. That freedom must be an internal freedom. The press must take a good look at itself It must become aware of its biases."

....

It was past midnight when Channing escorted the Tremaines from the back of the hall into the cold night. Large, lazy flakes of snow rocked gently back and forth before settling on a thin white carpet beneath the barren trees. Accompanied by members of the Secret Service, the Tremaines walked along the path that led across the quadrangle to the waiting cars. Students stood on either side and, as they passed, murmured their thanks and good-byes in the hushed night.

CHAPTER 18

It was evening when Aziz and Shamir arrived above Bent Jebail. Behind them the great ramparts of the mountains were golden in the setting sun. Through the gloaming, lights twinkled while smoke from the cooking fires rose to hang in great flat rivers on the evening stillness. Shamir heard the sound of dogs barking and watched as people made their way home. She was tired. The walk from Rachaf wasn't long, but the terrain was rugged.

Six months had passed since she had left Nassir's home, the cave that she shared with him after the death of her family.

"Why do we have to go?" she'd asked when he told her they were leaving the following day.

"Because we must," was all he would say.

"I like it here," she'd protested.

"I know."

"Forgive me for asking, Nassir, but can't I stay?"

"No. Your destiny lies elsewhere." Nassir had refused to be drawn into further discussion.

....

And so it was with a sense of sadness that Shamir left the cave that had been her home. With Nassir, she had climbed high into the mountains until at last they sat quietly and caught their breath on a rocky outcrop looking east. Below them, familiar valleys snaked down the side of the mountain to the distant ocean.

Then, as if on cue, they stood and continued along a faint trail that led through the mountains. Several hours passed when the sound of a shot broke the silence. Nassir reacted instantly. Pulling Shamir off the trail, he raced up the incline and leaped to a ledge, turned, grabbed her by the hands, and pulled her up beside him. Breathing hard, they lay side by side, peering down at the trail below. Nothing moved.

From where they were hidden, they had a commanding view of the surrounding area. If anyone came along the trail, they would see them. Holding his breath, Nassir listened, his ears tuned for the slightest sound. The sighing of the ever-present was all they could hear. Half an hour later, they cautiously moved on.

"We'll stay above the trail," Nassir explained.

"What do you think it is?"

"I don't know, but guerrillas operate in these mountains. It's best we not meet them."

Memory of her parent's death made Shamir shudder. For half an hour they moved slowly, keeping the trail below them, always in view. Climbing around a rocky promontory, Nassir caught a movement below. Instantly he froze. Shamir held her breath and watched, trembling. Beneath them a man had crawled off the trail and sat against the shattered trunk of an old tree. His head fell forward, his hands hung limp at his sides, and blood stained his shirt.

"Shamir, stay here. I'm going down to see what's happened."

Before she could respond, Nassir slipped away. Quickly yet cautiously he worked his way toward the man, taking care to stay out of sight. The sun was low, and the shadows in the depressions served as hiding places. Nassir checked the surrounding area for signs of life before he crept within ten meters of the wounded man.

Nassir studied the man. The black hair, wet with sweat, was plastered to his forehead, the eyes were closed, the breathing ragged and fast. He wore camouflage pants and a long-sleeved khaki-colored shirt. His feet were bare. A dark stain had spread down his shirt from a large, gaping wound in the upper chest. Suddenly the eyes opened, and Nassir, with a jolt, recognized Tariq, Kahlil's friend.

Nassir stood, and as he did Tariq's head turned toward him. Recognition spread across his face, light returned to the eyes.

"Nassir, is that you?"

"It is." Nassir knelt before the wounded man and examined him."

"I can't survive this, can I?" Tariq whispered.

Nassir looked into Tariq's eyes. "No, my friend, this is the final wound for this body."

Standing, he signaled Shamir to join them. In moments, the young woman was at his side, breathless. While Nassir cradled Tariq in his arms, Shamir unslung her water skin and carefully guided a small stream of water to the man's dry lips. His eyes caught hers, and a faint smile crossed his face. "Thank you," he whispered.

"What happened?" Nassir asked.

Tariq shifted his gaze from Shamir and looked out across

the desolate slopes. "Iranians joined our unit about a month ago."

Nassir and Shamir strained to hear him.

"We captured a young Israeli girl two nights ago and brought her across the border. I was ordered to kill her. I refused. The Iranians brought me here today and one of them shot me."

"Was Kahlil with your unit?" Nassir asked.

"He was, but was sent ahead; we were to rendezvous in Bent Jebail."

"Is that where he is now?"

"Yes," came the hoarse voice.

Shamir raised the water skin to moisten Tariq's lips. His eyes focused on her momentarily, and once more the hint of a smile spread across the ashen face.

Nassir adjusted Tariq's position. "It's almost over, Tariq, soon you'll leave this place of suffering."

"Yes. Will you see my mother for me?"

"Yes." Nassir bent his head to catch the words.

"She's a good mother, please tell her for me." The words had come slowly. The eyes stared, no longer seeing. Nassir knew that in Tariq's mind his mother stood before him, her arms tenderly encircling the son she had loved. "I love you." Nassir heard the dying man's final words.

Shamir watched intently, her heart still pounding. She felt the bond of love between the two men and watched through her tears as consciousness faded from the body of Tariq. With a deep, rasping shudder, he drew one last breath, his head falling forward on his chest.

....

Shamir and Nassir had stopped for the night, far from where Tariq died. It was late, and Shamir, exhausted, fell asleep at once. She awoke once during the night and realized Nassir was gone. Long before dawn, he was shaking her by the arm.

"We must leave at once," he whispered.

In moments she was ready.

"What's going on?" she asked

"There's an Israeli unit nearby, they must be looking for the young girl Tariq mentioned. We must get as far away as possible."

Shamir had trouble keeping up with Nassir. Despite his age, he was agile and strong. They climbed a ridge and descended the other side into what seemed like a shallow valley. Against the stars she could see ridge lines all around. She could tell from the stars that they were moving in an easterly direction. They stopped only once for a brief rest.

"Where are we going?" Shamir asked when she'd caught her breath. They sat on a low hill. From there they would know if someone was coming. If patrols operated in the region, Nassir did not want to run into them.

"Once we reach the head of the valley, we'll climb back into the high country again. From there it's not far to the village of Rachaf. The Israelis will stay clear of settled areas. I've friends there. We'll find out what's going on."

....

Dawn found them standing before an old wooden door, entrance to a small, tidy dwelling on the outskirts of the village. In response to Nassir's knock, the sleepy face of an elderly man with a stubbly beard and white hair that stood on end, had appeared. As he peered out into the morning light, his eyes lit up with recognition.

"Come in, come in."

With that they were welcomed inside. A small oil lamp

sat on a wooden table, shedding a warm light in the little room.

"Have a seat."

Nassir and Shamir sat in the chairs at the table, glad at last to be off their feet.

"Shamir, this is my old friend Aziz; Aziz, this is Shamir."

Aziz gave Shamir, a radiant smile. The smile and the disheveled hair struck her as funny. She found herself laughing.

As Shamir watched, Aziz moved quickly to get some coffee brewing. Soon the smell filled the room. From an old barrel he took out dates and placed them in a wooden bowl. Bananas along with a loaf of bread, a round of cheese, and a knife were placed on the table.

"Eat," he said.

....

Shamir awoke, and from the slanting rays of the sun knew it was late afternoon. Outside she heard the murmur of voices. When she was ready, she opened the door. Aziz sat on the step and patted the space beside him. The warmth of afternoon had peaked and passed. Cool currents of air wafted down from the lofty peaks. Nassir sat on his blanket beneath an old tree, its gnarled, leafless branches twisted at odd angles. In front of him four men sat cross-legged, engrossed in conversation. A breeze sighed in the branches, providing a soft counterpoint to the melodic sound of voices. The scene bore a dreamlike quality.

"One man was speaking, in the language of the educated. I've been searching for truth many years," she heard him say. "I've been told that you are a holy man, a sage, one with whom I can speak concerning spiritual matters."

She heard Nassir saying, "I am merely a shepherd who takes care of his flocks; I have done so since I was a boy."

"Why do you hide from me?" responded the man.

"Why do you hammer on my door?"

"I told you, I seek the truth."

"Would you know the truth if it was before you?"

"Of course."

"What of truth do you seek to know?" Nassir asked, "Is it to add to your storehouse of knowledge?"

"To acquire real knowledge, spiritual knowledge, is the only undertaking worthy of a man."

There is arrogance in that educated, refined man, Shamir thought to herself.

Nassir continued, "Real knowledge cannot be acquired; it happens spontaneously, and only to a few. It's a gift of the Divine; it's either there or it's not, and in your case, it's not."

The man recoiled as though he'd been slapped. "Why do you say such things?"

"Because they're true," came the quiet response. "You said you would recognize truth when it was before you, so start with this."

"You insult me and my family."

"No, what takes insult is not real. Who you are lies behind the mask you present to the world."

"What are you talking about?"

"You wanted to know the truth; you pressed for it, and now I've taken you at your word. When does a mango drop from the tree?"

"When it's ripe, of course."

"The understanding you seek is not something that can be forced. Like the mango, the so-called person cannot fall from the tree of illusion until the necessary ripeness has been achieved."

"How can I achieve it?"

"You cannot; it comes only as a by-product of living."

"I have lived, maybe not as long as you, but more than this man beside me."

"Wisdom, the ripeness of which we speak, is not a matter of age in the way that you understand it. Who can measure the unfathomable experiences of the ancient soul? How many times has it dressed to enter this vast hall of life for the feast of the senses?

"Your time will come, my brother. Never fear. Walk abroad in the world, and no matter what you do, pay attention. Find wherein lies the happiness that does not disappear. That search will turn your life into a great adventure, and one day, when the time is right, you'll sit before the one who will shake you into wakefulness. Then you will know the truth you seek."

"It was a mistake coming here today."

"No mistake. From deep in the dream, the consciousness that you are heard the voice of the Divine and responded, drawing you near. It is but reassurance that is needed by the sleeper enmeshed in life's dream. Now you may go your way, relieved. Step back into life. After all, is it not the greatest story ever told?" Nassir stood, reached down for the man's hand and helped him to his feet.

"Aziz, give him dates, bread, and cheese for his journey; make sure his skin is filled with water." Nassir embraced the man, who suddenly seemed uncertain. Aziz did as he was told.

Shamir watched the man walk slowly up the road and disappear. She wondered, was it sorrow she sensed in those stooped shoulders?

"I'm so sorry for bringing him," Shamir heard one of the men saying.

"It was something you had to see for yourself," Nassir responded. "These teachings have nothing to do with converting anyone. Who can improve on the handywork of the Divine? So where is the necessity of conversion? It is the antithesis of truth."

"I'd heard him say many times how much he wanted to

know the truth. He's always reading. He's a learned man, while I am not. I was sure he'd love to meet you; and when I told him of you, he was excited. I didn't know where you were, and so it was coincidence that brought us to Aziz's house. I thought he might know when you'd be back, and there you were."

"Timur, I know that in your heart is generosity and love, but you must understand what I said about the mango. Until the human being is ripe, the presence of a master does no good. Those who are compelled to seek the Divine cannot help themselves. The seeker does not choose to be a seeker. How could he? It is the action of destiny, the love of the Divine for itself."

"But what about the mullahs who teach that the only way is the way of the prophet?" one of the young men asked.

Nassir turned to face the young man and spoke. "A wagon wheel has many spokes, surrounded by a wooden and steel hoop. At the center is the hub, to which the spokes are attached. In the center of the hub is a hole around which everything else revolves. The spokes come from the four corners of the world and arrive at the center. The center is the nameless and formless. Out of necessity, we have given it the name of Allah. The spokes represent the many paths that lead there. The farther they are from the center, the more distinct and separate they appear to be. At the outer limits, beliefs are rigid, and those found there believe that their particular spoke represents the one and only true way. Those close to the hub already sense that all spokes lead to the same place; their beliefs are less rigid. Those who've arrived at the hub can discard belief altogether; they know that all the spokes, though coming from different places, arrive at the same place. When this is known, it's not long before each one dissolves into the formless center. This is the end of the journey, the union with the Holy One, which words cannot describe."

"Why is there so much conflict at the outer edges of the

spokes?"

"Because the world is divided into right and wrong. This division is a kind of mistake, a misunderstanding, something superimposed upon the creation by the mind of man himself."

"I don't understand."

"What we see around us can only be seen by the combination of its presence and absence. The tree can only be distinguished when seen against that which is not tree. This is known as duality. Everything has two aspects to it. Inside and outside, beauty with ugliness, good with bad. As two banks define a river, so does duality give rise to the perception of the world. Believers in religions the world over have not understood the nature of reality. They have sought the good without the bad; they struggle and strive, prisoners of their own beliefs, unable to see the obvious truth."

"How foolish we are."

"Yes, in a way, but on the other hand, nothing is out of place. All is as it is, and so brings about the divine dance known as life. This is the way it is. This is life; it could be no other way, nor should it be."

"Then why are we here?"

"Because the fruit is ripe."

....

Later Nassir, Aziz and Shamir sat eating around the table in Aziz's home.

"Where are you going, Master?" asked Aziz.

Until today, Shamir had never heard Nassir called "Master," yet she realized she felt the same way toward him as did Aziz and the young men under the tree.

"I'm going to Bent Jebail tomorrow, leaving in the afternoon."

"Are you going by road? Maybe I can find someone to take you."

"No, I think I'll stay off the road. It's not far."

"Can you see Tariq's mother in the morning? She heard you were here and sent word this evening, asking if she could come and see you."

"Yes, let her come."

"Karima wants to see you as well. She came by just yesterday, asking for you."

"How is she?"

"As well as can be expected. Ibn Saud has wanted to marry her, but she confided that she cannot go to another man's bed. She's heard the reports of her husband's death; but even after three years, she's still convinced he's alive. If he's dead, she says she wants no other man. One loss like that is enough for a lifetime."

In the morning, Durri, Tariq's mother, knocked on the door. She immediately reminded Shamir of her own mother. Once more the sorrow in Shamir's heart stirred, and tears came to her eyes.

Nassir embraced the woman then held her at arm's length and looked her over. "It's good to see you again, Mother."

"It's good to see you again, too," came the response in soft mellow tones.

Shamir's heart went out to the woman; she knew what was to come.

"Durri, this is Shamir."

The two women acknowledged each other.

"Let's sit under the tree. Aziz, come and join us."

Durri sat on a carpet that Nassir spread for her beneath the tree. Her long black dress covered her crossed legs. "Have you any news of Tariq?" she asked.

"I have," Nassir said. "Shamir and I saw him yesterday."

"Was he well?" came the eager inquiry.

Nassir, sitting directly in front of Durri, took her hands in his. "Beloved Mother, your son is dead."

Shamir felt the shock like a blow. She watched the eyes moisten as the woman bowed her head.

Nassir kissed Durri's hands and watched as the silent tears fell into her lap. Aziz knelt behind her and placed his hands on her shoulders for support. Suddenly, like the bursting of a dam, huge, racking sobs shook Durri's frame, and from the depths of her sorrow came a long mournful cry.

....

It was late in the morning when Nassir accompanied Durri home. When he returned to Aziz's little house, it was mid-afternoon. Shamir and Aziz joined Nassir beneath the tree, the sunlight warm in the cool air.

"Shamir, I want you to stay with Durri. I've made the arrangements. You'll take care of her for a little while. She's a good woman, and you'll be good for each other. If you need any help with anything, you can speak with Aziz. He will help you."

"Where are you going?" Shamir asked.

"To Bent Jebail. I have business there."

"Will I see you again?" she asked, suddenly inexplicably afraid. She sensed something in Nassir she hadn't felt before.

"Yes, you'll see me again."

"What's happening? Something's changed. Tell me." Suddenly chilled, she shuddered involuntarily. "You know, don't you?" she demanded.

Nassir looked directly at her. His eyes no longer danced with humor; they were clear and tranquil.

"My dear Shamir, you are precious to me. You are like my own daughter. Destiny decreed that in this lifetime I would not have children of my own. My family has always been very important. And now, only you and my brother remain."

Shamir found herself crying. Yes, she thought, you and your brother are my family.

"What do you mean?" she said through her tears. "You frighten me."

"I am merely a bridge to help you along your way. Your life stretches where mine cannot go. My time is short."

"Nassir, this kind of talk frightens me. I don't want to lose you. What's happening?"

"Life is so vast that no one can ever know the whole. Each of us must play our appointed part. We're born where we're born of parents we did not choose, with gifts and skills that come with a birth. Most people live out their destiny not knowing ahead of time what is to happen. There are some, however, who have the gift of seeing. They know ahead of time, as it were, what is to take place. Time is an illusion, part of the great dance we call life. The seers are not subject to time, and so they know things others do not. This gift was instrumental in saving your parents' lives many years ago. It brought me to the well where we met. Through this gift I knew to bring you here."

"Are you going to die?"

"Yes."

"When?"

"Within a year, this body will return to the earth."

"Oh, Nassir, I can't stand to lose you. Everyone I've loved is gone, and you're the only one left."

"Beloved daughter, I do understand; and that is why you must stay with Aziz and Durri. They are your family now." Leaning over, he took Shamir's hands in his. Tears streamed down her face. "Though I'll be gone in form, the love we shared will remain. When the time is ripe and wisdom matures, the honey of that love will drip from the hive, and you'll be compelled to give to those whom Allah sends your way."

"Why does this have to happen?" Shamir sobbed, despair in her voice.

"So much sorrow for someone so young." Nassir said quietly, as though to himself. "It takes a hot fire to melt the ore and release the imprisoned gold. Nothing is wasted in life; all is essential. There are some, however, who look upon their lives with sorrow and despair. That attitude alone makes sorrow unbearable. Your destiny is to bring healing. It is Allah who has set in motion the preparation of his holy vessel, Shamir." Nassir had taken her in his arms and held her as she cried.

"Is there any way out?" she finally asked.

"No. Even the master Jesus in the Garden of Gethsemane asked if the cup of suffering could pass from him, knowing there was no other way. Life is not as it seems, little one. In the West, people go to watch movies. The movies are life stories projected upon a screen, and as such they are not real. But they can so involve those who watch them that they feel deeply the love, hatred, and sorrow as if it were their own. Although it may not seem so at the time, life is much like a movie. It's real only in a certain sense, unreal in another."

"I don't understand."

"You dream, don't you?"

"Yes, of course"

"In your dreams, do you experience love and sorrow, happiness and joy? Do you see people and events?"

"Yes."

"And what happens to them when you wake up?"

"They vanish."

"Yes, and what happens to the sorrow and pain? Was it real?"

Shamir was crying softly. "Why Nassir, why are you telling me this? I can't stand it! Let me die with you."

"It's not your time."

"I don't care," she wailed. "I can't stand the thought of losing you."

"Your task right now is to help Durri. I know how she affected you. You need her for a mother; she needs you for a daughter. Such unions as this are not made from flesh and blood, as are mothers and daughters on the physical plane. This union is born of the heart. Sorrow has prepared the ground. Love will flourish here. This will be. You sensed it when you heard Durri's voice; it reminded you of your beloved mother. Durri, for her part, felt a strange stirring in her heart when she first saw you. It was as though she'd been waiting for you."

"I know what you're saying, but I don't want to lose you."

"You can't lose me, Shamir. I am love, and love is without form. Don't be too attached to the form. Feel instead the love that is here in Aziz, feel the love in Durri, and know that it is me that you feel. I will never leave you. I am with you always, to the very end."

"Oh, Nassir," Shamir sobbed.

Nassir and Aziz sat silently while Shamir cried. There was no hurry, and when she'd finished, Nassir spoke again.

"Shamir, this world is a dream; it's not real because it doesn't last. When you wake up, the sorrow and the pain will vanish. You will remember it, but it will no longer affect you. Then you will understand that you have always been home, you could never have gone away, you were just sleeping."

They had gone into the house and, sitting around the table, had eaten in silence. The silence soothed Shamir. When they finished, they stood, and Nassir gathered together what he needed.

"Aziz," he embraced his friend, "take care of my daughter."

Aziz nodded, tears obscuring his sight.

"Daughter, take care of this father."

Shamir was on the verge of tears again.

Nassir held her tight, and then pushing her away, took her hands. "I will see you one more time before I leave. Never forget, my beloved daughter, that this body cannot contain the love I am. When the time comes leave it behind, do what is before you. Enjoy the dream until the time comes and you awaken."

....

Now, months later, as she looked down at Bent Jebail, she wondered if Nassir was somewhere in the town. Would this be the time of which he'd spoken?

CHAPTER 19

Miguel shuffled along the pavement. An observer would have seen a shambling derelict scavenging in the gutted ruins of the abandoned buildings. The old man, for so he appeared, was dressed in a dirty raincoat and wore a battered, sweat-stained fedora, the brim covering his face. A filthy scarf wrapped his neck, and a pair of old woolen gloves covered his hands. It was nine o'clock Tuesday morning. The area was deserted. He stopped to light a cigarette, and under cover of shielding the match from the wind, made sure no one was around. Suddenly he stepped between two buildings and with swift purposeful strides walked fifty yards down the alley.

Empty ruined houses rose on either side. He ducked into an opening and waited five minutes. Then, in complete silence, he slowly made his way through the rubble to an battered door. He tapped three times, and it swung open. He entered and descended the stairs. One guard remained at the top while a guard at the bottom opened the door and closed it behind

Miguel. Not a word passed between them.

Miguel took off his outer clothes and threw them on the back of an old chair. He lit the hurricane lamp, opened the metal cabinet, and took out a 9mm pistol and screwed a silencer in place. Taking down the maps, he set them on fire. They burned quickly to a pile of blackened ash, which he crushed beneath his feet. With a cloth he carefully cleaned the handles to the cabinet, the door handle, the edges of the table, and the old metal chairs. He carefully cleaned the unlit lanterns. Taking his time, he looked around the room, his eyes covering every inch. Then he went to the door and signaled the guards to enter. The guard outside waited for his companion to reach the bottom of the stairs before they entered.

"Put your guns on the table," Miguel ordered

The men looked at each other, then unholstered their guns and placed them on the table.

"You've done a good job." Miguel smiled. The men visibly relaxed.

"Everything went well; the Scarlatis no longer exist."

The men nodded and smiled.

Miguel pulled out a chair and sat down. "There's cash for you in there," he said, indicating the steel cabinet behind them. "There's one bundle for each of you. You'll find a bottle of wine in the back, too. Bring it out and we'll drink to a successful operation."

As the two men turned toward the cabinet, Miguel pushed his chair over, sending it crashing to the floor. He jumped to his feet. The two men, startled, spun around. Each received a bullet through the heart. The last thing they saw was the cold look on their killer's face.

Miguel took the two pistols from the table and dropped them into a bag. Once more he cleaned the chair, removing all fingerprints. He lifted down the hurricane lantern and, taking his time, dusted it and left it on the table, still burning.

....

    An old man shuffled slowly into a bus station and bought a ticket for Oklahoma City. It was five in the afternoon, an hour before the bus was to leave. Entering the cafeteria, he ordered coffee and a pastry. The speaker blared a last call for passengers bound for Memphis on platform number four. A few minutes later a man in his late twenties entered the bus station. He was dressed in a three-piece pin-striped suit of navy blue. In his hand he carried a small briefcase and over his arm a thick coat. He stepped up to the ticket counter and bought a ticket for Oklahoma City. Half an hour later a young marine stepped up to the window. He too, bought a ticket to Oklahoma City. In his hand he carried a newspaper. The headline read, "GANG WAR ERUPTS."
    Six well-dressed men entered the train station from different points between ten and eleven the following morning. During the course of an hour they also bought tickets for Oklahoma city. As they boarded the train, each entered a different carriage.
    At a U-Haul office that afternoon, two men and a woman rented a small moving van. The wall clock showed two thirty.
    "Yes, our main office is in Oklahoma City," the man at the desk responded to the woman's inquiry. "You can leave it there when you finish."
    Later that afternoon a priest, in the company of five nuns, dressed in habit, rented a large van from Hertz and set out for a convent just outside Oklahoma City.
    The same evening, three men wearing blue jeans, high-heeled leather boots, warm plaid jackets, and Stetsons unlocked the door of a new Ford F250 extended cab. Loading their bags

behind the seat, they got in and started the engine. As the truck emerged from the underground parking facility, the street light reflected off the Oklahoma license plate.

....

"Nothing? You must be shitting me. What the hell are you talking about?" Brigadier General Clint Duval exploded. His chair scraped on the concrete floor as he got to his feet. Before him stood two men. One wore the uniform of an officer in the Green Berets, the other the uniform of an officer in the Navy SEALS.

It was ten o'clock Wednesday morning and Duval had been up for two days. He'd already had reports from the police and the National Guard. Ten police officers dead, eighteen wounded, two firemen dead, fifteen National Guard killed and six wounded. Four civilians had been killed, and forty-seven of the Scarlatis. The police had rounded up fifty of the Capones for questioning which was still continuing. No one had a single lead.

....

Jonathan Makarios and Doug Kersey arrived at the White House early Wednesday morning. It was still dark. Morgan was already present when they entered. The three men sat in the comfortable chairs; Tremaine stood with his back to the fire. "Let's get down to business," he said. "This could be a long day. Let's start with the Middle East trip. Where do we stand?"

"The arrangements have been finalized," Doug Kersey began. "You leave for Israel December twelfth. You'll be there till the fifteenth, then two days in Jordan with the King, two days in Syria, and two days in Lebanon. You'll be back just in time for Christmas."

"Now, what about this thing in Chicago? Is there any more news? Morgan was telling me seventy-eight people had been killed."

"Yes, that's what we understand, too," said Jonathan. "Travis talked with Clint Duval, and they're at a total loss. The special units that went in Tuesday night came across nothing. In fact, there's been no more confirmed gunfire since seven o'clock Tuesday morning.

"The Capones were rounded up, and the preliminary questioning has been completed. According to the police department, the Capones claim that none of them were involved in this whole thing. For some of them, the statements check out, but it'll take more time to thoroughly investigate. It's also difficult to know who their members are; they don't keep written records and they don't volunteer information"

"What about the Scarlatis, those still alive?"

"So far as we can tell, only six survived the firefight and there are another sixteen who weren't there that night. Their report supports what the Capones have said. The six who survived the fight said they didn't see any of the Capones that night. But they're convinced it was them. They may be right, but so far there's no evidence to support what they say."

"I spoke with Mike Jackson late last night," Morgan added. "He mentioned the same thing. He said they'd questioned the Scarlati survivors. One of them insisted that when he got outside, he was surprised to see another Scarlati gang member across the street. He wondered how he got there so fast."

"Are there no other leads?" David asked.

"There are. The Chicago police think that some members of the Capones' gang have vanished. But it's difficult to confirm when gang members cover for each other and are so hostile. There's also a report that several dogs in the area were killed the week before. The FBI thinks they were killed deliberately. Poisoned meat may have been used. Anyway, they're still checking. The power company verified that all the lights in the area within six blocks of the Scarlatis headquarters were shot out. Police investigators found air pellets in the vicinity that they think were used."

"Anything else?" David asked.

They all shook their heads.

"Then we must wait and see what happens. Is Travis back yet?" David turned to Jonathan.

"He's due in this afternoon."

"Tell him I want to see him as soon as he gets in."

....

It was six o'clock and Travis sat before the fire, Tremaine to his right.

"What time did you get in?" David inquired.

"A little after five, I think."

Travis looked tired.

"Thanks for coming. Let's make this brief so you can get home to your wife."

Travis smiled his appreciation.

"So what have you got?"

"Not a hell of a lot," Travis responded. "The finger seems to be pointed at the Capones, but I'm not sure that's where it belongs. Jackson won't say either way. He likes to play his cards close to his chest."

"What's your hunch?"

"I don't really know what to say."

"C'mon, Travis, I know that brain of yours must have some thoughts running around in it."

Travis smiled.

"Don't worry, I'll not hold you to it, but I want to know

what you think."

"Okay. My hunch is that whoever carried this out was highly skilled. There may have been fewer involved than we initially thought, but they were exceptionally well trained. Whoever they were, they threw us a curve ball, distracting us by leading us to believe it was a gang war. While we took the time to discover that was not the case, they slipped away."

"Any ideas as to who it might be?"

"No, but something about this whole thing has been niggling away at the back of my mind. On the flight back this afternoon, I remembered that when I was in Vietnam, there were rumors of a special unit of mercenaries funded by the CIA whose sole function was to operate outside the law."

"What do you mean?"

"Well, I'm not sure whether it really existed or not. If it did, however, this unit's job was to kill selected South Vietnamese politicians and military personnel. Sometimes even American support staff at the Embassy in Saigon were targeted. It was always made to look as if it was the Viet Cong. When this happened, it usually precipitated retaliatory strikes that would otherwise not have been justified. Although Cambodia and Laos were not officially in the war, the Viet Cong did operate there. We needed some pretext to set up operations in those countries and to make certain unspecified strikes where we otherwise would have been prohibited."

"Can this be checked into?"

"I'll do my best. We'll have to see."

"So are you suggesting that a similar kind of operation was mounted?"

"Maybe."

"Anything else?"

"Not for now."

"Thanks, Travis. Keep me informed."

"I will."

David got up and shook hands with the general and walked him to the door. "I'm going to the Middle East on the twelfth of next month," he said as he opened the door.

Travis turned. "Be careful. That part of the world is a dangerous place."

"So is Chicago. Maybe we're not so different after all."

"Maybe you're right."

....

It was December twenty-first. The trip had been worthwhile. David was pleased. He'd addressed the Knesset, stating his case clearly and concisely. Accorded a measure of politeness, he was aware that much of what he had to say did not, at first, go down well. The give-and-take following his speech had, in his opinion, opened a breach in the wall of closed minds. Following the speech, which had been broadcast nationwide, Tremaine received calls for further radio and television interviews, which he accepted. The polite hostility that initially greeted him had given way to a more thoughtful consideration of what he had to say.

Michael Levin and Joseph Goldstein expressed their appreciation. "You've opened some closed minds," they told him, "and you've drawn attention to the crux of the matter. We must, as you said, pay attention to the legitimate concerns of our adversaries."

"It looked to me as if they really heard you, even though there were some who didn't want to. We're convinced this is the key to peace, lasting peace that is." Michael Levin had told him privately.

David and Sandra had been the guests of the Levins, and such proximity afforded the two men more time to get to know each other. Joseph Goldstein had also participated in the talks.

At his insistence David met for several hours with Yigal Rabine, the leader of the opposition, and the strongest opponent of peace. David had found the diminutive man tough and straightforward, with a keen mind and pessimistic assessment of human nature. David had enjoyed the discussion. There'd been a wide-ranging exploration of the prospects for peace, and the prospects of continued war. Mutual respect for each other had emerged from three lengthy meetings. Rabine's sense of humor was quick and self-deprecating. Tremaine recognized in Rabine a man of high integrity, an honest man.

"Let us talk again upon your return. I'll be curious to know your views at that time," Yigal had said when they parted. David agreed. He planned to meet with Goldstein and Levin when he returned; he'd be happy to speak with Yigal as well.

....

Sitting in the hotel room in Tel Aviv, David and Sandra watched the evening news. The announcer was saying that the American President and his wife had left aboard Air Force One for the return trip to Washington after a successful trip to the Middle East. On the screen, the Israeli Prime Minister and his foreign secretary shook hands with David and Sandra, who then ascended the ramp to the waiting plane. At the top they turned and waved before disappearing inside.

The idea to stay had been David's. For all intents and purposes, they had returned to Washington. But in fact they remained behind to take a brief vacation in the warm weather. Four Secret Service agents remained with them, two unobtrusively accompanying them wherever they went. Sandra colored her hair for the first time in her life, as did David. Additionally, David hadn't shaved, and the stubble on his face was already visible.

By phone, David had spoken with Phillips, the chief of the Secret Service. He'd exploded. David listened patiently then quietly informed Phillips what he was going to do. Phillips had quickly seen that it was he, not the president, who had to follow instructions.

"I'll keep two agents with me," he heard David say.

Phillips balked, "Four!" he snapped.

David acquiesced, relieved that he'd done better than he expected. He smiled and agreed, "Okay, only four of them, two men and two women."

David had reasoned that if they created the illusion that the president and his wife had returned to Washington, he and Sandra would be relatively safe. Only Levin, Goldstein, and Rotstein, the head of Internal Security, were privy to the facts.

The three couples had been on holiday. To all appearances, they were American Jews visiting the Holy Land for the first time.

The day after Christmas, Sandra and David finished an early breakfast and left the restaurant with two agents. They walked leisurely along the street as the city came to life. Above the mountains, a fiery sun burned in a cloudless sky. The street, still in the shadow of the tall buildings, was a hive of activity. Local merchants opened their stores, sliding back the iron grates, removing shutters, and wheeling out display carts loaded with produce. Along the street, traffic was becoming heavy, impeded by trucks unloading fruit and vegetables from the kibbutz.

Sandra put her arm though David's, giving it a squeeze. He looked at her and smiled, thankful for the time of relative privacy and anonymity. His eye caught sight of bright red hair blowing in the open window of a passing bus. A young girl of about ten looked out. Their eyes met and they exchanged a smile. David waved and the girl waved back. The bus continued down the street, disappearing from sight several hundred yards away, behind two large trucks unloading produce from the kibbutz.

Suddenly there was a blinding flash and a thunderous roar. For a moment it seemed as though everything stood still. Sandra and David and the two secret service agents had been knocked to the ground by the force of the explosion, but were unhurt. Sandra was the first to regain her wits. Getting up, she checked David and the agents. Realizing they were fine, she turned and ran in the direction of the explosion. She saw at once what had happened. The bus was a twisted shell of metal and shattered glass. Lurid yellow flames flickered in the wreckage, giving off a black pungent smoke. Without thinking she had rushed to help, her training as a nurse immediately coming into play.

David and the two agents had run after her, and when she climbed into the bus they were right behind. Looking around the smoking remains, they quickly assessed the situation. Sandra looked for survivors and checked the seriousness of their injuries. Many hands worked to free the injured from the blackened wreckage. Amidst the smoke and sickening flames, they toiled until all who were alive were free from the wreckage.

Sandra climbed down and went to see what she could do for a woman who lay on her back nearby. Black powder covered her face and blood dribbled from her mouth. Her clothes were in shreds. She moaned as though in sleep. Sandra felt her pulse; it was still strong. The sound of sirens filled the air. People were rushing in every direction. Someone had put a coat under the woman's head, and Sandra adjusted it to give her greater comfort. As she stood, she felt a forceful blow to the back of her neck. At the same time, someone charged into her side, knocking her over. As she fell, strong hands grabbed her arms and pulled her back on her feet. A pair of intense dark eyes stared at her through a black ski mask. The man held a gun against her belly. On either side of her, men similarly attired held her by the arms.

"You're coming with us," said a heavily accented voice from behind her.

Before she realized what was happening, she was being pushed along the sidewalk. The gun had disappeared. Then she heard a grunt as though someone had had the wind knocked out of them. Then she felt something heavy fall against the back of her legs, tripping her. The men on either side of her had spun around. Both of them drew guns. She saw David step into the man on her left and with his right hand grasp the wrist behind the gun, and thrust it into the air. At the same time she saw him twist and strike the man's exposed side, sending him sprawling, the gun flying harmlessly through the air. The two Secret Service agents struck the other man and, knocking him down, twisted the gun out of his grip.

She watched, mesmerized. Six more attackers, each with a ski mask over his head, materialized. One of the agents went down under a fierce attack from two of the gunmen. A third had drawn a knife and lunged at David. She screamed a warning. David had stepped toward the man, letting the knife pass a fraction of an inch from his face. With a fierce yank, he pulled the wrist down. Simultaneously he drove his shoulder under the armpit of his attacker, and with a quick rotation of his hips, sent the man flying through the air. Before her husband could recover, Sandra watched as one of the attackers put a gun to the back of his head. She saw the hammer click back. David had begun to turn, and sensing what was happening, jerked his head down. At the same time she heard the crack of the gun. David dropped like a sack of potatoes to the ground.

With a vicious jerk, she found herself being propelled toward an alley. She struggled with all her might, her screams no longer audible above the din of approaching sirens. Before they reached the alley, the man at her right staggered from a heavy blow to the side of his head. From the corner of her eye she saw the Secret Service agent drive his heel into the man's knee and heard the cracking of the bones. At the same time she saw a dark red stain suddenly appear on the agents chest. A look of surprise crossed his face as he fell heavily to the ground.

Quickly she was rushed down an alley and emerged on the other side, propelled by the men holding her arms. Two men were in front, three behind. A small black panel-van stood nearby. As they approached, the doors opened and she was shoved roughly inside. In a matter of moments they were speeding down a narrow street. Then she felt a scarf tied around her eyes, and rough hands secured her wrists behind her back.

....

At the precise moment David felt the gun at the back of his head, he knew what it was. As he jerked his head down he heard a roar in his ears, and everything went black and silent. When he came to, he was in a hospital bed. Janet Merril, one of the agents, was beside him. A nurse stood nearby. To the right a doctor sat on a chair, a stethoscope around his neck; he peered at his watch while his fingers felt David's pulse. David noticed the armed guards at the door.

"Where's Sandra?"

"They got away with her," Janet responded.

"Who were they?"

"We don't know."

"Where's Robert?" David asked, referring to the other agent who'd been with them when the attack came.

"He's in critical condition with a chest wound. The doctors think he'll pull through."

....

Morgan was in his office when Travis knocked on the door. He was accompanied by Jonathan Makarios. He'd not called ahead. The smile on Morgan's face suddenly faded when Travis walked in. Travis was pale and shaken.

"Have a seat." Morgan motioned to a chair.

"Have you heard the news?" Travis asked.

"What news?"

"Sandra has been captured by Hamas, and David is in a hospital in Tel Aviv with a gunshot wound to the head. One of the agents who was with them is in critical condition."

"Good God." Morgan's face had turned pale, and he sat in his chair, stunned. "How did you find out about this?"

"A phone call from Michael Levin. Anyway, he thinks the group that captured Sandra may not know who they have."

"What happened?"

"Apparently a bus was blown up by a suicide bomber in Tel Aviv. David and Sandra were in the vicinity and went to help. During the commotion, she was captured. When David and the agents tried to rescue her, one of the agents was shot in the chest. David suffered a bullet crease to his skull; it was superficial, but he lost a lot of blood."

"What's being done?"

"I spoke with David just before coming here. He said the Israelis are following every lead. They've mounted a massive search but are trying to make it as unobtrusive as possible."

"What can we do?"

"David has asked that you take over in his absence and Jonathan is to be your assistant. He'll be able to help you. I'm going to Israel, leaving in the hour."

CHAPTER 20

Rotstein and Goldstein met Travis and his two companions at the Israeli airport. After the introductions, they were on their way to the Israeli control center. It took three hours to bring Travis up to date on what was being done. After the briefing, Travis and his two companions were driven to the U.S. Embassy.

Travis showered and changed, and in less than an hour was on his way to the hospital. He traveled alone.

....

Travis slipped quietly into the room. David looked up in surprise, then smiled.

"What are you doing here?"

"What do you think?"

David didn't respond; he knew why Travis was here, and he knew the man would not be dissuaded. The truth was, David was glad to see the Chairman of the Joint Chiefs. He'd come to respect this tough, wily old bird. He knew that Travis, being who he was, would do everything in his power to find Sandra; and he knew he was skilled and highly capable. The two men talked for an hour. After Travis left, David, weak from loss of blood, fell into an exhausted sleep.

When he awoke, he lay quietly, listening to the sounds of the city coming through the hospital window. He found his mind going back to a day seven years ago. He'd been sitting with Avinash in the front room of his light airy apartment in Bombay. Sandra was with him. Outside, the kites wheeled in the hot air that rose from the busy streets. The sounds of traffic and the cries of those selling their wares floated through the open windows.

He sat watching the Master as he spoke, answering the questions of two guests who leaned toward, him eagerly listening. He found himself crying silently, filled with a love that overflowed. The Master looked at him, and with a knowing smile said, "It's like the love of the lover for his beloved, isn't it?" Then he continued the conversation with the two men, never losing a beat.

David had been too choked with emotion to respond with words, but Avinash had accurately captured the feeling.

....

Sandra lay on an rusty cot in a darkened room that smelled of rats and urine. A chain fastened her foot to the wall. Her head pounded, and she was stiff all over. She couldn't get comfortable. She had enough room to stand and when she needed to, she could relieve herself in an old bucket against the wall. But at night she was so cold she shivered uncontrollably and curled in a ball to keep warm. She was not dressed for the cold, and her captors provided nothing for warmth.

All she'd eaten since her abduction were dried crusts of

bread and a little water. She had no idea where she was. Days passed, but she was uncertain how many.

After they'd put her in the van, they had travelled for three days. They hid in daylight and at night travelled without lights, the moon providing sufficient light for their need. On the third morning, they had continued to drive. It was slow going along seldom used trails. It was late afternoon when they finally stopped near some foothills leading into the mountains. Sandra was pulled out of the van. She watched four men unload and cover the vehicle with camouflage. Then they all set out on foot. Her hands had been untied. They walked in single file, two men in front of her, two behind. It was dark when they stopped. Above and to her left was the sea of stars laced the limbs of overhanging trees. Moonlight revealed shadowy shapes on the uneven ground.

"Try to escape and you'll be shot!"

She turned and stared at the short stocky man who'd spoken. In the light of the moon she saw he was clad in army fatigues and a short jacket. He was unshaven and smelled of stale sweat. His eyes, almost hidden in shadow, conveyed no emotion. At his waist, a holstered pistol was barely visible, and in his hands he held what she guessed was a high-powered rifle. Within half an hour, five more men had joined them. The men sat in a circle and a discussion had ensued, carried on in a language unfamiliar to her. From time to time, someone had looked at her, some with curiosity, all with hostility.

They traveled on foot for two nights more. Before dawn of the second night, she was blindfolded. She felt herself being led down a steep and uneven path. She slipped several times, and each time rough hands jerked her upright. She heard the cry of a rooster in the distance and detected the smell of smoke. Perhaps half an hour had passed before they reached even ground. She guessed they were close to a village. Her captors walked on either side of her now. It was another fifteen minutes before they stopped. She heard subdued voices and the sound of a door creaking on a hinge.

....

Hours later Sandra awoke. She felt as though she'd been chained to the bed for days. The blindfold had been removed and a gag was forced between her lips and tied behind her neck. There was nothing to see. The room was dark and empty and the only light came from tiny pinholes of light during the day. At night she was fed by a guard, one of the men who'd traveled with her. Whatever she didn't eat or drink when the gag was removed was taken away.

Alone in the dark, dingy room, she'd been enveloped by sorrow. She found her mind going back to the last glimpse she'd had of David, before the walls of the alley blocked her view. He lay on his side, unmoving. Blood from the head wound obscured his face and formed a terrible, widening pool on the pavement beneath him. In the intervening days, as she lay cold and shivering on the cot, the sorrow over the death of her husband had crested, then receded, leaving her suspended in a profound emptiness.

At the peak of her sorrow, she found herself recalling the words of Avinash. While visiting the island of Maui, he was taken by friends in a helicopter. They flew into one of the valleys with steep walls that rose several thousand feet on either side. Rivers disgorged into space, and it seemed the rotors would hit the sides. Avinash mentioned later that, as they flew further into the valley, it became even more narrow, and the thought crossed his mind that death could come easily. He said he'd suddenly felt a rush of emotion, a deep and abiding joy at the thought of going home. She had always wondered about that comment. Avinash had welcomed death. He was not afraid. Later she had questioned him about this.

"Your observation is correct, Sandra, I'm not afraid of death. Why would I be afraid?"

"What is it like? What is it that you know that makes you so unafraid?"

"Have you ever been to a theater?"

"Yes."

"When you see the actors on the stage, they appear to be sitting in a room talking with each other. The room seems real, as does the conversation of those in the room, doesn't it?"

"Yes."

"Have you ever been backstage?"

"Yes."

"When you're backstage you can see that the room the audience sees is really just an illusion. And the actors are really not who they appear to be either. Knowing that, one can hardly take what is being said with the same seriousness as someone who is convinced that what he sees is real. Death in life is no more real than death on the stage. It simply means the play is over and it's time to go home. Are you not glad to go home when the time comes?"

"Yes, I am."

"So now you understand."

Sandra found herself remembering a similar conversation with David. They were discussing the dangers inherent in his position, dangers for him and for her. The conversation had taken place over several days before they left for the Middle East.

"Sandra, if something should happen to either one of us, rest easy. Know that whatever happens is purely the play of destiny. Nothing can be done to avert it; whatever is to happen will happen."

Lying on the bed, Sandra was awakened by a strange noise and listened silently, trying to identify it. She had no idea how long she'd slept. Then she heard the bar being removed from the door. Have I slept all day? she wondered. Light from the lantern flooded the room as the door was pushed open. A man unfamiliar to her entered. His hair was white and his skin dark, and he wore a shepherd's clothing. At first glance, he gave the appearance of being elderly, but the suppleness and ease to his movements suggested otherwise.

Sandra found herself looking into eyes she would never forget. In the lantern's light they were completely peaceful yet alert, not missing a thing. For the first time in days she didn't feel afraid.

The thought crossed her mind that she was dreaming. She sat up and put her feet over the side of the bed, shivering. The man set the lantern down, and producing a small key, knelt down and unlocked the chain that held her foot. Looking down on the man, she saw he was dressed in soft but coarse cotton clothing. He straightened up and looked into Sandra's eyes.

"You must be very quiet," he said, his voice low.

She nodded.

Then, reaching behind her neck, he untied the gag. She could smell the lanolin of raw wool.

"Are you all right?" he asked.

"Yes," she said, her voice a hoarse whisper.

"Then follow me. We don't have time to waste."

With that he stood and, taking her by the hand, helped her to her feet.

"My name is Nassir," he said, "and yours, I think, is Sandra?"

She nodded.

Picking up the lantern, Nassir went into the other room. The guard lay slumped on the floor, no longer breathing. As she looked up, she saw man standing against the wall, almost hidden in the shadows.

"This is Kahlil," Nassir said. The young man gave a slight bow, inclining his head in her direction. He was tall and slim, with dark skin like Nassir's.

"We've a long way to go before dawn," Nassir said. Sandra noticed his voice had a melodic tone along with an accented English she was unfamiliar with.

"Who are you?" Sandra whispered.

"There's no time to talk; we can talk later," Nassir responded.

Kahlil, in the meantime, removed the jacket from the dead guard and handed it to Sandra. Then, turning, he opened the outer door, and the three slipped into the night. Above them the stars glittered while on the horizon the thin sliver of a crescent moon cast her waning light through the cold, silent night.

They'd traveled hard for hours, and just before morning, Kahlil knocked quietly on the small wooden door of a tiny house. Quickly they were ushered inside.

....

"Where is she?" Abdullah asked.

"El Quozah," Harith responded.

"Is she safe?"

"Of course. Why did you call me here?"

Harith had been rushed to Beirut from Bent Jebail after the abduction. He'd had little chance to rest and was feeling in no mood for idle talk. What he wanted was sleep. He looked around the hot, stuffy little room. Although it was midday, very little light entered from outside. An oil lamp flickered on a packing crate, casting an uneasy light, barely keeping the darkness at bay. Harith and six other men sat in a circle on old crates and broken chairs.

"Where did you capture the woman?" continued his interrogator.

"She was on the street, helping the wounded in the bus that was bombed. We knew she was American from her accent. She must be quite wealthy because it looked to us as if she had two servants accompanying her and a man we think is her husband."

"We lost four men in that action of yours. Hardly worth it for the life of some wealthy American." Abu spit the words out, his hatred spilling forth.

"Abu, hold your tongue."

Harith looked up at the powerful built Abdullah, who'd suddenly gotten to his feet.

"Whoever this woman is, she must be very important. In less than an hour, my sources tell me, a massive manhunt was launched by the Israelis. It's unlike anything we've ever seen before. There are even rumors that the American Chairman of the Joint Chiefs arrived in Tel Aviv the day after the kidnapping. Nothing has been reported in the press. That makes me suspicious; they don't want us to know who we've captured. We must find out, and quickly." Abdullah looked slowly at each man. "We'll meet tomorrow. Harith, get some sleep, and we'll see you in the morning."

....

"Travis, we've reason to believe she's been taken across the border into Lebanon."

"What makes you think so?"

"We managed to trace the vehicles. They used three of them, and the last one was found ten kilometers from Bar'am, right on the border. Hamas seems to be coordinating their activities with Hizballah. There's been a lot of guerrilla activity in this area the past year. The Lebanese security forces have been unable to control it, if they ever really wanted to in the first place," Rotstein ended cynically.

Travis looked at Rotstein. "You must have more than that."

"We've word from informants that a small group of men crossed the border and were headed toward Bent Jebail. They had a captive with them. It was night, so my sources couldn't be sure if it was a woman."

"Do you think they'll go to Bent Jebail? It seems to me they would avoid the populated areas, don't you think?"

"Yes, I think they would, but the guerrillas who operate in the area seem to have an excellent network. They're considered heroes by many of the locals."

"Do you have people up there?"

"Yes, we've inserted two commando units in the area. We'll be in touch with them regularly."

"Let me know what develops."

"Will do."

....

Travis left for the Embassy, frustrated at having to sit around and wait. But he could do nothing until he was sure of Sandra's whereabouts. *I'll bet it was Sandra the guerrillas had when they crossed the border*, he thought.

He was familiar with the area. In 1974, he'd spent time in Israel working with special forces. The Israeli government had hired him to train these highly skilled units in techniques of counter-guerrilla warfare, learned in Vietnam. For six months they'd worked in a section that stretched some twenty miles into Lebanon along the border. It was a rugged area, ideally suited for guerrilla warfare.

It had been a clandestine operation. During that time they had mapped the area, and become familiar with the mountains and valleys, all the places where small mobile units would tend to hide. They became familiar with the trails used by the guerrillas, their caves and hiding places and the most likely places from which they would launch their attacks.

That information had been invaluable when Israel crossed the border and later, twelve months ago, launched their own attacks, aimed at suspected hiding places and the villages that supported the guerrillas.

Back at the Embassy, Travis opened a map and spread it on the table. Peter Nevis and Kevin McCloud watched.

"This is where the Israelis think she is," Travis pointed at the map.

"Damn, that's wild, rugged country," Nevis whistled.

"We'd never find her without a lead," McCloud shook his head.

"Maybe we could go in, see what we can find—in disguise, of course."

The two younger men looked at Travis, shaking their heads.

"No sense, General. Without a better lead than we've got, we'd be at a complete loss; they could be anywhere in those mountains," McCloud responded.

"We could stay in touch with the Embassy," Travis continued, as if to himself. "We could be kept informed of developments. Who knows? We might get lucky." Travis knew he was grasping at straws, but he couldn't stand the waiting. He was a man of action. He was afraid his impatience was clouding his judgment. "It's late; we'll see what the morning brings. Let's get some sleep," he said.

The two younger men, looking relieved, wished him good night and left.

....

Travis had difficulty sleeping. He lay on the bed, between sleep and wakefulness. He'd brought with him the two ex-Green Berets because of their training and because they were masters of disguise and fluent in Arabic. He'd known them for years and trusted them implicitly. They'd jumped at the chance to come with him and only learned the purpose of their mission once they were airborne.

Travis could hardly believe what he'd done. When he received word of what happened, he began at once to make preparations to leave for Israel. The decision to go was like a compulsion; it never occurred to him that he should stay.

He'd become close to the President and his wife; he liked them very much and held them in the highest regard. Tremaine had impacted him like no other man in his life, and Travis had only known him a comparatively short time.

Over breakfast Travis told his wife he'd be out of the country for a few days, maybe a week or so, he said. She knew enough not to question him.

It took a long time before Travis finally drifted to sleep.

The sound of the phone jolted him awake, and for a moment he couldn't remember where he was. The loud ring came again, and he grabbed for the phone.

"Yes... I'll be right down.... Yes."

Travis slammed the phone down, and grabbing his clothes, pulled them on. Quickly he strode down the hall and knocked on one of the doors.

"Nevis and McCloud, get down to the conference room."

....

"It came in this morning?" Travis asked, looking at the clock. It was zero three hundred hours.

"Yes, about fifteen minutes ago."

"And you recorded it?"

"Yes, we record all incoming calls."

"Let's hear it again."

There was the sound of static on the line and then the voice of the Embassy operator. "U.S. Embassy, can I help you?"

"Listen carefully," came the response. The voice was accented. "Sandra Tremaine was abducted. She's been freed, and for the time being is safe. We will bring her to you."

"Who is this?"

"It's better that I don't give you my name for now."

"How can we be sure we can trust you?" asked the Embassy operator.

"You can't. But please listen carefully. Send some of your people to Bent Jebail; two or three are enough. More will attract attention. They must look like merchants traveling in the area. Go to the shop of Jabil and arrange to purchase three hundred pounds of dates from him. We'll take it from there." With a click the line went dead.

....

"The President's wife?" Harith was stunned. "No, it couldn't be. I saw them boarding the jet for the return flight. I saw it on television."

"I don't care what you saw, Harith, the woman you abducted is the American President's wife."

"Now we can break the will of the great Satan." Abu's voice cut through the silence like a whip.

"If we play our cards right. We must get her out of the country, at once."

"Why?" demanded Harith.

"The Israelis and the Americans will turn the country upside down looking for the woman. No hiding place will be safe."

"Where do you suggest?" interrupted Abu. "The leaders of Jordan, Syria, and Lebanon were impressed by the hard line the American President has taken with the Israelis. They were even more impressed by him when they met. The leaders of these countries won't help us; they'll expose us if they find out."

"That's right, so we have to get her out of the country and into Iraq. I'll make the arrangements. Harith, bring the woman to Ar Rutbah."

They'd spent the morning hastily planning a strategy, knowing that if they were going to pull it off, they had very little time to do so.

....

"She's gone?" exploded Harith. "How can that be?"

"We don't know what happened," Ali responded, afraid of Harith's anger.

"What do you mean, you don't know?" Harith demanded.

"When we got there in the morning to relieve Bayazid, we found him dead, lying on the floor. The door was open, and the woman was gone. We've scoured the area all day. We even got old Tambal to see if he could track them. It seems there were two men besides the woman. Tambal was able to follow the tracks for several kilometers but then lost them."

"Which direction did they go?"

"South toward the border."

"Bring Tambal here. I want to talk to him," ordered Harith. "In the meantime get me some food."

Harith had traveled hard all day without eating, and it had been late when he arrived in El Quozah.

Harith had just finished eating when there was a knock on the door and Tambal was ushered in.

"Sit," ordered Harith.

The old man sat down and looked at Harith. "What do you want?" Tambal despised the Iranian.

"Tell me all you can about the escape and where you think the woman is," Harith ordered.

"I'm not a seer, Harith, I'm a tracker."

"Don't fool with me, old man." Harith's patience was getting thin. "Tell me what you know."

"Two people got her out. They were headed toward Ramiye when I lost their tracks."

"Do you think they were heading for the border?"

"That's what it looks like, but that could be what they want you to believe."

"What do you think, old man?"

"I think they were trying to lead you astray."

"What makes you think that?"

"Whoever was leading them left only a hint of a trail, not obvious to the inexperienced eye. I followed it for five or six kilometers before the trail led up into some rocks along a ridge. Then it vanished completely. I followed the ridge for several kilometers in either direction and checked both sides, looking for the trail to start again. It didn't. This makes me think the people involved knew exactly what they were doing. They wanted you to follow the tracks in one direction. They're very familiar with the terrain."

"Who might it be?" Harith was from Iran and not as

familiar with the area as were the other men. "Who, besides you, knows this area that well?" he demanded. "Think!"

"There's an old shepherd who lives in these hills. His brother is retarded. They move their flocks from place to place, and he often picks up supplies in Bent Jebail," Ali suggested.

"What do you think, Tambal?"

"I've heard about this man and seen him from time to time. He keeps to himself, seems to be a hermit."

"I've heard it said he's a Sufi, not really a shepherd." Barat spoke for the first time. He was one of the older men in the cell. Twenty-five years he'd fought the Israelis.

Harith turned toward Barat. "Tell me what you know."

"I don't know anything for sure, but over the years some of the men disappeared into the mountains. They'd come back after two or three days. I heard rumors they'd gone to see the old Sufi. He seemed to have a strange effect on them. They'd lose their will to fight, would become soft. I think Kahlil and Tariq were two of the most recent ones to visit him."

"Kahlil?" Harith snapped. "Where is Kahlil?"

Ali looked at the others, suddenly frightened. "He left for Bent Jebail two days ago. He was supposed to be back tonight."

"He and that traitor Tariq were friends, you say?"

"Yes," responded Barat. "He and Kahlil were from the same village."

"Where's that?"

"Rachaf."

....

It was mid-morning when Nassir returned. Aziz was sitting on the steps. Kahlil came out of the house and joined them.

"I got through to the American Embassy. They'll send someone into Bent Jebail either tonight or tomorrow night.

They'll contact Jabil to buy dates. That's how we'll know them."

"So we're going to meet them there?"

"Yes."

"How are you going to get the woman there?"

"You and I will leave at sundown and meet whoever comes. Sandra will remain with Shamir and Durri. She can rest. Once we meet the Americans or their representatives, we'll go from there."

....

Travis and his two companions entered Bent Jebail from the east. It was late afternoon. Their disguise was impeccable, allowing them to mingle easily with those entering the town. Like merchants passing through, they attracted no attention. They made discreet inquiries and then made their way to Jabil's small shop. Pushing the door open, they entered and were greeted by a short, potbellied merchant.

"What can I do for you?" he asked politely.

"We'd like to buy some dates, three hundred pounds," Travis said.

"Good, good. Please, have a seat. Can I get you some coffee?"

"Yes, that would be good," Travis responded.

For an hour they drank coffee and haggled over prices, seemingly enjoying the exercise.

"You must come for a meal at my humble home," Jabil insisted when they were finished.

After he'd closed the shop, Travis and his companions walked leisurely up the road with Jabil. It was dark when they arrived at his home.

Jabil's wife, a short, portly lady with graying hair, had prepared a meal. Her face was hidden behind a veil. Making sure her guests were taken care of, she placed food on the table and, with averted eyes and a slight bow to the men, excused herself and disappeared.

....

They'd just finished their meal when Travis heard a light tap tap on the door. Jabil opened it. Travis heard the whispers of greeting and watched as two men were ushered into the room.

Jabil made the introductions.

"Coffee?" he asked.

"Yes," answered the older of the new arrivals.

While Jabil made the coffee, Nassir and Kahlil sat across from the three Americans.

Looking at Travis, Nassir spoke in his accented English.

"Sandra Tremaine is safe and well."

Travis recognized the voice on the tape.

"Where is she?"

"We'll take you to her. She's not far away."

....

It was past midnight when Kahlil, Nassir and the three Americans approached Rachaf. They'd traveled quickly but slowed their pace as they approached the populated area. As they rounded a bend, Nassir suddenly stopped, listening intently. The night was dark and moonless. High clouds hid the stars. They listened, holding their breath. There it was, the sound of small stones being dislodged above them. The sound carried easily in the cold air. Quickly the men melted off the road and waited.

Nassir and Kahlil knew that the trail from El Quozah entered Rachaf just in front of them. No one but guerrillas would be using it at this time of night.

"Nassir, take the men to Durri's. I'll meet you there," Kahlil whispered. "I'm going ahead to see what's going on. If I'm not there within an hour, get the Americans away." Before Nassir could respond, Kahlil vanished in the darkness.

Quickly he made his way to where the trail met the road; there he waited in concealment. Half an hour later he heard the distinct sounds of men traveling at night. They moved cautiously, but the weight of their equipment and the darkness made it difficult for them to be completely quiet. Kahlil knew what it was like. As the men left the trail and entered the road, Kahlil could make out ten altogether, all well armed. Once they were on the road they put down their equipment and stopped for a few moments to rest. Kahlil listened carefully. He heard whispering and, with great caution, moved closer.

"Which way is Tariq's home?"

"About three kilometers down this road there's a small trail which enters from the east. It's at the end of that trail, about five kilometers all together," came the whispered response.

Kahlil recognized the voices of Harith and Barat. This was his cell. He knew at once why they were here. Turning away from the voices, Kahlil moved back silently along the road. He'd take a shortcut to Durri's home and get everyone out. Suddenly he froze. He sensed someone directly in front of him, almost within arm's length. He held his breath, listening. A light flashed in his eyes, blinding him.

"So, Kahlil, what are you doing here?"

....

Nassir and the three Americans arrived at Durri's home and knocked on the door. Durri let them in. Inside, an oil lamp burned in front of an old picture of Tariq.

"Durri, this is Travis, McCloud, and Nevis. They've come for Sandra."

Durri, eyes averted, welcomed the men to her home.

"Sandra's sleeping," she said.

"You must wake her at once."

"Nassir."

Nassir turned to see Shamir standing just inside the door. Sandra, hidden in the shadow, stood beside her, holding her hand. The two women had been sleeping. "You've come at last," Shamir said.

"Yes."

"This is what you spoke of, isn't it?" Tears glistened in her eyes.

"Yes. Shamir, you and Durri must go with Sandra and these men. They'll take you safely away from here. I told you once that one day you'd go far away across the sea to another land. Now is the time for that to take place. You must help Sandra and Durri. There's not much time so you must get ready at once."

Shamir and Durri left the room.

Sandra had watched the interaction between Nassir and Shamir. She sensed something momentous was happening; but, unfamiliar with Arabic, she didn't know what it was.

Travis had watched as well. Shifting his gaze, he saw Sandra looking at him. At first he didn't recognize her. She'd lost weight, and her hair had been cut. She wore long pants and a loose-fitting shirt. In the subdued light, Travis had at first mistaken her for a man.

"Sandra, is that you?" Travis stepped forward. "It's me, Travis."

Sandra was stunned. "Travis?" She stared at him in disbelief. Suddenly she was in his arms. Like a giant bear, Travis held her. "Is it really you?" she said looking up into the big man's face.

"Yes, it is. We've come to take you home."

"Tell me about David," she said, almost choking on the words.

"He's in a hospital in Tel Aviv."

"He's alive?"

"Yes, he'll be fine."

Stunned, she stood transfixed. Her mind had difficulty adjusting, but her heart had leapt with joy at the news. Her legs suddenly weak, she sank onto a nearby chair and sobbed in relief.

Moments later Shamir and Durri came back into the room, dressed and ready to travel.

"You must hurry," Nassir said. "You and Durri must guide them to Bent Jebail. Can you do it?"

"Yes," she answered.

"We're familiar with the area, too," Travis added.

"You're not coming, are you?" Shamir directed her question to Nassir.

"No, daughter, I'm not. You must hurry. There's not much time, danger is approaching."

Sandra, sensing the agony in Shamir, took her hand and gave it a squeeze. With all her heart she wanted Shamir to know that she would do her best to take care of her.

"Durri, when you leave here, take the trail from behind Aziz's house and head south. Do you know where I mean?"

"Yes," Durri responded.

"Are you ready?"

"Yes."

"Then you must leave at once. Under no circumstances are you to return, no matter what happens. Understood?"

Durri nodded. Then she knelt in front of him and kissed his feet. "Master, I will ever remember you."

Nassir gently reached down and, taking her by the hand,

helped her to her feet. His eyes looked long and deep into Durri's, and she returned the gaze. "Good-bye, Mother, take care of this daughter of ours."

Nassir turned and placed his hands on Sandra's shoulders. "Shamir will need your friendship and guidance when you return to your country," he said in English.

"You need have no concern for her," Sandra responded, "I'll take care of her." Impulsively she hugged Nassir, kissing him on the cheek. "Thank you," she said.

Nassir smiled at her then turned and shook hands with the three Americans. "Take care of them," he said.

"They're in safe hands," Travis said in Arabic.

Nassir smiled. "God be with you."

Shamir stood in front of Nassir, wiping away the tears. He took her in his arms and held her. Then he gently pushed her away, and said, "You must go. Remember I will always be with you. God speed, my dearest Shamir. Now go." Nassir gently turned her around and, kissing the top of her head, guided her out the door.

Once outside, it took a few moments for their eyes to adjust to the dark. Shamir looked back and saw Nassir silhouetted in the light from the door, hand raised in a parting gesture.

....

Nassir traveled hard all night—just far enough ahead to keep the guerrillas following; never close enough for them to catch up to him. As he climbed, a light snow began to fall, making travel more difficult.

At first light Nassir entered a stand of ancient cedar, the glade carpeted with the droppings of the great trees, the snow absent. The scent of cedar filled the cold air.

Nassir had moved rapidly ahead of the advancing guerrillas for several kilometers now, knowing they could easily follow his trail in the snow when they were revealed by the light of dawn.

The stand of trees grew against the side of the mountain, which rose in giant ramparts two thousand feet above and to the west. Before him the land fell away in great rifts and canyons that opened to the valleys beneath them. Snow covered the peaks; silence reigned.

Nassir jumped onto a low ledge against the rock face four feet off the floor of the glade. With the blanket around his shoulders, he sat quietly with his back to the mountain and waited. For the last time, he watched the soft colors of the rising sun bathe the surroundings in purple and gold.

Savoring the beauty of this remote place, Nassir bid silent farewell to the mountains and the life he'd loved, glad at last to be going home.

He heard the sounds of approaching men long before they arrived. Unmoved, he watched as they slipped into the glade along the length of its curved perimeter, rifles at the ready, searching him out. It took only a few moments for their eyes to adjust to the subdued light in the grove. Then they saw him. Quickly they advanced and surrounded him, not more than ten meters away.

"You led us on a merry chase," Harith hissed. He was furious.

Nassir sat and said nothing.

Earlier on the trail, Harith had raged. With the coming light, he saw at once they'd been following only one man. Nassir had led them away from their quarry; he'd outsmarted them.

Harith knew the president's wife would now be far away. This round in the battle with the great Satan was lost; opportunity had slipped through his hands. He was bitter. He, of all people, had failed to do the bidding of Allah. Now he'd have to return to Iran in disgrace, his promising career in ruins.

Harith's men were unsettled. There was something strange about the man before them. He sat unmoving, seemingly unafraid, his eyes alert, taking everything in.

The fury in Harith suddenly burst and with three swift strides, he stood before Nassir, his fist drawn back ready to strike, the only thing in his mind was to smash the face of his enemy with his bare hands.

As Harith moved toward him, Nassir's eyes glittered. Harith stopped. Something in the gaze of the man before him caused Harith's mind to go suddenly blank. Harith lowered his hands.

"It's over," Nassir said quietly, as though to himself.

"What did you say?" Harith demanded, suddenly regaining his wits.

Just then a shaft of light from the rising sun struck the rock face above the trees to the west. The reflected light suffused the glade beneath it in soft golden light.

"It's time to leave," Nassir said, his voice barely audible.

"You'll never leave here alive," Harith screamed, spittle flying from his twisted mouth, rage once more taking hold. Jerking his pistol from its holster, Harith leveled it at Nassir's head and cocked the trigger.

Looking past the gun Nassir fixed his eyes on the would-be killer. Raising his hand, Nassir pushed the gun aside. "You'll not defile the temple of Allah this day," he said quietly. Then, shifting his gaze, Nassir looked into each man who stood before him. He felt their fear, anger and frustration; he saw in it the never-ending disturbance of the wind over the vast silent depths of the ocean.

The boundaries of normal consciousness melted away, and as the men looked on, Nassir closed his eyes, a slight smile playing across his lips. His breathing slowed, becoming shallow until at last it stopped. The men stood waiting and wondering, all lost in their own private thoughts, eyes fixed on the figure before them. Then, one by one, they lowered their rifles and bowed their heads.

Let us conclude.

"That was an interesting story. It made me wonder about a lot of things, but I have a question."

"And what is it?"

"It seems to me that Tremaine had opinions about things. How could a man who had awakened have opinions?"

"Why not? Opinions are mere preferences. Some love the sound of a saxophone, others the classical guitar. You may not like what another likes, and you can't help liking what you do. That is the level of an opinion. The truth is direct, obvious, and simple. It is right before the eyes."

"I must think about it. Anyway, I doubt anything like this would ever take place."

"In his day and age, who would have thought the philosopher Marcus Aurelius would ever become Emperor of Rome? But he did. And King Janaka was an elderly man when he met his guru. Anything is possible."

"Now I've one final question, and to me it's a pivotal one."

"Go ahead. What is it?"

"If one takes seriously what Tremaine and Nassir have to say, one would have to conclude that free will is a myth."

"Ah, that is the crux of the matter, isn't it?"

"You're serious, aren't you? You really do mean there's no free will? That's an awful lot to swallow. I'm not sure I can accept it."

"I understand."

"Then what can I do?"

"The truth is, there's nothing *you* can do."

"Why?"

"Because *you* do not exist. Who you think you are is really a conceptual illusion, that occurs when consciousness identifies with a particular human organism. Therefore, if you do not exist, who is to have free will?"

"But I do exist."

"You do, but not in the way you think. The shadow is real in the sense that it exists, we can see it! But the shadow's existence depends wholly upon the sun. Consciousness is the sun. It is present in eveything, everywhere. But like the sun, it is impersonal and without identity. The identity is the ego which plays in the world like a child with his toys. This is "maya," the grand illusion, the "lila" of God.

Separation from the whole is a concept. Concepts are unique to humankind. The animal does not feel separate; he has no such concept. It's only the human mind in action, which tries to join what was never separated in the first place."

Colin D. Mallard, Ph.D., was born in England during the Second World War. After immigrating to Canada with his family in the fifties, he grew up in Ontario.

From 1961 to 1971 he attended university in Boston. Those years brought the deaths of the Kennedys and Martin Luther King. As the war in Vietnam escalated, he found himself in active opposition to it.

Always interested in religion, but uncomfortable with Christian Theology with it's emphasis on sin, and it's narrow restricting dogmas, he entered the Unitarian ministry and served an inner-city parish and two rural fellowships before he left the church in 1981.

Convinced that sages the likes of Jesus, Yogananda, Lao Tzu, and Ramana Maharshi are alive today, he sought such a master. In 1990 his search ended at Hermosa Beach, when he met a retired banker from India.

Ordering information

This book may be obtained
<u>from</u>

Wild Duck Publishing
PO Box 909 Kapaau,
HI 96755 U.S.A.

E-mail: wilduck@ilhawaii.net
<u>from</u>

http://waking.com/waking/

U.S.A. Prices

Cost of book	$16.95
Shipping: Air mail per book	$4.00
Total Cost	**<u>$20.95</u>**
NOTE: HAWAII RESIDENTS ADD 4% EX TAX	$0.70
Total cost to Hawaii residents	**<u>$21.65</u>**

You may listen to the author read selections from the book by calling The Talking Book Directory
@
1-800/796-2665 or 818/788-9722 or 310/273-1134
Ask for Box 2977

Please make checks payable in U.S. funds
to: Wild Duck, Inc.

Thank you